Ethics and Electronic Information

Ethics and Electronic Information

A Festschrift for Stephen Almagno

Edited by Barbara Rockenbach *and*
Tom Mendina

McFarland & Company, Inc., Publishers
Jefferson, North Carolina, and London

Library of Congress Cataloguing-in-Publication Data

Ethics and electronics information : a festschrift for Stephen Almagno / edited by Barbara Rockenbach and Tom Mendina.
p. cm.
Includes papers originally presented at the 2001 "Ethics of Electronic Information in the 21st Century" symposium, held at the University of Memphis on Oct. 18-21, 2001.
Includes bibliographical references and index.

ISBN 0-7864-1409-X (softcover : 50# alkaline paper) 

1. Information science — Moral and ethical aspects— Congresses.
2. Library science — Moral and ethical aspects— Congresses.
3. Internet — Moral and ethical aspects— Congresses.
4. Electronic information resources— Moral and ethical aspects— Congresses.
5. Information technology — Moral and ethical aspects— Congresses.
6. Almagno, Stephen — Congresses.
I. Rockenbach, Barbara, 1974–
II. Mendina, Tom, 1944–
III. Almagno, Stephen.
Z665.E83 2003 174'.9092 — dc21 2002011644

British Library cataloguing data are available

Manufactured in the United States of America

McFarland & Company, Inc., Publishers
Box 611, Jefferson, North Carolina 28640
www.mcfarlandpub.com

Table of Contents

Preface by Tom Mendina vii

An Homage to Stephen Almagno

1. Stephen Almagno: Biography and Bibliography
   Barbara Rockenbach 3
2. Stephen Almagno: A Reminiscence
   Toni Carbo 13
3. *Ma Position Intellectuelle*
   Stephen Almagno 16
4. My Response to *Ma Position Intellectuelle*
   Nancy Zimmerman 25
5. *Ma Position Intellectuelle*: A Discourse-Specific Response
   Jeffrey Huber 30
6. Ethical Reflections
   Netiva Caftori 39

Library Issues

7. An Ethos of Trust in Information Service
   David Wildon Carr 45
8. The Ethics of Electronic Information in China and in Eastern Europe
   Lester J. Pourciau 53
9. The Organizations That Represent Information Professionals: Form, Function, and Professional Ethics
   Wallace C. Koehler, Jr. 59

10. Preserving a Secret Garden for the Mind: The Ethics of User Privacy in the Digital Library
Paul Sturges and *Ursula Iliffe* 74

11. Libraries in the World of E-Commerce: Technological Opportunities and Ethical Implications
J.B. Hill and *Eric W. Johnson* 82

12. Intracultural Reciprocity, Information Ethics, and the Survival of Librarianship in the 21st Century
Bill Crowley and *Deborah Ginsberg* 94

13. Universal Bibliographic Control—A Contradiction in Terms? A Reflection on the Ethical Problems and Dilemmas of Universal Bibliographic Control
J.J. Britz and *Retha Snyman* 108

14. It Is Not Just a Matter of Ethics II: An Examination of Issues Related to the Ethical Provision of Consumer Heath Services in Public Libraries
Nancy Zimmerman and *Feili Tu* 119

Topical Issues

15. The Internet: Plagiarism's Newest Accomplice?
J. Wayne King and *A. Dale King* 131

16. Watermarking: From Ethics to Praxis
Spyridoula M. Armeni, Sofia F. Lioli, and *Dimitrios Christodoulakis* 138

17. Ethical Hacking: The Security Justification
Bryan Smith, William Yurcik, and *David Doss* 148

18. Social Democracy and Information Media Policy
Alistair S. Duff 154

19. Internet User Dependence and the Duty of Loyalty
Ian R. Kerr 166

20. Clashes Between Businesses and Consumers Over Unsolicited Commercial E-Mails
Byung S. Lee and *Wonhi Synn* 177

21. An Ethics for the Electronic World: The Ethics of Dialogue
Maria Antonieta Lopes Vigário 196

About the Contributors 205

Index 211

Preface

Surely a large and happy part of being Chairman of EEI21–MEMPHIS is to say Thank You over and over again to the many who help.

Thanks go, first of all, to Barbara Rockenbach, Instructional Services Librarian, Arts Library, Yale University for taking initiative with arranging for the publication of this volume, which is in fact a *Festschrift* for the 2001 EEI21–MEMPHIS honoree, Professor Stephen Almagno, and for helping otherwise in an impressive number of ways. Martha Smith (Clarion University and the Center for Information Ethics, now Drexel University) boldly and capably led the symposium-wide discussion of "Information Ethics in the Post-September 11th World." Barbara Rockenbach, Wallace Koehler (Valdosta State University), and Thomas Froehlich (Kent State University) chaired symposium sessions with grace and fairness.

EEI21–MEMPHIS has benefited enormously from its friendship with the School of Information Sciences, University of Pittsburgh, an institutional leader in the cause of establishing Information Ethics as a critically important field of inquiry and reflection. In this connection I am grateful to the Dean of Pittsburgh-SIS, Toni Carbo and, of course, to Stephen Almagno. Though their respective organizational roles change soon, they remain absolutely essential principals in the EEI21–MEMPHIS enterprise. Pittsburgh SIS sent three students to EEI21–MEMPHIS—2001: Brianna Bedigian, Michael Clark, and Melissa Gotsch, and I trust that Brianna, Michael, and Melissa are forerunners for a steady stream of library-school and other student conferees in the future.

I want to thank Dr. Martha Smith of Drexel University and the International Center for Information Ethics for taking on the challenging job of moderating the symposium-wide discussion, "Information Ethics and the Post-September 11th World," which she did with characteristic erudition. While the substance of that discussion could not be included in the present volume, a rather full indication of the topics covered is available at the EEI21 Web site (www.memphis.edu/ethics21). In all likelihood the discussion of the aftermath of 9/11 will continue at EEI21–MEMPHIS—2002.

The Dean of Libraries of the University of Memphis, Dr. Sylverna Ford, as well as the university's new President, Dr. Shirley Raines, extended the warmth of their hospitality to conferees. I thank the University of Memphis and its Libraries for providing the setting in which EEI21–MEMPHIS can flourish.

I was assisted by a number of University of Memphis staff and faculty, and especially by Ms. Judith Broy of the Libraries' administrative office. Betsy Park, Head, Reference Department; Janell Rudolph, Reference-Instruction Librarian; Christopher Matz, Collection Development head; and Bess Robinson, Reference-Instruction Librarian all played important roles.

The support and good cheer of Lasley Dameron, Professor Emeritus, English; Pierre Secher, Professor Emeritus, Political Science; and Les Pourciau, founder of EEI21–MEMPHIS, never fail to sustain and motivate when the details of symposium preparation pile high. Ongoing repartee with Hanness Britz, member, EEI21–MEMPHIS Advisory Council and frequent conferee, oils the wheels as well. My thanks to all.

Tom Mendina
Chairman, EEI21–MEMPHIS

An Homage to Stephen Almagno

1

Stephen Almagno: Biography and Bibliography

Barbara Rockenbach

Upon the occasion of his retirement from the University of Pittsburgh School of Information Sciences after a distinguished thirty-year teaching career Professor Stephen Almagno is the 2001 honoree of the "Ethics of Electronic Information in the 21st Century" symposium held at the University of Memphis, October 18–21, 2001.

My first encounter with Stephen was in 1996 when I was visiting the University of Pittsburgh in search of a library science graduate program. I asked to meet with one of the professors to talk about the program and I was introduced to Stephen. I remember sitting in a wonderful leather chair in his office, surrounded by books on information, theology, ethics, poetry, and everything else imaginable. Stephen asked me what I liked to read and I listed my favorite fiction at the time. I could immediately sense his love for books and for teaching and it was this meeting that convinced me to study at the University of Pittsburgh.

I spent a year and a half studying under Stephen, taking his courses on the history of the book, resources in the humanities and most importantly, information ethics. I had not only the privilege of being a student of Stephen's, but also the Information Ethics fellow for two semesters. I left the University of Pittsburgh with many wonderful things, but I remember most distinctly these gifts given to me by Stephen: a deep understanding of ethics in relation to my profession and to my person, a sense of the importance of librarianship in culture and scholarly work, and a love of the humanities and the poetry of W.H. Auden.

When preparing for this volume I asked Stephen for his *curriculum vitae* and further information about his life. Not knowing we were preparing a *Festschrift*, he was suspicious about my request, stating that if I was writing about him, then, my text ought to be something far from a canonization ("I'm certainly not a saint!) and not yet an obituary (I'm still alive!"). Stephen may be leaving the academy after thirty years as a professor of Library and Information Science, but he is anything but retiring from his life as a scholar. He may not have formal classes every semester or a cadre of new students every year, but he will certainly continue to teach, mentor students, lecture, write, influence and inspire.

While reviewing some of Stephen's writings, I stumbled across a text that is a perfect description of Father and Professor Almagno. In a book entitled *Studies Honoring Ignatius Brady Friar Minor*, a book edited by Stephen in 1974, then Father (and now Bishop) Donald Wuerl wrote these lines:

> Scholar-priests abound, recognizable as such even when not internationally famous. But whenever you meet him, he is a recognizable type. He is sometimes a shade cantankerous, occasionally a shade eccentric, seldom neat and tidy in his personal habits; there tends to be egg on the front of his cassock, a general scent of tobacco ash in his room and books and papers piled high in hideous confusion. He is, characteristically, a man of humor and the light touch; deeply learned in some specialized field, he has come by a hard road to an understanding of how little it is that men can actually know, apart from what God reveals to them.

I repeat: a perfect description of Father and Professor Stephen Almagno! Although I have never actually seen egg on his clerical rabat or Franciscan habit, he always smells distinctly of pipe tobacco (shipped from his favorite tobacconist in Rhode Island) and cologne (Sonie Rykiel's *Homme*)—he is truly a scholar and humanist of great standing.

Biography

Stephen Almagno was born in Providence, Rhode Island, on August 5, 1939. He was the first of two sons of the late Stefano and Theresa (La Fazia) Almagno. His early education was in the Providence Public School system and his theological education began at the St. Francis Seminary in Lowell, Massachusetts. He entered the Franciscan order in 1956 at age 17 and was ordained a priest in 1965.

Soon after ordination, Stephen received a master's degree in library science from the University of Pittsburgh. It was there that he met his mentor and friend, Roy Stokes. Later he went on to teach all the courses Roy Stokes taught at the University of Pittsburgh, and, at the specific request of Professor Stokes, he finished editing the sixth edition of *Esdaile's Manual of Bibliography*, the which Stokes had to place aside in the period of the last illness before his death.

Stephen's early professional life unfolded between the priesthood and teaching. From 1966 to 1970 he was a professor and librarian at the Franciscan Seminary in Troy, New York, and a lecturer at the College of St. Rose and Our Lady of the Angels Seminary, both in Albany, New York.

In 1970 he was called to Rome by the International Franciscan-Dominican Research Centre where he spent the next ten years as a member of the Theology Section and as Head Librarian. During that decade, he worked in close collaboration with Cardinal John Wright, later becoming the Cardinal's literary executor.

Stephen's career as a professor of Library Science began in 1971 when the University of Pittsburgh invited him to be the Visiting International Lecturer. For the next nine years Stephen came from Rome each summer term to teach three courses: history of books, critical bibliography and rare books.

The University of Pittsburgh, in 1980, promoted Stephen to full professor of Library and Information Science. He then taught the summer and fall term at the university, spending the winter term reading, writing, and thinking in any of his favorite haunts: Providence, Boston, New York City, San Francisco, Oxford, Paris, the Italian Alps or Rome. He was the first Roman Catholic priest to be a full professor at the University of Pittsburgh and remained the only priest teaching full-time at the university for many years.

In his thirty years in the profession he has taught: History of Book Publishing and Printing, Rare Books, Critical Bibliography, Resources in the Humanities, Theological Librarianship, Information Ethics, and Latin and Greek Manuscripts.

Professional Contributions

Stephen has made vast contributions both within the church and the academy. He has served the church in Pittsburgh for more than thirty years and has traveled throughout the world giving clergy retreats in Canada, Central America, Latin America, Africa, the Philippines, and Europe. He has preached extensively throughout the United States. Additionally Stephen has served as a member of the Board of Regents of the Catholic University of America and a member of the Board of the American Teilhard Association.

Stephen's work for the church went on simultaneously with work in academia. It is not easy to measure the full impact of Stephen's thirty years in the academy. Besides his teaching one must take into account the many articles published and papers given around the country at library and information conferences; student reflections about their experiences with Stephen in and outside the classroom; and the national and international contributions Stephen has made in the area of information ethics.

In 1990, Stephen, coordinating with Dean Carbo, became the first professor in the United States to teach an Information Ethics course in a Library and Information Science program. Two years before (in 1989) Dean Carbo and Stephen — in an effort to lay some groundwork for and engender interest in Information Ethics— inaugurated the first *Dean's Forum on Information Ethics.* The forum continues to be held yearly, with one or sometimes two lectures, and attracts a wide audience. The Information Ethics program at the University of Pittsburgh has grown over the last 11 years, and more than 300 students have taken the ethics class. In 1996 Dean Carbo honored Stephen's twenty-five years at the University by initiating a program to support research and teaching in the area of Information Ethics. The Information Ethics Fund was established to support an Information Ethics Fellow. Out of this fellowship has come an Information

Ethics Web site, many articles by Fellows in journals such as *The Journal of Information Ethics, The Visual Resources Association Bulletin,* and *The Journal of Scholarly Publishing.*

Student Reflections

Many students and colleagues have benefited from their associations with Stephen; here are the comments of several

> "Having had the opportunity to study Information Ethics under the direction of Stephen Almagno has proven to be invaluable. Insights Professor Almagno presented in the classroom and in subsequent discussions continue to provoke ethical consideration in my current role as researcher, practitioner, and educator. Given the paradigmatic shift in information production, dissemination, and consumption, the importance of ethical deliberation cannot be overemphasized. Ethical reflection, where the information-knowledge-wisdom continuum is concerned, is no longer a luxury but a necessity."
>
> Jeffrey T. Huber, Ph.D.,
> Associate Professor,
> Texas Woman's University
> 1990 Information Ethics student
>
> In his *Letters of a Young Poet* Rainer Maria Rilke writes "…I would like to beg you, dear Sir, as well as I can, to have patience with everything unresolved in your heart and to try to love the questions themselves as if they were locked rooms or books written in a very foreign language. Don't search for the answers, which could not be given to you now, because you would not be able to live them. And the point is, to live everything. Live the questions now. Perhaps then someday far in the future, you will gradually, without even noticing it, live your way into the answer. At its heart, education is not about imparting information, although that is no mean task. What great teachers know is that asking students to read books and explore ideas is only the beginning and a means to a profound transformation in which students are challenged to live the questions that are the heart of life itself. Stephen Almagno did so much more than simply introduce me to the history of books and the salient writings of information ethics. He challenged me by giving me the hunger to ask, the resources to answer, and the courage to ask again, the questions that we must all live."
>
> Benjamin Moss, Assistant
> Manager of Information Systems
> & Technology,
> Yale Divinity School
> 1993 Information Ethics Student

Where to begin? With Stephen there are so many stories, so many interesting tales to tell. My fondest memories of Stephen have less to do with the classroom, although they have everything to do with him as a teacher. It was usually three o'clock when Stephen would come by the office. Sally Buchanan and I would be polishing a grant proposal, reworking a syllabus. In the back of our minds we were both thinking: coffee and cake, but neither of us wanted to admit to the other that we'd much rather be anywhere other than the third floor of SIS. Just then, Stephen would poke his head around the corner — pipe in one hand and our coats miraculously appearing in the other — and entice us to stroll to Craig Street for an afternoon coffee, or a glass of wine. We went. Our conversation would range from politics to literature, fiber arts, architecture, the latest exhibition at the Carnegie, or perhaps the best spot to get paella. Laughter.

More coffee (or wine). He sparkled and so did we. Conversation with Stephen was, and is, never boring; he is so urbane. He makes you feel that you are the most brilliant person to whom he has ever spoken. Stephen inspires you to extend yourself, to be a scholar. Seven years after my first class with him, Stephen remains a confidant, an advisor, and a cherished friend. And we still do coffee (or wine).

Kirsten Jensen, Archivist, Historical
Society of the Town of Greenwich
1994 History of the Books Student

"I don't think I can speak of Information Ethics without, first, mentioning Professor Stephen Almagno because he made the course meaningful to me; so for me to speak of Information Ethics is to speak of Professor Almagno and the tremendous impact he has made on my life. Of all my experiences in graduate school, the most enduring is the way in which Professor Almagno constantly challenged, encouraged, and guided his Information Ethics students "to love the questions." To me, that is precisely what the course is all about — being open and willing to examine life critically and to appreciate the process of ethical decision-making as much, if not more than, the decision itself."

Leslie A. Lee, J.D., Collection Services
Librarian, Jacob Burns Law Library
1995 Information Ethics Student

"I was once told by a classicist of my acquaintance that the purpose of learning Latin was not so much to learn the language, but to learn how to think. I can say the same about Professor Almagno's course in Information Ethics. As a medical librarian, I know that all the people involved in the information cycle bring their own particular biases and perspectives to bear on the information product. Information Ethics provides essential tools for producers, managers and consumers of information to assess, evaluate, and understand what they do. I consider this an essential course for survival in the new millennium."

Catherine Arnott Smith, MA, MLIS
Predoctoral Research Fellow, Center for
Biomedical Informatics
1999 Information Ethics Student

My first encounter with Father Almagno was in the summer of 2000 as I enrolled in his Information Ethics class; I subsequently audited his class on History of Books. Here was a man who knew his subject inside out; but he never began to suggest that he knew it all. On the contrary, he managed to convey an impression that he was still immersed in learning. Any questions that were posed were thoughtfully considered and the response was always logical and well based. And when he took a personal interest in my work, it did not take long for me realize that his knowledge was nothing less than vast.

The gulf between his knowledge and experience compared with mine was (and will probably remain) wide. But his gesture of fleetingly giving me the impression of being on a knowledge level with him, not only gave me a wonderful lift. From that day I worked harder than I had ever worked before. Suddenly, I felt more confident. I began to develop creative thoughts. This man had inspired me to travel difficult roads of knowledge that, without his encouragement, I would never have attempted. The ensuing discussions were equally uplifting. He was a good listener but in the end I was the one who was listening! The more I was in contact with Father Almagno the more I wanted to learn and aspire to perfection. The man was nothing less than an inspiration. From now onwards, although, sadly, he will no longer be amongst us in Pittsburgh, Father Almagno will always remain a source of wonderful inspiration and a friend like no other! Thank you, Father Almagno.

Andrea Everard, Doctoral
Candidate in Management
Information Systems
Katz Graduate School of Business
2000 Information Ethics Student

Stephen Almagno's tradition of teaching at the library school has had multiple threads: the history of the book, critical bibliography, the humanities, and information ethics. He was originally asked to become a member of the summer faculty, to come to Pittsburgh from Rome, to teach courses in the history of the book and in critical bibliography.

Over the years he came to stay full-time on the faculty and assumed the added responsibility for the course on resources in the humanities, and finally took on the project that resulted in the addition of coursework on information ethics to the curriculum. By the end of his twenty-fifth on the faculty, he was teaching in all four areas, as well as advising students interested in careers as academic and special collections librarians and supervising doctoral students whose research emphases lay in historical studies and in ethical issues.

His syllabi always emphasized readings from original texts and essays by scholars and his assignments often required the writing of many reflection papers on readings and class discussions.

Students would spill out from his assigned classrooms, and follow him into the corridor beside his office, continuing discussions and gathering more ideas from the informal post-class conversations, sometimes extending into lunch.

Almagno's office was invariably the neatest and most organized of the faculty's space; not for him the traditional piles of papers awaiting filing, the blinking computer screens, and pink "while you were out" slips everywhere — his office was an oasis of calm and orderly bookmanship. Beautifully bound volumes, pictures of his mentors and honored colleagues, an armchair, and faint hint of fine leather marked his area, while some of his colleagues were better-known for offices that functioned as archeological digs! He would invite a colleague or student in to sit down, relax, and talk about whatever issues were pressing. He knew when to ask for help, usually with a bureaucratic form or some document for an advisee, and he also knew when and how to be the colleague to whom one could turn for advice and counsel. He was pastoral when needed; in particular, his presence and his words soothed and succored the School's community at several funerals for long-time colleagues.

Committee meetings were not his favorite faculty activity, but he attended those that he had to, and participated in them with good humor and frequent wit. He could argue vehemence with a colleague over a fine point of academic politics, and then immediately go out for a friendly lunch with the same colleague in appreciation of the bonds between them.

He will be missed.

Ellen Detlefsen
Associate Professor, DLIS
School of Information
Sciences Core Faculty
Center for Biomedical Informatics
School of Medicine Project Director
Highmark Minority Health Link

Works by Stephen Almagno

Books and Monographs

A Basic Teilhard Bibliography 1955–1968. New York: The American Teilhard de Chardin Association, 1968. 10p.

A Basic Teilhard Bibliography, 1955–1970. New York: The American Teilhard de Chardin Association, 1970. 21p.

Bibliografia Teilhardiana 1955–1970. Presentazione di Alessandro Dall'Olio, S.J. Firenze: Centro di Studio e di Ricerca Teilhard de Chardin, 1970. 60p.

S. Bonaventurae 1274–1974. Volumen Commemorativum Anni Septies Centenarii a Morte S. Bonaventurae. Cura et studio Commissionis Internationalis S. Bonaventurae. Grottaferrata: Collegio San Bonaventura, 1974. 5 volumes. Member of editorial team.

Saint Thomas and Saint Bonaventure in the Vatican Library. Exhibit on their Seventh Centenary 1274–1974. Catalogue by Fathers Guyot, Bataillon, Brady and Almagno. Citta del Vaticano: Biblioteca Apostolica Vaticana, 1974. 121p.

Studies Honoring Ignatius Brady Friar Minor. Edited by Romano Stephen Almagno, O.F.M., and Conrad Harkins, O.F.M. St. Bonaventure New York: The Franciscan Institute, 1974. 496p.

The Teaching of Christ. Catholic Catechism for Adults. Noll Plaza, Ind.: Our Sunday Visitor, 1974. Member of editorial team.

Bibliography of Articles Published in English on Pierre Teilhard de Chardin S.J. from 1955–1975. New York: The American Teilhard Association for the Future of Man, Inc., 1976. 32p.

Days of Our Years. Preface by Cardinal Wright. Providence: St. Bartholomew Parish, 1976. 61p.

Cardinal John Joseph Wright the Bibliophile. Pittsburgh: The Pittsburgh Bibliophiles, 1980. 15p.

Mary Our Hope. A Selection from the sermons, addresses and papers of Cardinal John J. Wright. San Francisco: The Ignatious Press, 1984. 227p.

Resonare Christum — Volume I: 1939–1959 — The Boston and Worcester Years. A Selection from the sermons, addresses, interviews and papers of Cardinal John J. Wright. San Francisco: The Ignatius Press, 1985. 419p.

The Saints Always Belong to the Present. A Selection from the sermons, addresses and papers of Cardinal John J. Wright. San Francisco: The Ignatius Press, 1985. 221p.

Words in Pain. A selection from the sermons, addresses, and papers of Cardinal John J. Wright. San Francisco: Ignatius Press. 1986, 147p.

Resonare Christum, Volume 2: The Pittsburgh years, 1959–1969. A selection from the sermons, addresses, interviews and papers of Cardinal John J. Wright. San Francisco: Ignatius Press. 1988.

Resonare Christum, Volume 3: The Rome years, 1969–1979. A selection from the sermons, addresses, interviews and papers of Cardinal John J. Wright. San Francisco: Ignatius Press. 1995.

A Sketch of the Franciscan Order by Fr. Panfilo Pierbattista. Anastatic reproduction. Bergamo, Stamperia Editrice Commerciale, 2001. 462p.

Esdaile's Manual of Bibliography. Edited by Roy Stokes and R. Stephen Almagno. Lanham, Maryland: Scarecrow Press, Inc., 2001.

Contributions to Books

"Introduction." *There Shall Be One Christ.* Michael D. Meilach, O.F.M., ed. St. Bonaventure New York: The Franciscan Institute, 1968. Pp. i–ix.

"Imprimatur," *Encyclopedia of Library and Information Science.* New York: M. Dekker, 1968–c2001. Volume XI. pp. 264–265.

"Incunabula," *Encyclopedia of Library and Information Science.* New York: M. Dekker, 1968–c2001.Volume XI. pp. 265–284. With Dr. J.P. Immroth.

"Limited Editions," *Encyclopedia of Library and Information Science*. New York: M. Dekker, 1968–c2001.Volume XVI. pp. 184–186.

"Miniature Books," *Encyclopedia of Library and Information Science*. New York: M. Dekker, 1968–c2001.Volume ZVIII. pp. 138–141.

"Prudentius Marcus Aurelius Clemens," *Encyclopedia of Library and Information Science*. New York: M. Dekker, 1968–c2001. Volume XXIV. pp. 256–257.

"Saint Anselm — College Library, Rome," *Encyclopedia of Library and Information Science*. New York: M. Dekker, 1968–c2001. Volume XXVI. pp. 267–268.

"Saint Bartholomew's— Heritage and Vision Within a Parish," *Saint Bartholomew's Church*. New Jersey: Custombook, Inc. 1970. PP. 8–9, 12–13, 16 and 22.

"Preface," *My Conversations with Teilhard de Chardin on the Primacy of Christ*. By Gabriele M. Allegra, O.F.M. Translated by Bernardino M. Bonansea, O.F.M. Chicago: The Franciscan Herald Press, 1971. pp. 1–4.

"A Basic Teilhard Bibliography 1955–1972," *The Meaning of Teilhard de Chardin*. By Alice Knight. Old Greenwich, CT: The Devon-Adair Co., 1973. pp. 145–165.

"The Eucharist — Center of Life." *The Teaching of Christ*. R. Lawler ed. Noll Plaza, Ind.: Our Sunday Visitor, 1974. pp. 419–456.

"The Chronology and Bibliography of Father Ignatius Charles Brady, O.F.M.," *Studies Honoring Ignatius Charles Brady Friar Minor*. St. Bonaventure New York: The Franciscan Institute, 1976. pp. 479–495.

"Some Notes for the History of the Quaracchi-Grottaferrata Library," *Collegium S. Bonaventurae Ad Claras Aquas*. Grottaferrata: Collegio S. Bonaventura, 1977. pp. 307–315.

"The Sectio Internationalis Bibliographie Franciscanae 1933–1947," *Collegium S. Bonaventurae Ad Claras Aquas*. Grottaferrata: Collegio S. Bonaventura, 1977.pp. 523–526.

"Summary," *Sermonse Dominicales*. S. Bonaventurae. Studio et cura I.G. Bougerol, O.F.M. Grottaferrata: Collegio S. Bonaventura, 1978. pp. 127–128.

Translations from English to Italian

"Amo le Aquile — Ricordo di P. Efrem Longpre, O.F.M. 1890–1965," *Vita Minorum* (Nov.-Dic. 1970): 463–477.

"La Testimonianza dei Laici. Del Cardinale Wright," *Palestra del Clero* (Gen. 1975): 3–18.

"Anno Santo e Sacerdozio Cattolico. Parte I. Del Cardinale Wright," *L'Osservatore Romano* (Apr. 12, 1975): 5.

"Anno Santo e Sacerdozio Cattolico. Parte II. Del Cardinale Wright," *L'Osservatore Romano* (Apr. 18, 1975): 5.

"Anno Santo e Sacerdozio Cattolico. Parte III. Del Cardinale Wright," *L'Osservatore Romano* (Apr. 20, 1975): 5.

Translations from Italian to English

"Giorgio Scarpati — The Franciscan Artist. By Gian-M. Polidoro, O.F.M.," *The Franciscan Herald* (May 1967): 137–138.

"Remembering Teilhard de Chardin. By Gabrielle M. Allegra, O.F.M.," *The Franciscan Herald* (October 1967): 306–313.

"The New Spirit Toward Islam. By Guilio Basetti-Sani, O.F.M.," *World-mission* (1967): 27–52.

For China Another Jerome. By Domenico Gandolfi, O.F.M. Translated and edited by R. Stephen Almagno, O.F.M., and Melody Mazuk. San Francisco: The Ignatius Press, 1984. 61p.

Translations from English to French

"Le Cardinal Danielou Devant la Souffrance. par Cardinal Wright," *Bulletin de Amis du Cardinal Jean Danielou*. (Juin 1976): 86–

90.

"Entrevue avec le Cardinal J.J. Wright relative au don de sa collection Johannique a la Bibliotheque Publique de Boston," *Bulletin de la Societe des Amis de Vieux Chinon*. (1977): 17–22.

Translations from French to English

"The Priestly Heart of Pere Teilhard de Chardin. By Pere Frederic-M. Bergonioux, O.F.M.," *The Cord* (June 1967): 171–177.

"Bonaventure the Churchman. By Jacques Guy Bougerol, O.F.M.," *L'Osservatore Romano*. English edition. (May 2, 1974): 6.

Journal Articles

"Dante the Franciscan," *Zeal*. (Nov.-Dec., 1965): 13–15.

"Quaracchi Flood Appeal," *The Franciscan Herald* (July 1967): 199–200.

"Professor Louis Massignon on the Fifth Anniversary of His Death," *Kenosis* (October 1967): 2–4.

"Guest Editorial: Statistics as Statistics Go." *The Cord* (Nov. 1969): 322–324.

"Emmanuel de Breuvery, S.J.," *Acta Teilhardiana* (1970): 89.

"A Predilection for Eagles— Some Notes on the Life and Work of Ephrem Longpre, O.F.M., 1890–1965," *The Cord* (April 1970): 104–112.

"Un Appello ai Frati Bibliotecari: Se Svendete Vendete a Noi." *Fraternitas* (April 30, 1971): 22.

"Listen to the Voice of Your Father — Interview with Fr. Constantine Koser, O.F.M., Minister General," *The Cord* (August 1971): 226–239.

"Tabor: Primato della Preghiera U.S.A.," *Fraternitas* (Dec. 15, 1971): 78.

"From the Pilot's Seat — Interview with Father Bougerol, O.F.M.," *The Cord* (Dec. 1971): 364–371.

"That Sacred Duty," *The Cord* (Feb. 1972): 36–47.

"Fraternitatem Franciscano-Dominicam de Grottaferrata Visitat Em.mus D. Ioannes Card. Wright," *Acta Ordinis* (Jan.–Apr. 1974): 102–103.

"Specialis Conviventia Fratrum Praedicatorum et Fratrum Minorum apud Cryptam Ferratum die 31 Iannuarii 1974," *Fraternitas* (Mart. 10, 1974): 98.

"Magister Generalis Ordinis Praedicatorum ac Minister Generalis Ordinis Fratrum Minorum S. Bonaventurae Collegii Internationale de Grottaferrata Insimul Visitant," *Acta Ordinis* (Jan–Apr., 1974): 102.

"That Sacred Duty — Franciscan and Dominican Friars Dedicated to Scholarship," *The Priest* (Oct. 1974): 41–45.

"U.S.A. — St. Bonaventure and the Ninth Conference on Medieval Studies," *Acta Ordinis* (1975): 389–390.

"Notae Bibliographicae," *Archivum Franciscanum Historicum* (1975): 539.

"Centenario Bonaventuriano: Precisazione," *Vita Minorum* (Gen-Feb., 1975): 81.

"Notes and Comments— Libraries and Archives," *The Catholic Historical Review* (Jan. 1977): 158.

"A Laying on of Hands— Cardinal Wright donates his Joan of Arc Collection to the Boston Public Library," *Religious Media Today* (Fall 1977): 3–5.

"Information Ethics: The Duty, Privilege, and Challenge of Educating Information Professionals." *Library Trends* (Winter 2001): 510–518.

Book Reviews

Teilhard de Chardin and the Creation of the Soul by Rober North S.J. *The Cord* (Apr. 1967): 120–121.

The Religion of Teilhard de Chardin by Henri de Lubac, S. J. *The Cord* (Oct. 1967): 313–314.

The Mystery of the Supernatural by Henri de Lubac, S.J. *The Cord* (July 1968): 218–220.

Letters to Two Friends 1926–1952 by Pierre Teilhard de Chardin...*The Cosmic Christ* by George A. Maloney, S.J. and *An Intro-*

duction to the Thought of Teilhard de Chardin by Norbert M. Wildiers. *The Cord* (Sept. 1969): 281–284.

Un Prophète en Proces: Teilhard de Chardin par René d'Ouince, S.J., and *Bibliographie Générale des Oeuvres et Articles sur Pierre Teilhard de Chardin* par J.E. Jarque. American Teilhard de Chardin Association News-letter (June 1971): 5.

The Church and the Two Nations in Medieval Ireland. By J.A. Watt. *Archivum Franciscanum Historicum* (1972): 632.

Why the Church? By Cardinal Jean Danielou, S.J. *L'Osservatore Romano*. English edition. (Jan. 15, 1976): 5 and 12.

The Inner Elite: Dossier of Papal Candidates by Gary Mac Eoin. *The Providence Vistor* (Aug. 24, 1978): 8.

Newspaper Articles

"The Prayer of the Church," *The Evangelist* (August 6, 1970): 7-B.

"The Rarest-Veined Unraveller: Scotus," *The Evangelist* (October 8, 1970): 8-B.

"The United Nations—A Teilhardian Meditation," *The Evangelist* (October 22, 1970): 1-B.

"A Mountain Ministry," *The Evangelist* (Oct. 29, 1970): 1-B.

"Vir Ecclesiasticus—or What Makes a Cardinal Tick?" *The Evangelist* (November 1, 1970): 1-B.

"Farewell All Hawking, Hunting and Old Pastimes!" *The Evangelist* (December 3, 1970): 8-A.

"John Henry Cardinal Newman—Unseen Father at Vatican II," *The Evangelist* (December 10, 1970): 7-A.

"Saint and Martyr Still Rule from the Tomb," *The Evangelist* (December 15, 1970): 1-B.

"Father Emmanuel A.S. de Breuvery, S.J., Priest, Scholar, Scientist, Diplomat and Citizen of the World," *The Evangelist* (February 25, 1971)

"When Truth Appears—Teilhardian Thought Sixteen Years Later," *The Evangelist* (April 22, 1971): 8-A.

"Another View of Vatican Diplomacy—The Church Speaking to the World," *The Evangelist* (June 15, 1971): 8-A.

"Synod Perspective-I," *The Evangelist* (October 14, 1971): 1-A.

"Synod Perspective-II," *The Evangelist* (October 20, 1971): 1-A.

"Synod Perspective-III," *The Evangelist* (October 28, 1971): 3-B.

"Prisoner 16670—A Man For Our Times," *The Evangelist* (October 28, 1971): 1-A and 6-A.

"Synod Perspective-IV," *The Evangelist* (November 4, 1971): 6-A.

"Mindszenty—A Modern Becket," *The Evangelist* (November 4, 1971): 3-A.

"Synod Perspective-V," *The Evangelist* (November 11, 1971): 6-A.

"Synod Perspective-VI," *The Evangelist* (November 18, 1971): 6-A.

"According to the New Rite," *The Italian Echo* (September 8, 1976): 9.

"Remembering Pope John Paul I," *The Freeman of Cebu* (The Philippines) (October 9, 1979): 3 and 13.

"Working for Peace ... Excerpts from the Sermon delivered by Father Almagno at Sts. Peter and Paul Cathedral," *The Providence Visitor* (August 23, 1984): 24.

2

Stephen Almagno: A Reminiscence

Toni Carbo

The dedication of the 2001 "Ethics of Electronic Information in the 21st Century" Symposium held at the University of Memphis and of this *Festschrift* to Professor Stephen Almagno, O.F.M. could not be more appropriate. I believe that, without Stephen Almagno, Information Ethics would not exist at the University of Pittsburgh. When I first came to the University in 1986, at a small gathering of faculty members, Professor Almagno asked me about my personal goals as the new dean of the School. When I told him that I had long had an interest in examining what I then called "The ethics of information in society," he said the magic words: "I will help you."

Of course, he did much more than help; he led our efforts to explore the entire area of information ethics and to acquire support for it. While I had somewhat naively called for a Code of Ethics for Information Professionals back in 1980,[1] I had not really explored the subject, nor did I understand, in fact, what a code of ethics should be. In the more than twenty years since that statement and the more than fifteen years at the University, thanks to the wisdom and guidance of Stephen Almagno, I have started to learn about information ethics. (I say, "started," because, no matter how much I read and study, I continue to learn how much I don't know and how long the journey to understanding is.) I am only one of hundreds (perhaps thousands) who have benefited from the teaching and mentoring of Stephen Almagno.

In Chapter 1 of this book, Barbara Rockenbach describes Stephen's background, publications, and teaching, including quotes from many former students and colleagues, and I don't want to duplicate any of her fine work. Trying to describe the impact Stephen has had on the study of information ethics, on scholarship more widely, and, most importantly, on individuals is an impossible task. I can only respond to the challenge by citing a few, selected examples. I know of countless examples of his counseling individuals through the most difficult of personal circumstances, including some of those in my own life. He helped members of my family and me through the long illnesses and deaths of both my mother and my sister, officiating at the simple memorial service my mother requested and assisting at the funeral mass a family member needed on the same day, carefully and sensitively bringing the two services together to help the family heal. In a much happier time, he fit into a very busy schedule a trip to Canada to bless the marriage of my daughter, again bringing family members together.

Stephen has helped many of us at the School through very hard times when we have lost family members and friends. He has counseled us through enormously challenging problems, providing perspective and a sense of balance, and sometimes humor just when it was needed. He has performed so many similar roles for many students, faculty members, colleagues and friends around the world, the list alone would fill pages. The kindness and humanity, just when we have most needed them, are especially memorable for all of us.

Of course, he has been an excellent scholar and teacher. His publications are well respected around the world and cover a range of subjects and languages. It is especially fitting that his former teacher, Roy Stokes, asked him to complete the editing of Esdaile's *Manual of Bibliography*, which Stokes had been asked by his teacher, Esdaile, to edit. This is both a tribute to Stephen's abilities and knowledge and to his understanding of how to carry forward a tradition of excellence, while building on that tradition and taking it to a new level. He understands the importance of intellectual and human legacy.

In thinking of Stephen's legacy, I first think of the many human lives he touched and changed. Not a month has gone by over the past fifteen years in which someone, often, but not always, a graduate of our program or a former colleague, tells me about the difference Stephen made in his or her life. Usually, the person says: "He (or the course) changed my life." They then relate to me a specific (and often dramatic) change made in career, family, or personal situation that occurred. While sometimes the course referred to is "The History of the Book" or "Critical Bibliography," it is usually "Information Ethics." Each term that the course is taught, I participate in at least one class and I tell the students that they will work very hard; that Stephen will provoke their thinking and probably make them angry; that they will learn; and that it is the most important course we teach. At the end of one term, I remember one student from our Telecommunications Program saying: "At the beginning of this course, I thought information consisted of bits and bytes to be shoved across networks; I now have a totally different understanding of information and an appreciation of the ethics involved in our field." Others write to me years after they have graduated to tell me that they didn't fully appreciate the course when they took it, but each day they are understanding what a difference it has made in their lives. Students taught by Stephen think differently than many others do; they ask questions and probe more deeply; they challenge ideas more rigorously; and they struggle to understand themselves. In the words of Rainer Maria Rilke, whom Stephen quotes frequently, they learn to "love the questions."

As we prepare for our friend and colleague to close this chapter in his life and begin a new one in Italy, we are all very sad to see him retire from our School. We know, however, that he will never stop teaching, because he lives to teach and teaching is like breathing to him. I have told him that I am very afraid to try to teach the course—his course—even with many years of his advice and guidance. After all, I haven't read Plato in the original Greek as he has. He has kindly told me that I must make it my course and—those magic words again—that he will help even from afar.

His legacy is in the people whose lives he has touched and changed. It is in his many scholarly works, and it is in the great service he has provided to his communities. His leadership in Information Ethics has set our School apart from others, and he has forged the path for many to follow. We, his followers, are immensely fortunate to have known him and learned from him.

Notes

1. Bearman, Toni Carbo. 1981. "Do We Need a Code of Ethics for Information Science?" *ASIS Bulletin* 8:36.

3

Ma Position Intellectuelle

Stephen Almagno

Introduction

In New York City, during April 1948 — almost eleven years to the day of his 10 April 1955, Easter Sunday, death in that same city — Pierre Teilhard de Chardin, Jesuit-priest-scientist-explorer-writer-mystic, wrote the text entitled *Ma Position Intellectuelle*.[1] Today, as I near the close of my teaching career, thirty years at the University of Pittsburgh School of Information Sciences, I stand here before you (in the spirit of Father Teilhard "who of all men most sways my spirits to peace") to present *Ma Position Intellectuelle* on and about the privilege that has been mine, these last eleven years — teaching Information Ethics.[2] And, I do so in and with the hope — as another mentor, Ronald Knox, wrote at the close of thirty years of work on his masterpiece *Enthusiasm*, that "there is some truth here worth the telling; or, if not that, tinder at least to catch the sparks of your fire."[3]

Background

The history of the Information Ethics course and program at Pittsburgh's School of Information Sciences has been thrice documented — 1998: Barbara Rockenbach's "Information Ethics at the University of Pittsburgh" published in the fall issue of the *Journal of Information Ethics*[4]; again, in 1998: Rockenbach's, Dean Carbo's and my four page brochure on our Information Ethics Fellowship; and, this year 2001: Dr. Carbo's and my article "Information Ethics: The Duty Privilege and Challenge of Educating Information Professionals" published in the winter issue of *Library Trends*.[5] So, here, brief chronological highlights will suffice.

1986–1988: Dr. Carbo is named Dean of the University of Pittsburgh School of Information Sciences. Soon after arriving, she expresses interest in promoting education, reflection and action on the moral issues facing information professionals.

She and I, then, work on actualizing her vision.

Coincidentally—theologians might say: providentially—I was going through an intellectual-spiritual sea change. Long periods in West Africa (Ghana and Liberia: 1976), the Far East (Philippines and Hong Kong: 1979), Central America (Honduras, Guatemala, El Salvador: 1981) and South America (Brazil: 1981) with previous years in Canada and Europe had made me keenly *aware* of the world as extraordinarily one despite its extraordinary diversity, *sensitive* to the demands of human rights (especially for women and minorities) in all cultures, *convinced* (especially with the onset of AIDS) that intolerance had returned in some fashion everywhere in the world, and *sadly aware* (especially as a priest) that religions remained in fact the most significant factor in xenophobic divisions and suspicions.[6]

I was, also, deeply influenced by the thinking and writing of Robert Muller,[7] Hans Kung's *Projek Welethos,*[8] and the writings of America's "most prominent female philosopher," Dr. Martha Nussbaum.[9]

And, I was becoming more and more disenchanted with the academy. The world of information was *once again* exploding. And, as with the printing press—there was much social change.[10] Most were singing the praises—and kneeling at the shrine—of what was new. Not a few predicted the demise of the book. (For a *sane* evaluation, see the important article by my colleague Dr. Richard Cox.[11] And few, indeed, were asking the vital questions voiced by T.S. Eliot in 1934:

> Where is the Life we have lost in living?
> Where is the wisdom we have lost in knowledge?
> Where is the knowledge we have lost in information?[12]

With Robert Muller, I was becoming more and more convinced—most especially as I sat in faculty meetings—that we were prepared to feed our students only half a loaf of bread. Muller loved to quote Jon Rye Kinghorn's *Parable*—let me do the same:

> Once upon a time there was a class and the students expressed disapproval of their teacher. Why should they be concerned with ... what others were thinking, feeling and doing?
>
> And the teacher said she had a dream in which she saw one of her students fifty years later.
>
> The student was angry and said, "Why was I not warned? Why was I not better educated? Why did my teachers not tell be about the problems and help me understand.... You helped me extend my hands with incredible machines, my eyes with telescopes, radios and sonar, my brain with computers, but you did not help me extend my heart, love and concern to the entire human family. You, teacher, gave me half a loaf."[13]

At this point I was happy as ever in the world of historical and critical bibliography. (The Rowman & Littlefield Publishing Group has just issued the sixth revised edition of Esdaile's classic *Manual of Bibliography.* Arundell Esdaile was Roy Stokes' professor and Roy Stokes was my professor. Shortly before his death, Stokes called me to his home in Vancouver, British Columbia, and asked me to complete his most recent revision of Esdaile.) Notwithstanding that happiness, and deeply concerned about "The half loaf of bread," I felt not only drawn, but obliged, to get to work in and on Information Ethics.

1989: In an effort to lay some groundwork — i.e., engender interest in the School, university and wider community — the School of Information Sciences hosts its first *Dean's Forum on Information Ethics*; with Jesuit-priest-lawyer-U.S. Representative from Massachusetts and Georgetown University professor Robert Drinan inaugurating the series.

1990: Dean Carbo and I teach the first Information Ethics class — the first course in Information Ethics ever offered in a U.S. Library School. The class, with fifteen students, was taught in the fall (September–December) semester.

1991–1995: The class grows in popularity; as our students (library science, information science and telecommunications) are joined by students from other disciplines (law, medicine, humanities and fine arts) and local universities. The course is now offered twice a year: during the fall (September–December) and summer (May to August) semesters.

1996: An Information Ethics fund is established to support an Information Ethics Fellow. The Fellow — Barbara Rockenbach was the first selected — is chosen by three of our faculty and two information specialists (external to the School). The Fellow is provided with full tuition and a $5, 000 stipend.

1997: Our Information Ethics Web site is set-up.

1998–2001: The class and the Dean's Forum enjoy steady growth and attract wide interest. At the School's 100th Anniversary an editorial in the *Pittsburgh Post-Gazette* states: "Toni Carbo ... founded the Information Ethics program ... that's the kind of progressive thinking that puts the School on the frontiers of Information Science."[14]

Behind all of this — the dates and facts — is, of course, our attempt to respond to a sad reality; the then *and now* persistent and appallingly scant amount and serious attention given by information professionals to information ethics.

To date, only three or four of the many U.S. Library and Information Science programs dedicate an entire course to Information Ethics. Our school, the first, was quickly joined by Kent State and Simmons, and the vision-encouragement-efforts and accomplishments of Alfino, Capurro, Froelich, Hauptman, Mendina, Piece, Smith and Woodsworth are well known. But, by and large, information ethics is not a high priority in our schools and profession.

Yes! Other schools claim to include information ethics in all courses — a fact, which I very much doubt. And, Yes! both national and local professional organizations do do information ethics things — and in some cases (e.g., The New York Library Association and the Long Island, New York, LILRC, and this symposium especially) do it well, indeed! But, in both cases and, not infrequently the presentation is so poor that cynicism and/or paralysis are the resultants. An example from each area will make my point.

In the academy: A class is presented with a moral quandary. Here, let me pause to make the fundamental and essential distinction between morals and ethics. Simply put; morals/morality is what we do. Ethics is reflection on what we do.

So, a class is presented with a moral dilemma. Let's say: two employees are frequently late for work. One, because she/he is habitually tardy. The other, because he/she is a single parent whose responsibilities often cause lateness. *Question/Dilemma*: are both to be penalized for tardiness? The teacher solicits opinions, questions each student: yes? no? And the *majority opinion* is often the basis for the resolution of the question/dilemma. Forgetting — and democracy is at the heart of the matter — that majority may (but does not necessarily) carry with it correctness. The majority may, in fact, be wrong — and in Plato's opinion, often is wrong.

In national and local professional organizations: Look at the sorry state of the *ALA Code of Ethics* and the *Library Bill of Rights*. A profession that is thousands of years old ought to be able to do better than that.[15] Compare the *ALA Code of Ethics* with the *Code of Professional Conduct* (British Library Association) and you will be amazed.

In the face of these realities— the Question/Dilemma example is given from firsthand knowledge and the codes of ethics are there for you to read — I have a reaction, conviction and a challenge. *Reaction*: on what basis does the student form/proffer his/her opinion? On what basis does the ALA formulate its *Code of Ethics* and *Library Bill of Rights*? *Conviction*: unless the teacher, student and information professional has been educated in the philosophical foundations of ethics (as applied to Information Ethics) then all efforts towards the resolution of a moral question/dilemma either miss the mark or get there by happenstance. *Challenge*: because ethical reflection is our heritage ... because as Martin Buber said "all real education is education of character" ... then ethical reflection is the sine qua non of an examined life and the non-negotiable ingredient in preparation for and activity in the information profession. Why? Because if you accept, as I do, the following description/definition of any profession (our included) ... then it is clear that, as I have said, ethical reflection is the sine qua non of an examined life and the non-negotiable ingredient in preparation for and activity in the information profession. Listen to the description/definition:

> A profession is a calling requiring specialized information and knowledge, long and intensive preparation (including instruction in skills and methods), as well as scientific, historical and scholarly principles underlying those skills and methods, maintaining by force of organization or concerted opinion high standards of achievement and conduct, committing its members to continued study and a kind of work which has for its prime purpose the rendering of a public service.

In all professions— the information professions *included*— education in general and applied ethics is an absolute.

Essential Components: Let me now set out for you what I believe are essential components— both in and outside the classroom —for the instruction and education which Cardinal Newman called the "true enlargement of mind and heart."

I stress: *in and outside the classroom*— because instruction and education in ethics cannot be something required only of our profession's newest members. If you haven't studied information ethics— you must! It will enlarge your mind and heart. And without it you can *never* hope to become (or be) a good teacher, manager, or leader.

So, all that I say concerning the classroom can be a map for *personal-ongoing-instruction-education* in information ethics.

1. *The Teacher:* The question is not: can ethics be taught? Of course it can! Rather, the question is: who can teach ethics? And here my answer is simple: anyone who "loves the questions" as Rilke put it ... anyone who *listens* as the Bible says ... anyone who is on the journey as Dag Hammarskjöld explained ... and anyone who sees wisdom and thinks of the baobab tree. Listen to the texts:

> *Rilke*:
>
> I would like to beg to ... as well as I can, to have patience with everything unresolved in your heart and to try *to love the questions themselves* as if they were locked rooms or books written in a very foreign language. Don't search for the answers, which could not be given to you now, because you would not be able to live them. And the point is, to live everything.
>
> *Live the questions now*. Perhaps then, someday far in the future, you will gradually, without even noticing it, *live your way into the answer.*[16]
>
> *Bible*:
>
> Shema', Israel ... Hear/Listen
>
> *Dag Hammarskjöld:*
>
> The longest journey
> Is the journey inwards.[17]
>
> *Baobab Tree*:
>
> In Swahili there is an ancient proverb equating wisdom with the enormous baobab tree: one person cannot get his/her arms around all of it.

Plato worried, as must we all, about teachers who are mere hucksters.[18] But, he was firmly convinced that those who seek wisdom (philosophy) could find some of it and pass it on to others.

2. *The Student:* In order to effectively teach ethics (in general) and information ethics (in particular) the teacher must quickly and at the very outset deal with three vital issues: self, religion, and others.

Self: The common tendency is to immediately apply ethical reflection to the actions of others. The teacher must, in my opinion, make the student aware that ethical reflection and moral action must be, initially and fundamentally, an intensely personal concern-quest-and-goal. I must engage in ethical reflection and moral action. I ... here ... before others.

Religion: Not uncommonly religion and ethics are confused. The same is true of religion and moral actions. Here, too, the teacher must immediately get to work. One can be highly ethical and not religious. One can be very religious and not ethical.

In both areas—the self and religion—I have found the writings of Stephen Carter and the Dalai Lama to be very useful. And before anything else I require my students to read-reflect-and-write on Carter's *Integrity* and the Dalai Lama's *Ethics for the New Millennium.*[19]

Now, Carter's book—while excellent in so many ways—hints that in order to really be ethical and moral one needs to be religious. So, I require the students to read the Dalai Lama (a religious figure) who appeals "for an approach to ethics based on universal rather than religious principles."[20]

Finally, this is also the place where I introduce the student to the enormously valuable contributions of Hans Küng.[21]

Others: While ethical reflection is about myself — it implies, of course, the presence of and relationship with others (God, persons, animals, nature and institutions). In class, and this in this paper, I briefly touch on God, animals and nature. But, I deal — in great length and depth — on the other person and on that *basic, essential, fundamental moral experience* without which real ethical reflection and moral action is impossible.

That experience is, and it is often true, best described by the poet rather than the philosopher. And few have done so as well, and beautifully, as the beloved poet W.H. Auden. In his essay "The Protestant Mystics" — an introduction to Anne Freemantle's, *The Protestant Mystics.*[22] Auden described what he experienced as the Downs School in June 1933:

> ... For the first time in my life I knew exactly ... what it means to love one's neighbor as oneself.... My personal feelings towards them were unchanged — they were colleagues, not intimate friends — but I felt their existence as themselves to be of infinite value and rejoiced in it. I recalled with shame the many occasions on which I had been spiteful, snobbish, selfish, but the immediate joy was greater then the shame, for I knew that, so long as I was possessed by this spirit, it would be literally impossible for me deliberately to injure another human being.... The memory of that experience has not prevented me from making use of others, grossly and often, but it has made it much more difficult for me to deceive myself about what I was up to when I do.

Still, the danger in Auden's text rests in the fact that the reader might understand that *basic, essential, fundamental moral experience* to be a *mystical experience* ... limited to the few. But, the *basic, essential, fundamental moral experience* is — with instruction and education — available to all.

When I learn to see the other person as the *same as me (=basic, essential, fundamental experience)* ... when I understand that because the other is the *same as me*, then she/he has the *same rights* I claim for myself *(=basic, essential, fundamental experience plus justice)* ... *then and only then* am I ready/able to engage in ethical reflection and moral action.

And basic to each area — self, religion, and others — it is essential and vital that the student be exposed to the *Universal Declaration of Human Rights*, the writings of Dr. Martin Luther King and Nelson Mandela.

The Universal Declaration of Human Rights — adopted and proclaimed by the General Assembly in 1948 — is so very important ... and yet it is largely unknown. Both teacher and student ought to have a copy of the text. Both student and teacher need to read, reflect and act on its thirty articles.[23]

3. *Modus Procedendi*: A careful, step-by-step reading of six basic sources gives the student a firm foundation in ethics (in general) and information ethics (in particular). I refer, of course, to Alfino and Pierce's magnificent text: *Information Ethics for Librarians*; supplemented by Stichler and Haupman's *Ethics Information and Technology Readings*; Mason and Culnan's *Ethics of Information Management*; Baldwin's *The Academic Librarian's Human Resources Handbook*; plus articles in the *Journal of Information Ethics* and the journal of *Ethics and Information Technology.*

But, these texts—in my opinion—require an essential substructure and launching ... especially as provided by Martha Nussbaum and Thomas Berry. A word on each.

4. *Modus Cogitandi et Modus Agendi*: In the "Introduction" to her tremendous study; *The Therapy of Desire—Theory and Practice in Hellenistic Ethics*, Dr. Nussbaum specifies that:

> The Hellenistic philosophical schools ... all conceived of philosophy as a way of addressing the most painful problems of human life. They saw the philosopher as a compassionate physician whose arts could heal many pervasive types of human suffering. They practiced philosophy not as a detached intellectual technique ... but as an immersed and worldly art of grappling with human misery. They focused their attention, in consequence, on issues of daily and urgent human significance ... issues that are sometimes avoided as embarrassingly messy and personal....

She stresses that:

The central motivation for philosophizing is in the urgency of human suffering, and the goal of philosophy is human flourishing or *eudaimonia*.

That:

Philosophy is above all the art of human life; and engagement in it that is not properly anchored to the business of living well is empty and vain

That:

Philosophy is an act that secures the flourishing (*eudaimon*) life by arguments and reasoning

And that:

Philosophical reflection and teaching on ethical and philosophical topics have a practical goal.[24]

Now, for us—in the Information Profession—ethical reflection must lead, among other things ... but also, especially ... to the practical action of decision making. And so, I spend a lot time teaching my students about both "the hidden traps of decision making" and how to make ethical decisions.[25]

And, then, there is the larger picture and the greater questions: *the great work facing us today*. How do we apply ethical reflection and moral action to that great work and greater questions? Do we even know that work and the questions?[26] Or do we simply go round-and-round-and-round with filtering and censorship and the printed book versus the e-book—boring ourselves and our students, engendering cynicism, pessimism and that paralysis which is convinced that information ethics has no practical value or use?

To help my students ask the bigger questions ... and to prepare them for the great work of our professions ... I introduce them into the thinking and writing of Thomas Berry—especially his book: *The Great Work—Our Way Into the Furture*.[27] Thomas Berry is a cultural historian.[28] He likes to call himself a "geologian"—an adjective flowing from his work as a theologian, philosopher, biologist and ecologist.

For Berry our present and new understanding of humanity (within the larger community of life) highlights the need (great work) for a comprehensive reform of our culture and institutions. And, I try to show the students where and how the information professional fits into this great work.[29]

Conclusion

So there you have it: *Ma Position Intellectuelle* on and about the privilege that has been mine, these last eleven years—teaching information ethics.

I have not recorded which effects my efforts have had on my students. That is for them to say.

What I have done is to share with you my convictions and experience; in and with the hope—as I stated at the very start of this paper—that "there is some truth here worth the telling; or, if not that, tinder at least to catch the sparks of your fire."[30]

Notes

1. Teilhard de Chardin, Pierre. *Oeuvres 13: La Coeur de la Matiere*. Paris: Seuil, 1976. pp. 173–174.

2. Bridges, Robert, ed. *Poems of Gerard Manley Hopkins*. London: Oxford University Press, 1930. p. 40: "Duns Scotus's Oxford."

3. Knox, Ronald. *Enthusiasum*. Oxford: Clarendon Press, 1950. p. vi.

4. Rockenbach, Barbara. "Information Ethics at the University of Pittsburgh." *Journal of Information Ethics* (Fall 1998): 13–18.

5. Carbo, Toni, and Stephen Almagno. "Information Ethics: The Duty Privilege and Challenge of Educating Information Professionals." *Library Trends* (Winter 2001): 510–518.

6. I strongly urge my students to a careful reading and a close study of the writings of Harvard's Samuel P. Huntington. "Le Nouveau Breviaire American" in *Lire* (October 2001): 26–27. And, were I again teaching ethics, I would require an equally careful reading and close study of Umberto Eco's, *Cinque Scritti Morali*, English translation: *Five Moral Pieces*...if only to have them exposed to Eco's conviction that tolerance is the ultimate value in today's world.

7. Muller, Robert. *New Genesis*. New York: Image Books, 1984.

8. Kung, Hans. *Global Responsibility. In Search of a New World Ethic*. London: SCM Press, 1991.

9. Boynton, Robert. "Who needs Philosophy?" in *The New York Times Magazine* (Nov. 21 1999): 67–69. And, McLemme, Scott. "What Makes Martha Nussbaum Run?" *The Chronicle of Higher Education* v 48 no 6 (Oct 5 2001): A14–A16.

10. Eisenstein, Elizabeth. *The Printing Press as an agent of change*. Cambridge: Cambridge University Press, 1979.

11. Cox, Richard, "Taking Sides on the Future of the Book," *American Libraries* (February 1997): 52–55.

12. Eliot, T.S. Choruses from "The Rock."

13. Muller, Robert. *New Genesis*. p. 9.

14. "Information Please—Pitt's School Has a Record Worth Celebrating," *Pittsburgh Post-Gazette*. (June 6, 2001); A-14.

15. Stichler, Richard N., and Hauptman, Robert. *Ethics Information and technology Readings*. Jefferson, N.C.: McFarland. 1998. pp. 307–308.

16. Rike, Rainer M. *Letters to a Young Poet*. New York: Norton, 1934. pp. 33–34.

17. Hammarskjöld, Dag. *Markings*. London: Faber, 1964. p. 34.

18. Protagoras. 313c–314b.

19. Carter, Stephen. *Integrity*. New York: Basic Books, 1996. And Dalai Lama. *Ethics for the New Millennium*. New York: Riverhead Books, 1999.

20. Dalai Lama. *Ethics for the New Millennium*. New York: Riverhead Books, 1999. p. xiii.

21. Haring, Hermann. *Hans Kung—Breaking Through—The Work and Legacy*. New York: Continuum, 1998. pp. 326–361, "A Global Ethic and Responsibility for Humankind."

22. Auden, W.H. *Forewords and Afterwords*. New York: Vintage International, 1989. pp. 49–78: "The Protestant Mystics."

23. Important resources: *Les Nations Unies et les droits de l'homme: 1945–1995*.

New York: Department de l'information Nations Unies, 1995 and *Basic Human Rights Instruments.* Geneva 1998.

24. Nussbaum, Martha. *The Therapy of Desire.* Princeton, New Jersey: Princeton University Press, 1994. pp. 3, 15, & 48.

25. Hammond, Keeney and Raiffa. "The Hidden Traps in Decision Making," *Harvard Business Review.* (Sept.–Oct. 1998): 190.

26. See especially: Paré, Michele and Desbarts, Peter. *Liberté d'expression et nouvelles technologies.* Paris: DEQ, 1998.

27. New York, Bell Tower 1999 and Greene, Herman F. *Understanding Thomas Berry's Great Work.* Teilhard Studies Number 41. (Autumn 2000).

28. His most recent book: *The Great Work,* follows his 1998 book, *The Dream of the Earth* and his 1992 book which he co-authored with Brian Swimme, *The Universe Story: From the Primordial Flaring to the Ecozoic Era.*

29. Were I teaching this course in the 2002 spring and fall terms, I would have my students read David Toolan's *At Home in the Cosmos.* In this new and important book — published by Orbis this year — Fr. Toolan, editor of *America* magazine, develops and expands Thomas Berry's insights.

30. Knox, *Enthusiasm.* vi.

4

My Response to *Ma Position Intellectuelle*

Nancy Zimmerman

I have a hero. I don't mean a hero in the way most often used, to refer to a celebrity, an idol, or a caped crusader of some sort, but rather my hero is just a man, albeit a charismatic one, who goes about his business of living, working, and most of all teaching. My hero is a man who ministers to his students, not through the religion his collar represents, but by inspiring his students to "love the questions." My hero is a man that has been an important figure in my life and although they don't know it, the life of my students. My hero is Stephen Almagno, who has shared with us his "Position Intellectuelle" of teaching Information Ethics (above).

When Stephen asked me what I thought of his paper, I told him I wished he had shared more of his personal "story" because not only does he have a gift for storytelling as any of his students will avouch — but because his IS a story loaded with "tinder to catch the sparks of our fire." Today, I am, like Stephen, a professor in a college of library and information science. Although my favorite course to teach is Introduction to the Information Professions— and I'll share my reasons for that a little later — my recognized areas of expertise are school library media and resources and services for children, including storytelling. The art of telling stories is interactive and common to every world culture. A story told is shaped by the skills of the teller and the participation of the listeners. Just as the role of the storyteller and listener are inextricably linked, so is my story linked with that of my hero. Stephen says he can't record the effect of his efforts on his students— that it is for us to say — so as a student who first entered his classroom nearly 30 years ago, I gratefully accept this invitation to relate my piece of his story and to give testimony to his heroic efforts. I ask you to participate in our story.

In the classic mythical story structure, the story begins with a "call to adventure"—the point in a person's life when something important happens to send the person in a new direction. For me, that point was entering the then Graduate School of Library and Information Science at Pitt and attending the school's sherry party on the building's terrace that was their customary welcoming for new students. I, like many before and since, fell into library school, but that lucky serendipitous occurrence changed my life's direction. It was at that party that I was introduced to Stephen, then called Romano—a young visiting instructor. And so our story begins: "Once upon a time, a young graduate student met her hero, a gentle scholarly instructor...."

I don't remember exactly the content of that first party conversation, just that we identified a common Italian heritage and love of wine, and that our conversation was immediately easy and comfortable. Several days and conversations later, even though I was in the school media track which Stephen didn't teach, it somehow became agreed that whenever I could I would sit in and unofficially audit Stephen's classes—mostly to explore options of the library world beyond school media—but I learned much more than just about library opportunities. After all these years, I don't remember much of the content of those audited classes either, but what I do remember is the passion, the enthusiasm in my hero's voice as he shared a world of ideas new to us and forced us to think and, dare I say, reflect. He challenged us and endeared himself to us. I can't speak for all his students, but this one worked very hard to win his approval—never wanted to disappoint him, never wanted to let his confidence in us be misplaced. Now, looking back, I realize just how young my hero himself was then and how remarkable he was to be able to motivate us that way.

This young hero was a softer, gentler version of today's. He was himself accepting the "call to adventure," beginning his own journey as teacher. He had not yet entered, or if he had, it wasn't apparent to us, his students, what we call in classic storytelling, the "road of trials"—performing those tasks or ordeals that a person must undergo. Teaching was not task or ordeal to him. To us, his students, it was obvious that teaching brought him joy, that WE brought him joy. He made himself available to us in and out of class. He sought, maybe needed, our affirmation. His passion was contagious. He kindled the sparks for us.

Sometimes in the classic story structure there is a "refusal of the call," where the person called refuses to go because they might not feel strong enough or smart enough. In that once upon time, this is often how I felt. In the face of all I was being called to do in this profession and, as a 21-year-old, in life, I often felt inadequate. It was the early '70s and expectations were high that we could make a difference, make the world better, freer. It is here that Stephen assumed the story role of the helper—the guide or magical being who appears to provide aid. My hero never failed to help me or support me, to tell me that I had, as he puts it, "the right stuff," no matter whether the advice and guidance I needed was personal or professional. His unwavering confidence and belief helped me to believe in myself and to accept the calls coming my way, made me aware of my responsibilities, challenged me to meet them, and modeled for me the meaning of "teacher."

As time passes, Stephen continues to be the hero of my story. He introduced me to the Teilhardian world and encouraged me to seek meaning and happiness in my life. In fact, he gave me these two books, *The Meaning of Teilhard de Chardin* and *On Happiness*,[1] back then, 1974 — and you'll note he is the bibliographer of the first and that his distinctive blue signature notation was included even then — that sent me searching for more to use to inform my life choices. Over the years he has introduced me to the works of Muller, Nussbaum, and Küng to name a few. He has shared happy and not so happy moments—from officiating at my wedding, to consoling me after my Mom's death, to celebrating with me the accomplishments of my children who think of him as their "Godfather" in all the meanings of that word, to agreeing to travel and be a speaker for me at professional association meetings when he is reluctant to do both — but it is his uncompromising support of me and the choices I've made that has meant everything. Whenever I'm in "the belly of the whale," the point in any story where the adventurer is between two worlds or directions and is really frightened of the challenges to come, my hero is there for me, as I suspect he is for many of his former students. But what is truly amazing about my hero is that he not only introduces his students to new ideas and demands that they think critically, but he empowers them to make better decisions and choices, enables them to grow both personally and professionally. He models for them the commitment to lifelong learning. He allows them to progress from a mentoring student-teacher relationship to one of colleague and friend. Now some of my moments of greatest joy are when I know he respects me for the person I've become and what I've accomplished — respects me enough to seek out my opinion and thoughts— even though we sometimes fiercely disagree. In return, he has shared his joys with me. One of those times was when the Information Ethics fund and fellowship became reality. How I wish you all could have heard his voice that day!

Which brings me to our later chapters. Several summers ago I was able to teach a course at Pitt. While it felt strange to return as teacher to the place where I was once student, it was an opportunity to experience again Stephen's power teaching and audit his class— this time the Information Ethics course. Just as I am much changed from that young woman who first sat in his classroom, so is Stephen. The smooth, easy delivery and the charisma are still there. The pipe is ever-present and he still brings his coffee to class in a dirty stein that he insists enhances the flavor. He still relishes a good intellectual sparring match with a bright student, and years of continued study have strengthened his power to dazzle. But there is a difference in his classroom demeanor. Today, when he enters the classroom he commands attention by his mere physical presence. He exudes a confidence born of experience and survival. He is much less tolerant of lazy scholarship and students without the "right stuff." There is an acute quality to his teaching. Gentler has been replaced by tougher. Not meaner, not less a teacher. Just different, and definitely still effective. Perhaps this change is born of his growing disenchantment with the academy and/or perhaps from his conviction of the urgency and necessity for professional education in information ethics.

For me, this return was my " meeting of the Goddess." The time in the story when after surviving the trials, the adventurer may experience a great romantic love or may have her heart filled with the love of true friends from which she gains strength to continue. She is filled with a wonderful sense of well-being. I spent that summer on the other side of the desk basking in the warmth of Stephen's friendship and engaged in reflective practice. I participated in the Information Ethics course not only as learner, but also as an observer of the other learners. I watched their faces as the light bulbs illuminated and dimmed pondering the art and the science. I watched as they probed and sought meaning. I watched as Stephen inspired and awed them. I watched as they grew to "love the questions." And as I watched, a new plan for the course I love to teach, Introduction to the Information Professions, began to take shape. After so many years of teaching, my summer of peace and reflection gave me the strength to completely change my approach.

While Stephen is adamant that the Information Ethics course not be required because students need to have a certain openness for moral education and ethical reflection (and I agree to a point), I still think it is our responsibility as library educators to introduce our students to what they don't know they need to know. In Stephen's words, "Ethical reflection, where the information-knowledge-wisdom continuum is concerned, is no longer a luxury, but a necessity."[2] The course has been designed to make them aware, lead them to that openness. The course begins by exploring what it means to be a professional beginning with the definition Stephen just quoted in his paper. Supplemented by outside readings and situations clipped from the news, Michael Gorman's book, *Our Enduring Values: Librarianship for the 21st Century*,[3] is the text. It not only covers the enduring values of the professions, but it contains a good deal of author bias, which is discussed as an entry to examining multiple sides of a dilemma. The student conducts a self assessment using instruments like the Myers-Briggs personality indicators, by reading Daniel Goleman's book, *Emotional Intelligence*,[4] by reviewing the skills and competencies demanded in job announcements, and by examining their own beliefs and values. How to read research articles and gather data and information from the literature is included. A study of the history of the profession is made through "bio bits," brief examinations of the people of the profession, alive and dead, and their situations, circumstances, contributions, and significance. These "bits" provide tie-in to the issues, beliefs, and values of the profession and to lessons learned. They also infuse the class with a sense of story and of the great work in this profession that has "gone before." The usual discussion of library and information agencies by type and function is covered, including the roles and responsibilities within a democratic society. Discussions of justice, equity, and civil and human rights lead to the recognition of what Stephen describes as the "fundamental moral experience" and the need for a method for the discernment of moral values. Using, with Stephen's permission, his wheel model, they begin an investigation of an ethical dilemma/issue within the profession, researching and writing a paper, presenting multiple perspectives, and proposing an informed solution/action. This is the third semester that I have taught the course with this approach, carefully watching, as I did Stephen's students that summer, for the bulbs to glow and dim. While this is not a course in information ethics (although I hope someday to have enough understanding and knowledge to develop one for our college), I am convinced that this is an effective way to inaugurate them into the information professions, to give my students a "nibble from the whole loaf." From this approach, they gain insight into the tough complex questions. They must confront their own biases and weaknesses, and acknowledge their strengths, beliefs, and values, and that ethics is about THEM. It requires them to think. It requires them to make connections. It requires them to reflect. It requires them to examine whether they are made of the "right stuff" and, hopefully, they come to understand that their degree is the entry, not the terminal, degree. And I think they will be better human beings and better librarians for it, which is why I said right at the beginning of this story, that Stephen is their hero, too. For without him and his wonderful Information Ethics course, this Intro course wouldn't be nearly as dynamic. Without his incredible support, their professor would not have reached the "ultimate boon," reached what she set out on her adventure to get, wouldn't be the teacher she is. Hopefully, I now kindle the sparks, pass something on to them as Stephen passed it on to me.

A new chapter begins. Stephen, sets out on another adventure—this time to Rome, to a wonderful new position. My wish for him is that he become, as in the classic story structure, the "master of two worlds," comfortable with the old and embracing the new. I also wish for him that the additions to his story and ours be happy, productive ones. Today, I am pleased that I can speak to his efforts, that I can tell him publicly that he is my hero, and say how grateful I am that our stories are linked. I also thank you for your patience with the skills of this teller and for your participation in his story, a "truth worth the telling."

Notes

1. Knight, Alice Vallé. *The Meaning of Teilhard de Chardin: A Primer*. Old Greenwich: Devin-Adair, 1974. Teilhard de Chardin, Pierre. *On Happiness*. Translated by René Hague. London: Collins, 1973.

2. Rockenbach, Barbara. "Information Ethics at the University of Pittsburgh." *Journal of Information Ethics* 7 (Fall, 1998): 16.

3. Gorman, Michael. *Our Enduring Values: Librarianship in the 21st Century*. Chicago: American Library Association, 2000.

4. Goleman, Daniel. *Emotional Intelligence*. New York: Bantam, 1995.

5

Ma Position Intellectuelle: A Discourse-Specific Response

Jeffrey T. Huber

My former professor, Stephen Almagno acknowledged that the practical application of information ethics has been questioned. Some doubt the value of ethical reflection and its relevance to the information professions. With that in mind, I frame my response within the confines of a particular discourse — the discourse of homosexuality.

Background

Ideology framing homosexuality has matured over time. As is true with other bodies of knowledge, the content of thought has changed. And as the ideas, notions, and perceptions founding the body of knowledge have grown, categorical structures have adjusted. Much of this metamorphosis is a direct result of society, since "...the dominant modes of thought are supplanted by new categories when the social basis of the group, of which these thoughtforms are characteristic, disintegrates or is transformed under the impact of social change."[1]

For modern man, societal delineation of homosexuality, like that of madness, was born out of the construction of deviance. And like madness, sexuality has been historically juxtaposed, in part, with the frenzies of passion. Deviance may be thought of in terms of any act or behavior that is perceived as violating expectations or departing from the norm. These expectations are socially defined, subject to individual perspective, and may evolve over time. Deviant behaviors— those which are believed to yield consequences that are negative and harmful — are generally perceived to flow from immoral practices. Equating the departure from "normative" behavior with immoral practices promotes the notion of a moral economy, an economy in which punishment is a justifiable repercussion stemming from violation of the rules of morality. The foundation for much of what is considered normative was laid during the Age of Reason and refined during the Victorian era, both historical periods when man sought to inflict order upon his world and distance himself from the uncivilized. At times such as these when construction and control were, and still are, central to maintaining social hierarchies and structures, any condition, episode, person, or group opposing societal authority may trigger moral panics. More, that which is perceived as deviant often elicits moral panics, since the act or behavior threatens socially defined values and interests.

Madness in its varied forms— melancholia, hypochondria, mania — often has been displayed with passion and determination not associated with what society has deemed "reasonable" human behavior.[2] Rather, this "unreasonable" behavior has been suggested to be more akin to animal in nature, for "reason" was decreed synonymous with human intelligence, logical thought, and cultural development. In much the same way that homosexuality has been defined as being diametrically opposed to societal norms, the animality of madness— defying civilized society's moral and behavioral code as defined by the body politic — yielded an inherent immorality of the unreasonable. "Madness threatens modern man ... with that return to the bleak world of beasts and things, to their fettered freedom."[2] To seventeenth and eighteenth century man, madness revealed a freedom or liberty festering in the monstrous forms of animality. The body politic demanded that this "threat" be medicalized and confined, and further ensured this control with the rigorous organization of an impenetrable armature in the form of a discourse. This discourse was applied to banish madness to a neutral world — that of the asylum — and eliminate it from the social order by subjecting it to confinement, thus deeming those affected as immoral. Madness, however, was not the only candidate to inhabit confinement or be exposed to societal regulation. In constructing deviance — and in establishing religious, legal, and medical authorities— the body politic positioned all behaviors not conforming to the accepted norm within its jurisdiction to administer, govern, constrain, punish, and control. As with madness, it is not surprising that homosexuality was deemed a pathology— medicalized, in fact, in a similar vein and eventually classed a psychiatric disorder. Similarities in the construction of madness and homosexuality are not by chance.

Homosexuality has been constructed in much of the world as a negative label, stigmatized largely because of perceived deviation from a broader societal norm. Stigmatization of this sexual orientation is not surprising, however, given the "threat" it poses to accepted social order. In fact, much of the construct circumscribing homosexuality is entirely dependent upon stigma. Stigma may be thought of as a language of relationships, resulting in the construction and application of deeply discrediting attributes.[3] Stigma represents a deviation from some socially-constructed ideal or expectation, such as adhering to an accepted sexual orientation or practice.[4] However, deviation itself is not intrinsically immoral or pathological; rather, it is inferred from a culturally-defined meaning. To assure a purely negative connotation and the application of stigma, the construction of homosexuality has been modeled around issues involving morality and disease. The social construct within which stigma exists allows stigmatized attributes to be discredited and tainted, resulting in prejudice and discrimination. The conception of deviance and application of stigma where homosexuality is concerned have resulted in discrimination against, and repression of, individuals seeking to engage in same-sex unions. Defining homosexuality as a pathology allowed the establishment to carry stigma to its extreme. And in its extreme, stigmatization of "disease" withholds legitimate privileges afforded non-stigmatized maladies and imposes special obligations on those affected, thus resembling crime more than illness.[5] The body politic sought to ensure the regulation — if not elimination — of homosexuality by placing it well within the administrative scope of the medical, legal, and religious establishments. In addition, moral panics and crusades relative to the practitioners of homosexuality historically have attempted to foster the perception of this population's being devoured by demonic, deviant behavior. For homosexuality, the social construct within which this sexual orientation exists is built largely upon politics of the body and the confines of conformity.

Politics of the Body and the Body Politic

For issues involving sexuality and homosexual sexual orientation, the strife between bio-politics and bio-power cannot be more obvious, with regulation of individual sexual practices perhaps being the best illustration. Societal normalization of sexuality is an instrument of power.[6] By defining what is normal, the body politic creates a tool that can be applied to control individual sexual behavior. Discourse binds physical actions by rendering normative behavior. Social discourse is used and applied to define the rules of sexuality. The various standards, models, exclusions, limitations, and perversions of sexuality are derived from a particular discursive practice, based not on scientific discourse but in a system of values and prohibitions.[7] Organized religion's stance on the practice of homosexuality, the continued existence and enforcement of sodomy laws, and the lack of inclusion of homosexuality as a legitimate sexual orientation in sex education materials are only three examples out of many that are illustrative of the establishment's regulating or administering sexual practices.

Social policy and processes have been, and continue to be, used to shape the politics of the body, both individual and collective. In the United States, this socially-constructed platform is built largely upon individual perceptions and societal perspectives. Where homosexuality is concerned, much of this construction has been forged within the medical establishment and reinforced within mainstream society.

Homosexuality as Medical and Mental Illness

Homosexuality was diagnosed by the body politic as a boil festering deep within the flesh of society, a boil that demanded it be lanced, drained, cured. In essence, the body politic defined homosexuality as a disease in an attempt to control it. "It is beliefs that homosexuality is evil, sick, or undesirable — and the corresponding efforts to punish, cure, or prevent it — that make homosexuality deviant."[8] By defining homosexuality in terms of illness or disease, the body politic positioned "deviant" sexual orientation so that it fell within the realm of its juridical arms— those of the religious, legal, and medical establishments. Thus, by declaring the practice of homosexuality to be sinful, enacting laws that forbade the physical practice of same sex intercourse and unions, and medicalizing the pathological, the body politic established homosexuality as something that could be administered, governed, managed, and ruled for the good of society as well as in the interest of public health. Shock, aversion, and conversion therapies became common weapons in the therapeutic arsenal dredged up by the medical establishment, supported by religious rhetoric and legal sanctions, to lay siege on homosexuality and rid society of its existence. In addition to efforts on the part of the medical, religious, and legal establishments, individual conservatives have fought fervently to fuel the fires of homophobia. Operating on a wide range of fronts, these moral entrepreneurs are essential to creating societal rules and enforcing "normative" social order. Moreover, they are indispensable to the creation and maintenance of moral panics. And "moral entrepreneurs have toiled tirelessly in attempting to persuade society that homosexuality is abnormal and immoral."[9]

Late on the night of June 27, 1969, frustration felt by the gay community at the hatred, prejudice, harassment, and regulation directed toward it by mainstream society culminated in rioting at the Stonewall Inn, a gay bar located in the Greenwich Village section of New York City. Although the rioting was over by 3:35 AM the morning of June 28, thousands of people crowded the Village streets by nightfall, with police being unable to prevent the gathering. "Gay Power" was chanted openly and loudly. The Stonewall riots marked the birth of the gay liberation movement, and June 28 became Gay Pride Day. "Stonewall fostered optimism, discovery of self, disdain for received prejudice, and solidarity between oppressed people, social underdogs, and sexual outcasts."[10] The slogan "love is a many-gendered thing" graced banners carried by men confronting conformity and proclaiming their gay heritage. Stonewall yielded many outcries from the community regarding the treatment of gays, including open criticism of pathologizing same sex sexual orientation. "The medicalization of homosexuality that had occurred in the late nineteenth century became a target, in particular the sickness theories of the neo–Freudians."[11] By the time of the Stonewall Riots, some members of the scientific community and medical establishment were already sympathetic to the demedicalization of homosexuality. Stonewall helped carry the movement forward by giving voice to a community that, until that time, had been essentially silent. Nevertheless, deconstructing the medicalization of homosexuality was not achieved overnight or without heated debate.

In time, however, the idea of equating behavior that is perceived as being culturally deviant with evidence of mental disorder began to be questioned by the scientific community. Laying the groundwork for this movement, earlier scientists had begun to examine homosexuality, not as a pathology, but as an alternative human behavior. A cross-cultural survey published in 1951 found evidence of homosexual activity to be considered normal and socially acceptable in some societies for certain members of the community.[12] As early as 1957, work was underway that demonstrated homosexual men possessed essentially the same level of adjustment as their heterosexual counterparts. Not only did this research suggest that "homosexuality as a clinical entity does not exist" and that "homosexuality may be a deviation in sexual pattern which is within the normal range, psychologically," the author stated quite clearly that "...what is difficult to accept (for most clinicians) is that some homosexuals *may* be very ordinary individuals, indistinguishable, except in sexual pattern, from ordinary individuals who are heterosexual. Or — and I do not know whether this would be more or less difficult to accept — that some *may* be quite superior individuals, not only devoid of pathology (unless one insists that homosexuality itself is a sign of pathology) but also functioning at a superior level."[13] This early research was later replicated and expanded to include lesbians, with results similar to those found in the 1957 work.[14–15]

The American Psychiatric Association (APA), after much debate, removed homosexuality from its listing of psychiatric disorders contained in *Diagnostic and Statistical Manual* (DSM) in 1973. In 1981, the American Medical Association (AMA) officially embraced a more progressive view of sexual orientation in a report concerning patient policy recommendations.[16] In the ninth revision of the World Health Organization's *International Classification of Diseases*, the instructions regarding the statistical coding of homosexuality stated "code homosexuality here whether or not it is considered as a mental disorder" and did not state that homosexuality should be viewed as a disease.[17] Homosexuality was completely removed from ICD's tenth revision as a reason for contact. "It was a historic step to have homosexuality changed from a medical anomaly to a psychological impairment in the early part of the century, and an equally significant step to have homosexuality removed from DSM-3 and ICD-9 in the early 1970s and later 1980s."[18]

Removal from the various disease nomenclatures, particularly DSM, was not accomplished, however, without great division among the scientific community.[19] Despite the body of scientific knowledge that supports a nonpathological model of homosexuality, the roots of homophobia run deep in society's psyche. An essay published in 1972, summarizing the research questioning the existence of a biologic or psychologic basis for homosexuality and the medical establishment's position on homosexuality,[20] met with vituperation. This work advanced the premise "that unless one chooses to define homosexuality *per se* as an illness, [homosexuals] are healthy" and challenged the medical treatment of individuals engaging in, or exhibiting a tendency toward, same sex relations with the intent to alter mental state and modify behavior. These views received some support [21–23] but were diametrically opposed to the more generally accepted ones that promoted the notion of homosexuality's being a "medical disorder which has reached epidemiologic proportions."[24]

The essay generated a flurry of critical responses based, in large part, on the historically orthodox — if not scientifically supported — belief that homosexuality stems from psychosexual development and a child's relationship with the mother and father.[25–27] Much of this negative, homophobic sentiment — overtly and covertly — has been, and continues to be, used to shape societal delineation of homosexuality, despite its "official" demedicalization.

Although homosexuality was removed from DSM and ICD in the 1970s and 1980s, the ripples radiating from homosexual psychopathologic discourse have not been easily dislodged. For example, the United States Congress enacted immigration exclusion criteria in 1917, for the Immigration and Naturalization Service (INS) to enforce, based on the psychopathologic and deviant status of homosexuality.[28] The terms "homosexual," "gay," or "lesbian" did not appear in immigration law. Rather, Congress relied on medical discourse and psychological classifications supplied by the Public Health Service to refuse gay and lesbian immigrants. The INS enforced homosexual immigration exclusion until 1990 with passage of the 1990 Immigration Act. The 1990 Act repealed the ban on gay and lesbian aliens— more than a decade after the official demedicalization of homosexuality — and marked the demise of a federal policy tied to unscientific discourse perpetuating the medical model.

Discussion

However, one need look no further than the appalling torture and death of Matthew Shepherd in Wyoming or the bludgeoning death of Private First Class Barry Winchell as he slept in his barracks at Fort Campbell, Kentucky, to be assured that homophobia in the United States sometimes turns deadly. Such examples, and thousands of instances of less lethal prejudice that occur daily in workplaces, social settings, and families, make it clear "that social and mental distress [in the gay population] is rooted within the structure of society and not within the individual."[29] The U.S. military's beleaguered "Don't ask, don't tell" policy further illustrates this point.

The message of such events falls chillingly on the psyches of adolescents struggling with their own sexual identity. High-profile crimes, and the fear they engender, coupled with the mindless taunts teens received from their peers in schoolyards and neighborhoods, family rejection, and self-doubt lead a significant number of gay and lesbian teens to contemplate suicide, even if they do not actually make an attempt. At the very least, keeping the secret of a socially-stigmatized sexual identity leads to both internal homophobia and inability to express emotions, both of which result in low self-esteem and difficulty maintaining relationships far past adolescence.[30]

Likewise, high rates of alcoholism and other drug abuse, depression, and unsafe or promiscuous sexual practices may also be reflective of the kind of behavior that can result when society pronounces an entire group marginal and effects stigma ranging from social ostracism to prison to murder for openly declaring and living one's identity. Social tolerance does not equal societal acceptance. Though the closet is less ubiquitous than it once was, it still exists, and the harm done to an individual who must live a lie extends to all who are associated with him or her, magnifying the damage. Despite laws, executive orders, and an overall more tolerant stance on homosexuality in many strata of society, the prejudice that still exists leads to significant morbidity, mortality, and suffering for gay men and lesbians, their families of origin, their community, and society as a whole.

Directly affecting the gay and lesbian health care movement in the 1980s was the emergence of the AIDS pandemic and its close affinity, in the United States, with homosexuals. In the wake of its devastation, HIV has brought a visibility—for better or worse—to the gay community never before seen. With the intense media blitz initially focused on the epidemic, the gay community could not help receiving heightened attention, given the number of its members infected with HIV and stricken by AIDS. While the close association of the disease with a particular population cemented the notion of "homosexuality equals AIDS" in the minds of many, others seized the opportunity to respond.

Indeed, the gay community has not remained quiescent in the face of the HIV/AIDS epidemic. In major cities like Washington, D.C., where the Whitman-Walker Clinic has been in existence since 1973 to provide health care and supportive services to gay men and lesbians, the foundation for meeting the needs of individuals affected by HIV/AIDS was well in place. Where that foundation did not exist, community-based organizations sprang up quickly. Three of the most notable are the Gay Men's Health Crisis (GMHC) in New York in 1981, AIDS Project Los Angeles (APLA) in 1982, and the San Francisco AIDS Foundation in 1982. Significantly, these and other community-based organizations have long been in the forefront of educating the public about the prevention of HIV transmission and in providing programs for affected groups outside of the gay and lesbian community. Many of the community clinics—like the Michael Callen-Audre Lorde Community Health Center in New York, the Howard Brown Health Center in Chicago, and the Nelson-Tebedo Clinic in Dallas—provide general health care, special screenings, and supportive services to the gay and lesbian community in addition to fulfilling their HIV/AIDS mission.

Professional organizations and new journals have emerged to deconstruct the equating of homosexuality with deviant or pathological behavior. Professional organizations such as the National Gay and Lesbian Health Foundation (NGLHF), the Gay and Lesbian Medical Association (GLMA), and the Association for Gay and Lesbian Psychiatrists (AGLP) have been instrumental in this process. The movement to provide professional support has been mirrored by the emergence of information resources. The *Journal of Homosexuality* began publication in 1974, the *Journal of Gay & Lesbian Social Services* in 1994, and the *Journal of Gay, Lesbian, and Bisexual Identity* in 1996. With assistance, guidance, and perseverance, the discourse of homosexuality has been forced to evolve beyond classifying this sexual orientation as a pathology—overtly, if not covertly.

Conclusion

With the release of Healthy People 2010, the nation's prevention agenda, gay and lesbian health issues other than HIV/AIDS are openly on the table for the first time in the history of the United States. This and other proactive steps, taken both within and without the gay community, represent encouraging signs of a shift away from homophobia. However, individual attitudes are remarkably slow to change. Excerpts from Dr. Laura Schlessinger's radio program indicate that the voice of homophobia is alive and thriving.[31] Schlessinger has used her program to promote the notion that gays and lesbians are "deviants" and "mistakes" who can be cured with reparative therapy, despite scientific evidence to the contrary. And in the wake of the recent devastation inflicted on the United States by terrorist, the Reverend Jerry Falwell declared that gays and lesbians bear partial responsibility, based on their lifestyle, for the attack on the World Trade Center and the Pentagon.[32]

Perhaps, over time, the discourse of homosexuality will evolve to the point that it reflects social equality for gay men, lesbians, and their partners and families. Until that time, however, I would contend that encouraging ethical reflection affords one means to aid in countering homophobia and its repercussions.

Bibliography

1. Mannheim, Karl. 1936. *Ideology and utopia: an introduction to the sociology of knowledge.* Translated from the German by Louis Wirth and Edward Shils. New York: Harcourt Brace.

2. Foucault, Michel. 1965. *Madness and civilization: A history of insanity in the age of reason.* New York: Vintage Books.

3. Goffman, Erving. 1963. *Stigma: notes on the management of spoiled identity.* New York: J. Aronson.

4. Alonzo, Angelo, and Reynolds, Nancy. 1995. Stigma, HIV and AIDS: an exploration and elaboration of a stigma trajectory. *Social Science and Medicine* 41(3): 303–315.

5. Freidson, Eliot. 1970. *Profession of medicine: A study of the sociology of applied knowledge.* New York: Dodd, Mead.

6. Hewitt, Martin. 1991. Bio-politics and social policy: Foucault's account of welfare. In Mike Featherstone, Mike Hepworth, & Bryan S. Turner, eds., *The body: social process and cultural theory.* London: Sage Publications.

7. Foucault, Michel. 1972.*The archaeology of knowledge and the discourse on language.* Translated from the French by A.M. Sheridan Smith. New York: Pantheon Books.

8. Greenberg, David F. 1988. *The construction of homosexuality.* Chicago: University of Chicago Press.

9. Huber, Jeffrey T., and Gillaspy, Mary L. 1998. Social constructs and disease: implications for a controlled vocabulary for HIV/AIDS. *Library Trends* 47(2): 190–208.

10. Thorstad, David. 1995. Homosexuality and the American left: the impact of Stonewall. *Journal of Homosexuality* 29(4): 319–349.

11. Ibid.

12. Ford, Clellan S., and Beach, Frank A. 1951. *Patterns of Sexual Behavior.* New York: Harper. Translated from French by Richard Howard. New York: Random House.

13. Hooker, Evelyn 1957. The adjustment of the male overt homosexual. *Journal of Projective Techniques.*21:18–31.

14. Armon, Virginia. 1960. *Some personality variables in overt female homosexuality. Journal of Projective Techniques.* 24: 292–309.

15. Saghir, Marcel T., and Robins, E. 1973. *Male and female homosexuality: a comprehensive investigation.* Baltimore: Williams & Wilkins.

16. American Medical Association. 1981. *Health Care Needs of the Homosexual*

Population. Report of the Council on Scientific Affairs. (c, I-81) Chicago, Ill: American Medical Association.

17. Van Drimmelen-Krabbe, Jenny J.; Ustun, T. Bedirhan; Thompson, David H., l'Hours, Andre; Orley, John; and Sartorious, Norman. 1994. Homosexuality in the International Classification of Diseases: a clarification. *JAMA* 272(21):1660.

18. Patton, Cindy. 1990.What science knows: formations of AIDS knowledges. In Peter Aggleton, Peter Davies, and Graham Hart., eds. *AIDS: individual, cultural and policy dimensions* (1–18). London: Falmer Press.

19. Stoller, Robert J.; Marmor, Judd; Bieber, Irving; Gold, Ronald; Socarides, Charles; Green, Richard; and Spitzer, Robert L. 1973. A symposium: should homosexuality be in the APA nomenclature? *American Journal of Psychiatry* 130(11):1207–1216.

20. Green, Richard. 1972. Homosexuality as a mental illness. *International Journal of Psychiatry* 10(1):77–98.

21. Bell, Alan. 1972. Human sexuality—a response. *International Journal of Psychiatry* 10(1):99–102.

22. Hoffman, Martin. 1972. Homosexuality as a mental illness;. philosophic, empirical, and ecologic remarks. *International Journal of Psychiatry.*

23. Marmor, Judd. 1972. Homosexuality—mental illness or moral dilemma? *International Journal of Psychiatry* 10(1):114–117.

24. Socarides, Charles. 1970. Homosexuality and medicine. *JAMA* 212(7):1199–1202.

25. Hatterer, Lawrence J. 1972. Homosexuality as a mental illness: a critique. *International Journal of Psychiatry* 10(1): 103–104.

26. Karlen, Arno. 1972. A discussion of "Homosexuality as a Mental Illness." *International Journal of Psychiatry* 10(1):108–113.

27. Socarides, Charles. 1972. Homosexuality—basic concepts and psychodynamics. *International Journal of Psychiatry* 10(1):118–125.

28. Turner, William. 1995. Lesbian/gay rights and immigration policy: lobbying to end the medical model. *Journal of Policy History* 7(2):208–225.

29. Robertson, Anne E. 1998. The mental health experiences of gay men : a research study exploring gay men's health needs. *Journal of Psychiatric and Mental Health Nursing* 5:38.

30. Ibid.

31. Barrett, Jon. 2000. Disc jockey: as criticism mounts against her popular radio program and upcoming TV show, Dr. Laura discusses her opposition to gay rights. *The Advocate.* February 15:28–35.

32. Musbach, Tom. 2001. While on TV, Falwell links gays to attacks. *PlanetOut.com.* Accessed September 15, 2001. http://www.planetout.com/news/article-print.html?2001/09/14/1.0.

6

Ethical Reflections

Netiva Caftori

Ethics according to the dictionary is:

1. **study of morality's effect on conduct**: the study of moral standards and how they affect conduct. *Also called moral philosophy*

2. **code of morality**: a system of moral principles governing the appropriate conduct for an individual or group.

In *Ma Position Intellectuelle* Professor Stephen Almagno has expanded on this definition and has shared his convictions and experience teaching information ethics in the past eleven years, being a trailblazer in this venture and opening the path for others to follow. This paper is a motivational exercise that succeeds in awakening in the reader/listener the desire to learn more about ethics and philosophy and pass it on to disciples and students.

Before reading *Ma Position Intellectuelle* I thought myself pretty knowledgeable in the matter of ethics, being an ethical person, having read much in the subject, and having participated in numerous related conferences. I thought that having written a few papers and editing a newsletter dedicated to ethics in computing made me an expert on the topic. This assurance was well shaken by the wealth of material Stephen Almagno has presented us. In his paper he shows me how much more I have to read and digest before I am ready to guide novices into the subject matter. This paper has stimulated me to read and learn from the proposed readings and share them with future students. Almagno has paved the road in preparing a curriculum for me to follow in my first course of ethics

The question that Almagno poses is not "Can ethics be taught?" but "Who can teach ethics?" He finds the answer in Rilke's writings: Anyone who loves the questions, and listens can teach. The answers will come on their own.

According to Almagno, one is ready to engage in ethical reflection and moral action only when one sees the other the same as one-self.

It is no wonder then that ethics is not taught in many schools. Very few people fit the above description of possible ethics teachers.

In his paper Almagno enumerates authors who influenced his thinking and ideas. He proceeds to compare the teaching of ethics in many schools to *giving half a loaf to students.* The job is poorly done. I believe it is not such a bad idea. Half a loaf to the starved will stimulate his/her appetite. When a whole loaf is given, not much remains to be done by the student. Our new generation already is spoiled by the easier technology involved in learning and research. Let the young seek the other half of the loaf.

Among several other readings suggested, Almagno stresses the reading of the *Universal Declaration of Human Rights* of the UN, 1948, which is largely unknown, but a must-know. He laments the *death of the book*, which was caused by the birth of e-books and the like. True, our young generation reads less of the classics, but on the other hand is more involved in electronic mail and instant messages. It renders them more responsive and less reflective at the same time. If the right stimulation is there, some positive results may be seen. However if it is lacking, we may see many young people similar in their ways and thoughts. I believe our aging philosophers should go on-line and throw in the pot a few motivating thoughts that will propagate, as if by themselves, through the web of minds. The Internet may be the answer that Almagno is seeking.

Almagno recounts the history of the Information School of Ethics where he has been teaching from its inception in 1990, to today, his planned retirement. Almagno ponders the sad state of affairs where little attention is given to information ethics by information professionals. He laments the lack of schools that dedicate an entire course to ethics. He deplores the majority rule, which may be often wrong when answers are received to ethical/moral dilemmas posed to a class. He also criticizes ALA (American Library Association) code of ethics and the Library Bill of Rights but does not detail their shortcomings.

In previous presentations in this conference I talked about the role of informatics in educating the world youth in ethical practices such as non-violence. I talked about privacy that is a well-valued right in the United States, but not necessarily throughout the world. I mentioned many ethical issues professionals encounter in their daily lives such as gender differences. However, today in the aftermath of 9/11, I am left with many questions I do not know the answers to. Using Almagno's prescription for asking questions, let us also attempt a few answers:

- Shall we use "an eye for an eye" in our press to revenge for the killings of more than 3,000 people in NY, Washington, DC, and Pennsylvania?
- Shall we turn "the other cheek" and do nothing?
- Shall we try to appease all those angry at us so such acts will not be repeated, or would such behavior appear as a weakness?
- Knowing that US association with Israel may have contributed to the events of 9/11, shall the US dissociate itself from its old friend?
- Shall we give up our civil liberties to preserve our security? (Let's not forget Ben Franklin's words about those willing to give up their freedom for

the sake of security, may lose both, freedom and security.)

- Is peace ever possible? And if not shall we keep trying?

All answers to the above questions are maybe obviously NO, except the last one. Even if the last answer is a NO I believe it is in our interest to believe that peace is possible and to attempt to reach for it. We could turn our swords into plowshares if we only trusted each other. The key word is "trust." Unfortunately, trust is not *transitive* (if I trust you, and you trust him, then I can trust him.), according to Phil Zimmerman (Zimmerman 1995, 5). Also, trust is not *associative* (I may or may not trust you if I knew you trusted a certain third party) according to Ed Gerck (Gerck 1998, 2), therefore divine peace cannot be achieved. Trust has several layers. We need to learn to trust one another on all levels in order to facilitate transitivity. We need to agree to disagree and not impose our truth on others. Much work is ahead of us.

How do we create trust without becoming vulnerable? Can we afford to be vulnerable in the face of threats to our security? According to Einar Stefferud (Stefferud 2000, 4) we have passed through a new paradigm shift each decade since 1950:

- Computers;
- Inter-computer Communication;
- Networks of Computers;
- Internets of computers (Networks of Networks); and
- Application Layer Information Object Interchange (MIME).
- And now; for the New Millennium, we have Inter-User Trust Induction Across the Internet.

Would the Internet help create trust among people and thus nations? This is yet to be seen. For the moment we witness the proliferation of hate groups. Maybe we need to go from one extreme to get to the other.

I'd like to end with a quote from Vikram Singh (Singh 2001, 3),Colombo, Sri Lanka, September 12, 2001:

> The United States remains the greatest hope for the concept of mutual accommodation and tolerance. With many hiccups, we generally live together in tolerance and even celebration of diversity. We allow all people the pursuit of happiness. As the United States chooses a path after Tuesday's tragic loss, may the leaders find the wisdom to seek out justice, not vengeance, and to take any retaliatory action with care. May Americans remember to keep one hand ready for positive action if the other is striking destruction. May we confront enemies with strength and with kindness and avoid today's global patterns in which one wrong makes a wrong makes a wrong makes a wrong.
>
> May we realize the need to re-engage the world. The stakes cannot be higher.

References

Gerck, Ed (1998). Toward Real-World Models of Trust: Reliance on received Information. Available from http://www.mcg.org.br/trustdef.htm

Singh, Vikram (2001). *NY Times*, Sept. 2001

Stefferud, Einar (2000). www.neiu.edu/~ncaftori/Pardigms-sept2000.ppt

Zimmermann, Philip (1995). *The Official PGP User Guide*, The MIT Press, 1995.

Library Issues

7

An Ethos of Trust in Information Service

David Wildon Carr

Among all our cultural institutions— museums, libraries, botanical gardens, zoos, historical sites— the one most specifically charged with a responsibility for service in our culture, charged with conducting its users toward a fitting and personally crafted sense of independent inquiry and possibility, is the library. This charge is an enduring trust. Over time, this trust involves exchange, communication, confirmation, and authority; it requires strategy, an awareness of urgency, and the use of logics and sequences. At its end, a relationship for knowledge formed under this trust arrives at an artifact, a crafted or perhaps a provisional truth, grounded and confirmed in structures of knowledge. In all of these actions the dimension of trust is tacit, but no less essential to the experience of inquiry, the arrival at its constructive resolution, and the subsequent forward motion that a confident arrival allows.

Origins

♦ In 1996 or 1997, as the director of a master's-degree program in library service, I am asked to serve as a panelist for the state library association where the question is asked, "Why get an MLS?" It arises as expediency and cost argue for the use of non-professionals at the reference desk. No, I say; the issue is not economics but ethics: in the provision of information to a community, any compromise in professional response implies an insult to the public and a violation of trust. I say that everything librarians do in relation to an unknown ought to reflect a long view of knowledge and tools, an assessment of service and need, and a grounded model of professional thinking. Warming to the topic, I go on. A librarian is obligated by training and responsibility to forge connections between the present and the possible, and so is thinking *forward*, in search of resonance among nearby disciplines, likely but untried paths or tools, and ambient clues momentarily tacit in the user's pursuits. With the user's permission, the librarian is prepared to work on what lies in back of, or under, or before the unknown at hand. To do this is part of the trust.

♦ A reference librarian from somewhere in cyberspace writes to an academic listserv asking for advice. The circulation desk is supplying its own version of reference help when the reference desk is briefly unattended, as the professional librarian assists another user. The library administrator appears to be unwilling to assert the value of the professional in comparison to the (probably) shallow circulation staff member. Comments ensue online about better signage, perhaps, and some basic reference training for the staff. Wait a minute, I write, the issue is not situational, but ethical: a leader (and the circulation staff) ought to appreciate the difference in a user's life when deeper assistance is provided, and a nascent question is allowed to grow up a bit under a professional nurturer.

♦ Asked to write about ethics in museums,[1] I find a consensus of standards, including these values:

- The institution's mission drives its ethical policies and the duties of the professional.
- A fundamental altruism, attending to the common good, bars all personal gains for individuals.
- Cooperative professional practices emphasize mutual responsibility for ethical behavior: professionals consult, evaluate and review; they strive to assure fairness and consistency in practice.
- Scholarship and the free pursuit of knowledge imply integrity in the information given.
- The grounding values of the institution compose a compact with its users: living up to the public trust, acting for the public good, advocating for pluralism, attending to an entire audience, and assuring diversity in the profession itself.

Among museums, libraries, and like institutions, the codification of ethical values requires steady interpretation and attention.[2] Ethical codes imply the institution's assumption of responsibility for the experiences of its users. "Service" and "ethics" are identical. The institution's system exists in dynamic, continuous ethical balance, showing respect for the user, the user's situation, and the quality of the information given.

What follows is an information educator's perspective on the art of library helping as a form of trust, an extension of the institutional ethos. Here I strive to present a view of service that acknowledges the critical threads of trust woven into an extensive and enveloping professional fabric. The fabric *is* extensive; the ethical dimensions of information service go far beyond the provision of correct *versus* incorrect responses to reference questions. The ethical fabric will include services to a diverse community of users; development of responsive and inclusive collections; and respectful outreach to the information poor. In the library—where cooperative and altruistic relations among professionals and users define the possibilities of service—we can observe a verification of David Good's observation that "Despite its apparent fragility and our many attempts to do without it, it is clear that ... trust is remarkably robust."[3] In this essay, it is the principal indicator of professional vitality.

The Pervasive Dimension

In my frame of thought, it is fair to say that the primary dimensions of all interactions involving the exchange of information, including the critical dimensions of currency, accuracy and precision of fit, are ethical. All dimensions of information having to do with its integrity, authenticity, and the conditions of its origin, are ethical. It is especially true that the primary dimensions of individual professional transactions, the conversations where new information significantly alters the knowledge or state of being of the inquirer, are ethical. Every day, we see that even the primary dimensions of occasions when people seek information from media, from knowledge organizations, and public figures, are ethical. At this moment in our national lives, the hunger for information rises, and the salience of trust in is provision is clear.

All of these dimensions are predicated on the question of whether the given information, the human agent of inquiry, the processes and strategies modeled by the agent, and the tacit contract between the professional and the user, are worthy of trust. A library is a way of uncovering and engaging fragments of knowledge, and as in any setting where such connections are made, there is a tacit structure of testimony standing behind the evidence: a record of inquiry, experience, observation, formal research, scholarship, insight, exploration, documentation, and reflection. Regarding social trust, Trudy Govier writes, "Knowledge based on testimony is absolutely fundamental."[4] In her words, we need each other for knowledge. "Our constructed view of the world depends on many other people, and we can discover what these other people have experienced and what they judge to be the case only because we generally believe their testimony."[5] Shared or given knowledge can have meaning and application only when it can be regarded with trust.

We might apply a standard of safe conduct, as we might in acts of rescue, to the transactions of the library. Information should be given in the context of exploratory behaviors: *We are starting here. We are headed there.* The agent's communication should include explanations of *what's possible* and *what's variable* in the search. By indication or by modeling, the agent ought to communicate the recognizable indicators of proximity (*We're close to something*) and expectation (*It is likely to be here*). When they are not obvious, the characteristics of a useful discovery are worth citing. The steady control and adjustment of the search by the user in collaboration with the librarian ought to be explicit at every turn.

The crafting of truth depends on trusting the testimony of many others, and by extension, it entails an assumption of trust in what others have crafted for themselves. "We place our trust in that intersubjective account, thereby presuming honesty, competence, and reliability on the part of the people and social institutions who define it. Truth," Govier writes, "presumes trust."[6]

Trust, in my practice-based view, is not a relationship that can be established between a human being and a volume, a record, or an electronic tool or device. When we say that a device is "trustworthy," we are saying something like, "It tends to work" or "It has been previously useful in this kind of situation." But "trust" can describe relationships between similarly permeable entities: each must be capable of response, give and play, adjustment and communication. Similarly, an ethos of trust can develop only in situations where vulnerability and the making and keeping of promises are present.

Bernard Barber gives the idea of trust a central place in the configuration of professional life, and by implication in the configuration of information service. In *The Logic and Limits of Trust,* he writes:

> I define professional roles and behaviors in terms of three essential variables, each somewhat independent of the others: powerful knowledge, considerable autonomy, and a high level of fiduciary obligation and responsibility both to individual clients and the public welfare.[7]

As professional responsibility increases, so do the opportunities to display each of these characteristic elements. *Whenever* a professional is invested with both powerful knowledge and considerable autonomy, the level of fiduciary responsibility to be observed is critical. In libraries, powerful knowledge is systematic and regulatory; it has to do with resources, authorship, locations, strategies, structures and the relationships among them. The librarian also has extensive autonomy having to do with the selection, organization and display of information, as well as the design and evaluation of the inquiry at hand. The librarian cannot represent the structures of information without also representing their integrity and acknowledging responsibility for its authority. (For similar fiduciary reasons, librarians weed outdated materials, also an ethical act.)

Knowledge and autonomy are attributes of competence and power; they inspire expectations of trust. But this expectation of competence is merely one, and perhaps the shallower, connotation of trust. Barber describes its deeper value as "the expectation that some others in our social relationships have moral obligations and responsibility to demonstrate a special concern for other's interests above their own.... Trust as fiduciary obligation," he writes, "goes beyond technically competent performance to the moral dimension of interaction."[8]

In support of their communities and cultures, institutions comprise systems of tacit expectations grounded on a largely unarticulated contract. By definition, information services are provided under conditions of need and vulnerability; a situation of relative safety for the user is required. However fully she may be committed to an inquiry, the user cannot anticipate where, or how far, she must go, or the complexity of the work she must do. Entering the library, the user ought to assume that she has entered a place where trust is in robust practice.

For the agent of information, the librarian, to live up to this deeper quality of trust, the essential criteria for helping extend far beyond mere accuracy and currency. Trust is implicated in the original *motive* to help another, in the level of *attention* given to the individual inquirer, in the quality of *access* to information given, in the *criteria* for satisfactory helping acts, and in the *conditions* for helping and referral created by the institution. Clearly, without certain trust in its accuracy, any information given has no value; but without the user's trust in the situation of its transfer, the institution itself has no integrity.

What are the contexts of trustworthy transfer of knowledge? What are the conditions of exchange and communication that allow information to be useful, to fit, to function, to work for the user? What qualities of trust in institutions assure the private crafting of insights and truths? What is it conveyed beyond information, when information is given?

Three Contexts of Trust

The user, engaged in an entropic information context, is dependent on the institution and its agent, the librarian, for rescue. "Entropic," because the proliferation of information overwhelms the time needed to manage it; "rescue," because the user is in need of a guiding hand, an intellectual model of inquiry, and a useful approach to mastery over the glut. There are many reasons to think of library services as acts of rescue.

The situation of the user in our hybrid, paper/electronic world is precarious. Each form of information appears to proliferate in proportion to the other; each demands its own kind of cognitive energy, understanding, and skills. And each gathering of data, print or electronic, carries with it an array of secondary knowledge required for access or use, such as thesauri, vocabularies, search protocols, file structures, and understandings of scope. Apart from these tools, the user needs to have ways of determining the authority, currency, and origins of knowledge, and any constraints on its application.

While assisting exploratory searches early in my reference work, during the "age of paper," I would encourage students to identify and pursue only five citations at a time, given the high potential for the emergence of new themes as each item was recovered and read. Increasingly now, in a different age, I anticipate that even the new user must make immediate choices about limiting the search and hardening its vocabulary, lest a deluge drowns her spirit in that most fluid substance, information that *just might* be useful. And so, even before the user is required to make decisions about the scope of her inquiry and the value of information, the inquiry is already subject to reification, distraction, uncertainty, and artificial constraints.

Here is another reason for rescue. The interdisciplinarity of contemporary information structures and the critical thinking required for their exploration adds to the diffusion of energy in the user's world. Even a minor inquiry can evoke the themes, vocabularies, values, methods, and paradigms of multiple subject matters; the alternative formats in which raw or cooked data might arrive at a tabletop add complexity to the process of creating priorities and categories for use. The easy flow of information depends also on a user's literacy, her previous experiences with inquiry, and the diffuse unknowns that tend to pop up and confound us, even in basic scholarship.

Further, no question exists apart from others; asking is always a step in a private sequence, always connected to a process the institution cannot see. Among potential ambiguities and contradictions, and differences between origins and contexts of knowledge, the user is potentially at a loss. The first context of trust occurs when the librarian confronts the real life of the user: the "powerful knowledge" held by the professional can be used to create hand- and footholds in the sheer wall of information available in a contemporary institution. When a user has the will to pursue a challenging inquiry, the institution owes expert assistance from a perspective of mastery, toward its resolution.

The transfer of knowledge to the user is anti-entropic: it imports energy and possibility to a situation of indecision and uncertainty. The giving of information tools and access to knowledge in response to a question is always connected to the learner's thinking and becoming. Such direct intervention in the process transforms the user's horizon, often simply by making it visible. Visible here means "possible;" it is in the illumination of possibilities that the librarian inspires forward motion in the learner's experiences.

This is no shallow change; it allows the user, compelled by inexperience or confusion to ask for assistance, to proceed with an idea. The transfer of information in this way is typically conducted with efficiency, brevity and economy; but the interaction between librarian and learner holds implicit complexity. What is this interaction really about? The transaction is about the topic, of course; but it is also about the learner's academic or personal work; it is about the librarian's work and experience as well; it is about the library's resources, and resources nearby; it is about the community being served; it is about the nature and tradition of scholarship and inquiry in practice. Further, the transaction is about the librarian's empirical knowledge of tools, sources, and potential avenues of inquiry, and the librarian's guiding professional knowledge of process; in no small degree it is also about shelf-side manner and personal style. The inquiry is also about its cost to the user: asking requires the expression of need, the revelation of possible ignorance and vulnerability; it reduces privacy and makes the interior life of the mind somewhat public.

Consequently, the constraints on assistance are extensive. The professional provides information for a user whose awareness is on the edge of thought; the knowledge conveyed must be contextually appropriate, fit, relevant and useful; it must be grounded in an authority that implies its truth; further, it must be usable and compelling in the present moment. That is, usable information is immediate, but it is also implicative and suggestive: by its content and documentation, it is likely to lead the learner toward thoughts not otherwise possible. The conditions of transfer are also critical: assistance ought to be given unconditionally and flexibly, with sensitivity to the circumstance and respect for the intellect of the user.

Though they will vary with the many unpredictable conditions of assistance, the definitive ethical tensions of information service are clear. They do not go away, nor do they change their form over time. Their presence, and the ambiguity they carry, characterizes professional work. In order to import energy and possibility to a situation of indecision and uncertainty, information service needs to consider: (1) the boundaries of an inquiry as defined by the user, (2) the careful and fair assumptions to be made by the librarian, (3) the respect to be shown toward the user's engagement with the task, (4) appropriate attention to the user, without intrusion or unrequested help, and (5) the construction of mutual responsibility in the course of a helping relationship.

Each of these considerations has to do with power, and each is complex enough to be problematic to the ethically-careless institution. Yet each also characterizes the promise of excellent assistance under the control of the user. This promise is fulfilled only in human relationships. What the institution promises is a set of current, accurate resources; a professional agency to apply these tools to problems of inquiry; and time and space for this work to occur. The human engagement involves far more. *However critical the information given, the relationship between the user and the librarian is more artful than mechanical, more illuminating than definitive.* This is the relationship where an ethos of trust is developed.

In the library where an ethos of service and trust prevails, as tools and resources become increasingly automatic and less subject to the dynamics of choice and design, the need for a dynamically open, unfinished human relationship increases. "Unfinished" is here intended in the sense of a tentative venture that follows an ethical obligation to give the best possible attention to the user. This engagement is likely to be completed not on the librarian's terms alone, but on the mutual terms of the librarian and the user. An ethics of obligation is based on the user's state of need, the librarian's professional mastery over tools, and a mutual approach to the unknown.

I believe that the unfinished relationship is configured by four obligations:

- The obligation to attend, listen and engage with the expressed interests and criteria of the user in mind. (This obligation acknowledges the librarian's altruism and responsibility to take action to influence the life of another person.)
- The obligation to reflect the situation, engagement and urgency of the user in performing professional acts of helping. (This obligation reflects the agent's responsibility to enter the inquiry as a full participant, not to remain outside it.)
- The obligation to offer and pursue connections to further the possibilities of an inquiry, beyond the original question posed. (This obligation recognizes that the quality of assistance is measured in the ways it moves the learner forward, into territory previously unknown.)
- The obligation to complete the helping relationship as a contract drawn and determined by the user. (This obligation acknowledges the critical character of service, and the equation of individual professional goals—at least while helping—with the needs and aspirations of the user.)

An Enduring Trust

Communities empower and endow libraries with such obligations implicit in their charters; in turn, the library is challenged with interpreting such obligations in human professional behaviors. I contend that the library creates its most enduring trust by defining and meeting these obligations in public. In the presence of a community and its members, library professionals, collections, services, programs are bound to do these things: attend to the person, reflect on the human need, connect and confirm new information, and respect the integrity of the user. In places where this trust is articulated in public, users can anticipate an experience worthy of trust.

In practice we can assume that the librarian will encourage the user to define the contexts of information need and use, and the desired level of complexity. The librarian will address the fit between the information at hand and the outcome the user requires. And the librarian will recommend guidelines (such as strategies, alternative paths, significant landmarks), structures (vocabularies, hierarchies, disciplinary angles), organization principles (varieties of media, how information is differentiated and compiled, and how it changes), and authoritative, constructive tools. In this way, the librarian acknowledges the broad cognitive processes in the user's work, and confirms the potential participation of the user in the design and ordering of that process.

To speak personally, in an enduring trust, the institution and its human beings address my need, but they go beyond my need, in order to assemble the possibilities of inquiry related to it. These are possibilities I may not have imagined or considered, if I am lacking the tools and masteries of the institution. Libraries—and other cultural institutions—have an obligation to regard me as a learner, and to understand that I may want to go beyond my need, as far as I can, toward new ideas or unknowns. The enduring trust is captured in that assumption: that I may need all of the mastery I can command, that it is more than a mastery of tools, that it will move me forward, and that the process will attempt to resolve but is also more than likely to expand my problem.

The enduring trust also implies that a situation has been created where the continuous *becoming* of the user is primary. The characteristics of that situation include an open fabric of information under human control, recognition that each problem presented at the reference desk is new, and that the user is entitled to present her problem with a pervasive sense of safety and confidence when it is most needed. We need most to trust at moments of intellectual self-presentation and risk, in the midst of dense and complex knowledge, when the crafting of personal truth is required. As any learner knows, a crafting and critique of knowledge cannot occur without the prevalence of trust. In our libraries, an enduring ethos of trust allows the learner to construct an individually informed life; it also allows us to see how an ethos of trust influences and builds an entire community of inquiry as well.

Notes

1. David Carr, "Balancing Act: Ethics, Mission, and the Public Trust," *Museum News* 80(5, 2001):28–32, 71ff.

2. Jackie Weisz, compiler. *Codes of Ethics and Practice of Interest to Museums* (Washington, DC: American Association of Museums, 2000).

3. David Good. "Individuals, Interpersonal Relations, and Trust," in *Trust: Making and Breaking Cooperative Relations*, Diego Gambetta, editor. (New York: Basil Blackwell, 1988), 46. See also Niklas Luhmann, "Familiarity Confidence, Trust: Problems and Alternatives," 94–107 in this volume.

4. Trudy Govier, *Social Trust and Human Communities* (Montreal: McGill-Queen's University Press, 1997), 59.

5. Govier, 61.

6. Govier, 62.

7. Bernard Barber. *The Logic and Limits of Trust* (New Brunswick, NJ: Rutgers University Press, 1983), 135–136.

8. Barber, 14, 15.

8

The Ethics of Electronic Information in China and in Eastern Europe

Lester J. Pourciau

This paper will report on and discuss experiences and interactions which this writer has had during several visits to China and to several republics in Eastern Europe since 1990. These visits have been to libraries and to various conferences during which there were opportunities to interact with persons working in all capacities in libraries and in the implementation of various systems of automated information services. In summary, observations and impressions of views of and attitudes toward questions of ethical issues associated with electronic information development and use were positive.

Introduction

Since 1990,this writer had the good fortune to attend and to participate in five library/information science conferences in China and in several republics in Eastern Europe; republics which were members of the Former Soviet Union or which were dominated by the FSU. With the exception of five excursions into Ukraine and two into Russia, each of the other sojourns was but a single visit. Nevertheless, all of these allowed for interaction with local information professionals and for the accumulation of a variety of observations and impressions. The intent here is to portray some of these by way of a description of experiences.

China

We made our first venture into China in 1990, before the introduction of the Internet in that country. Our lectures were primarily about the organization and structure of colleges and universities in the United

States and, to a limited degree, about the existence of the Internet in the

U.S. There was much interest in this Internet topic and a large number of questions were asked. Some three years later in 1993, the implementation of the Internet in China was imminent when I spoke about the Internet at the Chongqing Institute of Posts and Telecommunications. Those gathered to hear my presentation were amazed that the President of the Institute had also chosen to attend. They told me that his attendance at lectures of foreign guests was virtually unheard of but that he was intensely interested in the topic. I remember very clearly remarking during the presentation that law in China was meaningless in Lithuania and that this enhanced the need to impress users of the Internet that the ethical use of this technology was of importance. That there was general agreement among the participants was of interest in that it was after 1990 that China was ever a party to any international copyright agreement and that, for the most part, the whole idea of intangible property rights was alien to a large portion of the Chinese population. Later, in 1996 I gave a paper at a conference in Shanghai titled "The potential for Chinese participation in the globalization of information." This paper reviewed the relative absence of any law or regulation in China speaking to the matter of intangible property rights. There was sufficient interest in this topic that this paper was translated into Chinese and published in the Chinese journal, *Information Science.* Throughout five trips to China from 1990 through 1999, impressions gathered about Chinese attentiveness to the ethics of electronic information were positive even though it seemed to be a relatively new concept for most Chinese.

Slovenia

The first venture of this writer into a republic in Eastern Europe was occasioned by my attending and participating in the Fourth International conference, "Information Systems Development" held in Bled, Slovenia in September of 1994. In that context, I presented a paper reporting on a survey of the thirty-one universities in the Southeastern United States whose library systems are members of the Association of Southeastern Research Libraries. This survey was an inquiry about Internet training offered to faculty, staff, and to students at these thirty-one universities. The paper, published in the Proceedings of the Conference, was entitled "Curriculum Content of Internet Training Programs in the United States of America." As I was the only librarian and the only American participating in the Conference, there was considerable interest in and curiosity about what sort of training efforts were being made in the U.S. My sense of the mood and attitude of the other participants was that they were all eager to be a part of an international group of scholars each interested in pursing similar goals. Several times during the informal discussions, which took place, I was asked about policies governing the use of information technology in the United States. Clearly, this interest can be interpreted as an interest in ethical standards associated with information technology. I was pleased that the Conference organizers were willing and eager to accept my offer to investigate the inclusion of the Proceedings of the Conference in the ERIC collection. ERIC is the Educational Resource Center, an agency in the United States which gathers and publishes various papers deemed to be of value to the general educational community. Indeed, ERIC did agree to reproduce the proceedings in its published microfiche files.

A Crimean Odyssey

In October of 1994 I attended and participated in the International Seminar on Information Technologies and Information Services held in Shanghai, China. I had served as a member of the Organizing Committee for the Seminar and presented a paper about the architecture of library buildings. It was at the Seminar that I first met Yakov Shraiberg. Among other things, he and I discussed Crimea '95, "Libraries and Associations in the Transient World: New Technologies and New Forms of Cooperation." One of the results of our discussions was that I became affiliated with the Crimea conferences and such has been the case to date.

My first Crimea Conference experience was that of the 2nd Conference which took place in Eupatory. Not only did I present a paper but also I co-chaired one of the presentation sections. This was an interesting and rewarding experience and one, which allowed me to establish collegial and collaborative relationships with several people. These relationships have continued and have grown since then.

In 1997, I made a brief study of Russian Institute and University WWW home pages searching for evidence of a publicly promulgated Code of Ethics or Acceptable Use Policy for computer use, wrote a paper on this topic, and presented my findings at the Crimea Conference in Sudak. I was surprised by the amount of interest shown in this topic and the variety of questions put to me about it. With the global development of computer and information technology, the uses of these resources raise a variety of questions that ignore political and linguistic boundaries. Thus, it is of paramount importance that local authorities delineate what is or is not acceptable for local use of computer and information technology.

In August of 1998, one of the Crimea Conference participants, Dr. Lyudmila Filippova sent an e-mail to me informing me of the establishment of an Internet Honor Code promulgated at Kharkiv State Polytechnical University. This document is in both English and Russian and can be viewed at http://www.kpi.kharkov.ua/Eng/et or at http://www.kpi.kharkov.ua/Rus/ethics. Dr. Filippova's doctoral dissertation, "Bibliographic Systems of Ukraine in Information and Computer Space: Theory, Organization, Technology" is a contribution to this overall theme of the ethical use of computer and information technology. Further, I am aware of additional work that she and a colleague, Victor Schehetinin, Head of the New Information Technologies Center of Kharkiv State Polytechnical University, are doing with regard to the legal regulation of relations connected with Internet access in Ukraine. I have nothing but the highest compliments for this work.

A Georgian Journey

In 1999, I received an e-mail from Nino Chkhenkeli, Information Resource Specialist in the USIS Library in Tbilisi, asking if I might be interested in attending and participating in the Second South Caucasian Regional Library Conference. I responded enthusiastically and was part of approximately sixty librarians and information professionals who gathered at the Conference Hall of the Ministry of Economics in Tbilisi in late April. The Conference was organized into a plenary session and then, into three separate workshops, one devoted to library standards for cataloging and electronic record exchange, another focusing on continuing professional education, and a third which reviewed the possibility of the establishment of a consortial effort among libraries and library associations of the South Cacausas. This particular workshop was the primary rationale for the attendance and participation of this writer. As was the case with the first two workshops, there were presentations made by representatives of Georgia, Armenia, and Azerbaijan. Then, I spoke about experiences with consortial endeavors and provided a rationale for the establishment of a consortium or confederation of libraries and library associations of the South Caucasus.

The remainder of the Conference was devoted to work on a draft policy statement about regional cooperation in the South Caucasus. Agreement was reached on a document, drafted by this writer, and which reads as follows:

Declaration

We, the participants of the second Regional Library Conference, "Library Associations— Regional Cooperation," approve the idea of the founding of the Confederation of Libraries and Librarian Associations of the South Caucasus.

We agree to select representatives of every country for preparing documents which will serve as guidelines and regulations and which will be presented to the library Associations and librarian organizations of each of the three countries for approval, with the goal of finalizing those documents at a meeting of the Confederation.

It was gratifying to observe representatives of each of the following associations affix their signatures to the declaration: Librarians Association of Armenia, Association of Developing Libraries of Azerbaijan, Association of Information Specialists (Georgia), Association of Automation of Libraries of Georgia, and Librarians Association of Georgia. Tbilisi '99 was organized and sponsored by the Association of Information Specialists in Georgia. It was funded by USIA and administered by IREX. The AIS is the professional organization in Georgia which, among other activities, conducts the continuing education program of the Association. Overall, Tbilisi '99 was well organized and, in the view of this writer, highly beneficial to participants from the three Republics of the South Caucasus. Implicit in all of the discussion, which took place, was a sincere regard what can be considered ethical standards applied to what was being considered.

BOBCATSSS on the Donau and the Danube

Again, because of collegial and collaborative relations established with various professionals in the FSU, I attended and participated in two BOBCATSSS Symposia, in 1998 and in 1999. BOBCATSSS is an acronym for a group of European educational institutions in library and information science. It takes its name from the cities in which the founding institutes are located (Budapest,

Oslo, Barcelona, Copenhagen, Amsterdam, Tampere, Sheffield, Stuttgart, and Szombathely). Since its inception, the institutes of Kharkov in Ukraine, Moscow in Russia, Sofia in Bulgaria, and Tallin in Estonia have joined BOBCATSSS. Its fundamental purpose is to promote educational and research assistance and cooperation among West and East European library educational endeavors. The annual BOBCATSSS symposia are perhaps unique in the world of librarianship in that they are entirely organized by library school students. This is what most impressed this writer. Such an experience is invaluable for any participating student. As in the previous discussion of experiences above, it was clear that participants in the BOBCATSSS Symposia were concerned with the ethical use of information technology.

The Intrigue of Samarkand and of Tashkent

Again, as a result of collegial and collaborative relationships formed, for the most part, during my five-time attendance and participation in the CRIMEA Conferences, I was invited to attend and to participate in "Central Asia — 99" held in Samarkand, Uzbekistan, in October of 1999. This was a most interesting and rewarding experience, and as before, I was most impressed by the enthusiasm and energies of library and information professionals in attendance. In fact, Marat Rakhmatullaev, one of this Workshop's presenters, has written a paper describing "Central Asia — 99" and this paper will be published shortly in *Library Hi Tech News*. He was the prime mover of the Conference and a large measure of its success is the direct result of his efforts.

Brief Excursions in Ukraine and in Russia

On three occasions, I had the opportunity to visit Kharkov and Kiev in Ukraine and Moscow in Russia, visiting libraries in each of these cities. Immediately before the 1999 Crimea Conference, I had the opportunity to visit and to lecture at the USIS Headquarters In Kiev, at the Kiev National University of Culture and Arts, and at the Lesya Ukrainka Public Library, speaking about Library Organization and Management, Conflict Management in Libraries, and Information Literacy. Following the Conference, I spoke as an invited lecturer at Kharkiv State University in Kharkov, presenting lectures on Conflict Management and Information Literacy. I was even honored by being asked to "cut the ribbon" at the opening of a computer laboratory at Kharkiv State University.

In an earlier visit to the Russian National Public Library for Science and Technology, I was impressed by the commitment which this library had made by providing an open classroom area, outfitted with computers, for the purpose of providing training for users of that library.

Summary Reflections

Anyone who has visited the Travel Advisory WWW page of the U.S. Department of State http://www.travel.state.gov/travel_warnings.html and has selected any country of Eastern Europe will invariably see language stating that this country is undergoing profound political and economic change or language to that effect. This change is largely the result of the single most prevalent problem throughout Eastern Europe, that of the relative absence of that legal and regulatory infrastructure that western democracies take for granted. Taking this into context, it is truly impressive to interact with and to observe librarians and information professionals in action. Their enthusiasm, their energy, their expertise and their spirit of cooperation is truly impressive when one reflects on the economic difficulties with which some of them must work. I have been most fortunate in my involvement and participation, however limited, in some of their work.

9

The Organizations That Represent Information Professionals: Form, Function, and Professional Ethics

Wallace C. Koehler, Jr.

Information professionals like other professionals organize themselves into organizations to represent their collective interests and concerns. These interests and concerns are also reflected — and often in great detail — in the codes of ethics, statutes, and organizational mission statements of these organizations.

These professional organizations exercise social influence in the resolution of and perhaps sometimes in the creation of conflict in the societies in which they are located.[1] Note for example the position the American Library Association (ALA) has taken on various censorship issues, particularly Internet filtering in public libraries and the response to that position from various segments of the public. The ALA has taken an ethical as well as a constitutional position that is supported in some sectors and rejected in others.

Different societies and different professional communities place different demands on the professional organizations that represent them. These social and professional demands affect the form the organization takes and, in turn, also affects the role of the organization in the governance and guidance of the profession. These roles are reflected in the organizational structure and the administrative, quasi-legislative, and quasi-judicial functions of these groups. Finally, these roles are defined in the statutes, codes of ethics, and mission statements of these professional organizations. These codes of ethics and codes of practice describe for practitioners the range of acceptable behaviors. These, according to Frankel,[2] may take one or a combination of three basic forms: regulatory, aspirational, or educational. We can add deontological codes to this list.

Regulatory codes can be both prescriptive and proscriptive. These rules define in explicit detail acceptable or unacceptable behavioral norms. They tend to be lengthy and legalistic. They may take one of two forms. The first lists specific required or prohibited activities. The other, the "small-l liberal codes" define the parameters of acceptable behavior. Behaviors between the defining norms are considered acceptable. The greater the "distance" between the norms, the more liberal is the system.

Aspirational norms are defined by abstract goals. These are the ends that professionals seek to emulate. They provide moral guidance. Aspirational codes may have some basis in utilitarianism. Utilitarians subscribe to a "pain/pleasure" thesis. Jeremy Bentham in his *An Introduction to the Principles of Morals and Legislation*[3] described "private ethics" as having a basis in maximizing pleasure and minimizing pain. Public action and public good works can be both described and explained in terms of both generalized and personalized.

Deontological codes have their roots in Immanuel Kant's *Groundwork of the Metaphysics of Morals.*[4] All good things are qualified good things except good will. Moreover, actors cannot be held responsible for their actions except where they have control over those actions. An actor of good will performs good acts because it is his/her *duty* to perform them. The concept of duty, good acts, good will, and ethics are therefore inextricably intertwined. According to Kant, the *Categorical Imperative* is an obligation to follow norms for their own sake consistent with a universalized set rather than for some higher good. A deontological response then consists of examining individual behavior with a set of universalized norms (a statute or code, perhaps). If the behavior in question is inconsistent with the universalized set, it is unethical behavior. In practical terms, deontological ethics codes describe the duties of the practitioner, often in day-to-day practice and often in great detail.

Educational norms provide both guidelines for behavior as well as instruction and explanation to the reasons for the value or norm. In a way, regulatory values prescribe or proscribe behavior, aspirational values provide targets to quest toward, and educational values describe the reasons for prescriptions and proscriptions but also the map toward desired ends.

The shape codes of ethics and related documents take (aspirational, regulatory, deontological, educational) is both a function of the obligations placed upon a professional organization by the larger society and of the internal dynamics of the professional organization itself. A professional organization required by law or custom to regulate that profession will necessarily develop a code of ethics, a constitution, and a mission that reflects the mandate. Organizations that seek to guide or educate their membership will reflect those goals in their organic documents. It comes as no surprise therefore that the organic documents for the American Library Association and the Colegio de Bibliotecarios de Chile, for example, are very different. Although both provide general representation for their librarian communities, their obligations are also very different.

Organization and Form

The role and function of different professions and their institutions can influence the norms that govern the conduct of the profession. Henry Mintzberg[5] suggests that there are four basic organizational structures for businesses: the simple or entrepreneurial startup, the machine bureaucracy, the professional bureaucracy, and the adhocracy. Librarianship best falls into Mintzberg's professional bureaucracy category. The category is less bound by formal institutional rules than by formal professional or standardized norms. Behaviors are guided more by professional/client standards rather than internal rules. The source of norms for professional bureaucracies by standards created outside the home institution and can and do include professional organizations. These standards are manifested through the statutes or constitutions, mission statements, and codes of ethics of the various organizations that represent the professional bureaucracies. These organizations include, we suggest, the many professional organizations representing the library and information science professions.

Organization and Purpose

One reason codes of ethics take different form is that professional organizations do not all serve the same purposes: Different purpose — different code of ethics. Library associations perform a number of different roles in different societies and for different groups. These roles can be divided into five basic types.

The first type is the association of associations and/or of libraries. Perhaps the best known of these is International Federation of Library Associations and Institutions (IFLA), drawing its membership from national library associations and from member libraries. IFLA also has a limited category for individual members, but their ability to participate in the functions of the organizations is restricted. There are also a number of national level library associations that limit membership to institutions and organizations. These include the Russian Library Association and the Association of College and Research Libraries in the United States. Others are comprised of individuals, but limit membership to *ex officio* participation. These include organizations for library directors, directors of state libraries, and so on.

The second type is the regulatory association. Many library associations, particularly those in Central and South America, have a legal mandate to regulate the profession. These associations, sometimes called *colegios* or colleges, establish minimum professional qualifications, license professionals, sanction those professionals for transgressions of the regulations and of the code, and provide general associational functions. These services include publication of newsletters and journals, the convening of meetings and conferences, and so on. In a number of countries, particularly in Latin America, professional organizations are charged in law to regulate and license the profession. The codes of ethics of these organizations read like statutes and are highly regulatory. In those countries where the professional organization has less of a quasi-judicial or quasi-legislative function mandated by law, the codes of ethics are often deontological and equally detailed.

The third are library associations that serve as trade unions to represent their membership to library management. These associations negotiate labor contracts, help establish work rules, and sometimes administer the retirement programs for their members. These organizations are typically found in the Nordic countries of Europe. They may therefore specify a wider range of member activities and behaviors than do national organizations elsewhere.

The fourth type is general membership organizations. These organizations represent librarians and other information professionals within a given country, region, state, province, and so on. They provide a wide range of services for their membership, including the convening of conferences, the publication of newsletters and journals, and represent their membership at regional and international organizations. Many but by no means all publish standards of practice and codes of ethics for their membership.

The fifth is a combination of or a variation on some or all of the first four. These are organizations for individual segments of the library professions. These can be separated into three basic categories.

These are those that represent a library specialty (medical librarianship, academic librarianship, records management, catalogers, and so on), those that represent librarians with certain interests (Chinese collections, toy libraries, children's librarians) and those that represent librarians with specific characteristics (racial, cultural, gender, sexual orientation).

A first rule might be that the kind of ethics code an organization promulgates, if indeed it promulgates one, depends in large part on the society in which it is located, the kind of organization it is, and the constituency it represents. Koehler and Pemberton[6] noted, for example, that the codes of ethics for the general library professional organizations in civil code countries tend to be more regulatory or deontological and in common law countries to be more aspirational. There are, as ever, exceptions to this "rule." The Code of Ethics of the [UK] Library Association is highly regulatory and specifies what librarians must and must not do.

Organizations that represent specific constituencies (archivists, records managers, catalogers, indexers, and so on) tend to develop codes of ethics, mission statements, and/or statutes that reflect those particular constituencies. For example the Association of Records Managers and Administrators calls upon its members to maintain good records management practices (http://www.arma.org///publications/ethics.cfm). That includes the development of schedules for records destruction. That may not be consistent with the goals and interests of archivists who have as an end the long-term maintenance of the historical record.

Interestingly, the Society of American Archivists recognizes both general principles recognized by professional groups and specific norms unique to each (http://www.archivists.org/governance/handbook/app_ethics.html).

Professional Organizations, Mission Statements, Ethics Codes

There are more than thirty library and information professional organizations in the world that publish their codes of ethics on-line. Many of these are listed in Table 1. In addition, there are hundreds of organizations that either do not have a code of ethics or that have not published them in machine retrievable format. For a more comprehensive list, see ***(WEBSITE).***

Not surprisingly, we find that many national level, general purpose library organizations have developed and published codes of ethics, while proportionately fewer regional (state or provincial) and "special area" organizations have done so.

Table 1. Library and Information Profession Organizations with Published Codes of Ethics

Professional Association	*Code of Ethics Name*	*URL for Code*
Academia Mexicana de Informática	Code of Ethics and Professional Conduct	http://amiac.org.org.mx/nuevo/amiac01.html
American Association of Law Libraries	Code of Ethics	http://www.aallnet.org/about/policy_ethics.asp
American Institute for Conservation	Code of Ethics and Guidelines for Practice,	http://aic.stanford.edu/pubs/ethics.html
American Library Association	Code of Ethics	http://www.ala.org/alaorg/oif/ethics.html
American Society for Information Science	Code of Ethics for Information Professionals	http://www.asis.org/AboutASIS/professional-guidelines.html
Asociación de Bibliotecarios Graduados de la República Argentina	Estatuto del Profesional en Biblioteclogia y Documentación,	http://abgra.sisbi.uba.ar/proy.htm
Association des Archivistes du Québec	Code de Déontologie	http://www.archivistes.qc.ca/fonctionnement/deontologie.html
Association des Bibliothécaires Français,	Les Bibliothèques en France: Thèmes et Débat.	http://www.abf.asso.fr/html/present.htm
Association of Canadian Archivists	Code of Ethics.	http://aca.archives.ca/publicat/general/code.htm
Association of Computing Machinery	Code of Ethics and Professional Conduct	http://www.acm.org/constitution/code.html

Professional Association	*Code of Ethics Name*	*URL for Code*
Association of College and Research Libraries	Standards for Ethical Conduct for Rare Book, Manuscript, and Special Collections Librarians	http://www.ala.org/acrl/
Association for Educational Communications and Technology	Code of Ethics, Mission Statement.	http://www.aect.org/AboutAECT/Ethics.html
Association for Library Collections and Technical Services Acquisitions Section	Statement on Principles and Standards of Acquisitions Practice	http://www.ala.org/alcts/publications/ethics/aesthics.html
Association of Independent Information Professionals	Code of Ethical Business Practices	http://www.aiip.org/purethics.html
Association of Information Technology Professionals	Code of Ethics	http://www.aitp.org/about/code_of_ethics.html
Association profesionnelle des informaticiens et informaticiennes du Québec	Code de deontologie	http://www.crim.ca/APIIQ/rapports/codedeon.html
Association of Professional Researchers for Advancement	Statement of Ethics	http://www.APRAhome.org/apra_statement_of_ethics.htm
Association of Records Managers and Administrators	Code of Professional Responsibility	http://www.arma.org/publications/ethics.htm
Australian Computer Society	Code of Ethics	http://www.acs.org.au/national/pospaper/acs131.htm
Australian Library and Information Association	Statement on Professional Ethics	http://www.alia.org.au/policies/professional.ethics.html
British Computer Society.	Code of Conduct	http://www.bcs.org.uk/aboutbcs/coc.htm
Canadian Information Processing Society	Code of Ethics and Standards of Conduct	http://www.cips.ca/membership/ethics.htm
Canadian Library Association	Code of Ethics Position Statement	http://www.cla.ca/about/ethics.htm

Professional Association	*Code of Ethics Name*	*URL for Code*
Colegio de Bibliotecarios de Chile	Codigo de Etica Profesional	http://www.bibliotecarios.cl/etica.htm
Colegio Nacional de Bibliotecarios de Mexico	Codigo de Etica	http://serpiente.dgsca.unam.mx/cnb/codetica.html
Conselho Regional de Biblioteconomia do Brasil	Código de Etica Profesional del Bibliotecario [not the original, it is located on a Mexican server, a translation from the Portuguese to Spanish].	http://serpiente.dgsca.unam.mx/cnb/brasil.html
Corporation des Bibliothécaires Professionnels du Québec	Code of Ethics—Not found	http://www.cbpq.qc.ca
Dutch Association of Professional Restorers.	Unofficial translation	http://palimpsest.stanford.edu/byorg/veres/vereseth.html
Hong Kong Library Association	Code of Ethics	http://www.hk.super.net/~hkla/
Information Processing Society of Japan	Code of Ethics	http://ipsj.ipsj.or.jp/english/codeengl.html
Institute of Certified Records Managers	Code of Ethics	http://mindspring.com/~dschewe/ethics.html
The Library Association [UK]	Code of Professional Conduct and Guidance	http://www.la-hq.org.uk/
The Medical Library Association	Code of Ethics for Health Sciences Librarianship	http://www.mlanet.org/about/ethics.html
Library And Information Association Of New Zealand Aotearoa	Code of Professional	http://www.lianza.org.nz/codes.htm
Records Management Association of Australia		http://www.rmaa.com.au/Rmaa.html
Society of American Archivists	Code of Ethics	http://www.archivists.org/governance/handbook/app_ethics.html

Professional Association	*Code of Ethics Name*	*URL for Code*
Society of Competitive Intelligence Professionals	Code of Ethics—no longer online	http://www.scip.org/

Table 2 is a select list of organizations shown in Table 1. The second column indicates the "code type" as aspirational (A), regulatory (R), or deontological (D). In addition, the organization's statement of purpose, objectives or mission is also provided. The mission statements, lifted verbatim from the association's Web site, show a pattern similar to the codes of ethics. "Aspirational" associations tend to have short, general mission statements, while the "regulatory" and "deontological" organizations tend to have longer and more complex statements. These statements tend to reflect, as they should, the purpose and place of the organization in the profession and in society.

Table 2. Professional Organizations, Codes, and Missions

Organization	*Code Type*	*Mission Statement or Objectives*	*Mission Statement Source*
American Library Association	A	The Mission of the American Library Association is to provide leadership for the development, promotion and improvement of library and information services and the profession of librarianship in order to enhance learning and ensure access to information for all.	http://www.ala.org/work/alaction2005.html
Australian Library and Information Association	A	ALIA will empower the profession in the development, promotion, and delivery of quality library and information services, through leadership, advocacy, cooperation, and strategic alliances.	http://www.alia.org.au/slideshows/199904/02.html
Canadian Library Association	A	Our mission is to promote, develop and support library and information services in Canada and to work in cooperation with all who share our values in order to present a unified voice on issues of mutual concern.	http://www.cla.ca/about/mission.htm
Colegio de Bibliotecarios de Chile	R	El Colegio de Bibliotecarios de Chile A. G.,tendrá por objeto promover el perfeccionamiento profesional, científico, y tecnológico de sus Asociados; velar por el prestigio, prerrogativas y ética de la profesión de bibliotecario; mantener la disciplina profesional de sus asociados y defender los derechos de los bibliotecarios asociados.	http://www.bibliotecarios.cl/estatutos.htm
Association des bibliothécaires français	D	Article 1 L'association dite "association des bibliothécaires français," fondée en 1906, a pour but, en dehors de toute	http://www.abf.asso.fr/organisation/statuts.html

Organization	*Code Type*	*Mission Statement or Objectives*	*Mission Statement Source*
		orientation politique, philosophique, confessionnelle ou syndicale : 1. de resserrer les liens de confraternité entre tous ceux qui travaillent dans les bibliothèques françaises ; 2. 2. d'étudier toutes les questions, d'ordre scientifique, technique et administratif concernant les bibliothèques et leur personnel; 3. de défendre les intérêts des bibliothèques et de la lecture ; 4. de promouvoir le développement des bibliothèques de toute nature ; 5. de représenter les bibliothèques françaises auprès des institutions e organismes français, étrangers et internationaux. Est considérée comme bibliothèque, quelle que soit sa dénomination, toute collection organisée de livres et de périodiques imprimés ou de tous autres documents, notamment graphiques et audiovisuels, utilisée par des usagers à des fins d'information, de recherche, d'éducation ou de récréation.	
Hong Kong Library Association	A	The objectives of the Association shall be: (A) To encourage the development of policies promoting the provision of information and library services in Hong Kong. This shall include the provision of guidelines and standards for such services. (B) To provide for librarianship and information work, a focal point as well as a network of formal and informal communication within Hong Kong and with China and other countries. (C) To unite and promote the interests of all persons engaged in library and information work in Hong Kong, and to ensure the effective representation of the interests of members. (D) To encourage professional education and training for librarianship and information work in Hong Kong.	http://www.hklib.org.hk/about-us.html#constitution
Japan Library Association	D	We recognize that it is our library's responsibility to preserve the fundamental right of intellectual freedom by making our resources and facilities available to the people. In order to perform this duty, our libraries support the following principles: 1. The freedom of libraries to select their materials. 2. The freedom of libraries to make their	http://wwwsoc.nacsis.ac.jp/jla/eth&free-e.html#ethics

Organization	*Code Type*	*Mission Statement or Objectives*	*Mission Statement Source*
		materials and facilities available to the people. 3. The right of libraries to protect the privacy of their patrons. 4. The right of libraries to oppose all forms of censorship. We are thus united in our determination to defend intellectual freedom.	
Colegio Nacional de Bibliotecarios—Mexico	A	Declaración de Principios Considerando que los profesionales de la bibliotecología tienen: a. La misión de apoyar a la sociedad en la búsqueda de alternativas que le permitan mejorar su calidad de vida; b. La obligación de mejorar la imagen de los servicios bibliotecarios y de información en apoyo del desarrollo de los ciudadanos y del país; c. La responsabilidad de promover el uso de la información en todos los sectores de la población; d. La obligación, al mismo tiempo que la oportunidad de fortalecer la imagen del servicio bibliotecario nacional	http://serpiente.dgsca.unam.mx/cnb/codetica.html
Library and Information Association of New Zealand Aotearoa	A	Vision — To be the vibrant, vital professional voice for those engaged in Librarianship and Information manage ment Values To realise this vision LIANZA will: 1. Be at the forefront of placing New Zealand in the global information network 2. Demonstrate commitment to the recognition of the Treaty of Waitangi 3. Promote equitable access to information for all New Zealanders, in a democratic society 4. Promote importance of an information literate society 5. Demonstrate ethical, legal practices 6. Promote ongoing professional training and development opportunities for the profession 7. Support the training of competent skilled professionals	http://www.lianza.org.nz/profile.htm
Library Association of Singapore	No Code	The objectives of the Association shall be: 1) to unite and promote the interests of all persons engaged in library and information work or interested in libraries and information centres; 2) to promote the better administration and management of libraries and information centres; 3) to encourage the establishment,	http://www.las.org.sg/constit.htm

Organization	*Code Type*	*Mission Statement or Objectives*	*Mission Statement Source*
		development and use of libraries and information centres in Singapore; 4) to promote professional education of persons engaged in library and information services; 5) to work towards the enhancement of the status and role of professionals in library and information services; 6) to encourage its members, through its programmes and publications, to increase their own professional capacities and performance; 7) to publish and disseminate such information and knowledge as will be of service of members; 8) to undertake such activities, including the holding of meetings and conferences, as are appropriate to the attainment of the above objectives.	
Union of Associations of Slovene	D/A	In the past people declared basic ethical principles and condensed them into short and clear life guidelines, which represent the basis for co existence among people. Slovenian librarians have created our own professional code of ethics as well. Its purpose is to form the personality of a librarian independently of the current political situation. The goal and importance of library work is to ensure a stable basis for the development of civilization, and is performed by preserving and transmitting written human knowledge. Being aware of our role and responsibility for the development of our society, nation and each individual, Slovenian librarians have accepted the code of professional ethics and pledge to form our personalities and our relationship to colleagues, users and entire social environment on its basis. -Preamble, Code of Ethics	http://193.2.8.11/english.html
Sri Lanka Library Association	R/A	Its objectives are: • to represent and act as the professional body for persons whorking [sic] in the field of librarianship • to improve skills, status and qualifications of librarians and information specialists • to conduct professional examinations and issue certificates of proficiency in librarianship • to establish liaison with national and international organisations in the field of librarianship • to promote and advance professional	http://www.naresa.ac.lk/slla/profile.htm

Organization	*Code Type*	*Mission Statement or Objectives*	*Mission Statement Source*
		activities in library and information science	
Ukranian Library Association	R/A	The Ukrainian Library Association promotes and defends libraries and librarians in Ukraine by helping to obtain positive legislation and appropriate funding. The Law of Ukraine on Libraries and Librarianship was passed in 1995. Now the development of standards and guidelines, evaluating materials and improving and extending service according to the Law are of great importance. The Association strives to be the chief advocate for the people of Ukraine to achieve and maintain high-quality library and information services (by protecting the right to read, educating librarians, improving library services, and making information available to everyone). The Ukrainian Library Association works on strengthening and developing the library profession, and library and information science education. It also contributes towards guaranteeing free access to information and intellectual freedom, and provides public awareness of this field.	http://www.ukma.kiev.ua/ukmalib/ENGLISH/uba.htm
[UK] Library Association	D/R	The mission of The Library Association is to promote the highest standards of professional practice and the highest quality of service delivery for the benefit of the public.	http://www.la-hq.org.uk/directory/about/plan.html#MISSION STATEMENT
Asociación de Bibliotecarios Graduados de la República Argentina	Statute R	Jerarquizar, dignificar y defender los intereses profesionales de sus asociados mediante el estudio y solución de los problemas inherentes a la profesión y como organismo técnico y consultivo colaborador del Estado; Prestar solidaridad moral y material a sus asociados; Mantener relaciones con entidades similares, dentro y fuera del país; Estimular mediante publicaciones y en toda otra forma posible la actividad profesional; Representar y defender ante el Estado, institutos de previsión, tribunales de justicia o empleadores los intereses profesionales colectivos o individuales de los asociados; Participar en los organismos estatales o inculados a la ordenación del trabajo; Promover la enseñanza profesional, la	http://abgra.sisbi.uba.ar/objeframe.htm

Organization	*Code Type*	*Mission Statement or Objectives*	*Mission Statement Source*
		organización y realización de congresos, jornadas bibliotecológicas, cursos, publicaciones, otorgamiento de becas, conferencias y demás actos análogos, como también concurrir a los que organizaren, en el país o en el exterior, otras asociaciones o instituciones afines.	
Namibian Information Workers Association	No Code	The Association strives to promote the development of information services in Namibia through the following functions: 4.1 To unite all information workers in Namibia in an autonomous and representative body. 4.2 To organise and co-ordinate the efforts of information workers in the promotion of the information services in Namibia. 4.3 To make and maintain contact with relevant international and national organisations. 4.4 To obtain and serve as a channel for national and international funding for information service projects or research. 4.5 To actively support programmes designed to meet specific community needs. 4.6 To promote the interests of information workers by making representations to concerned authorities regarding matters affecting the collection, preservation, or dissemination of information. 4.7 To raise the level of expertise of information workers by offering training courses, seminars, workshops, or other relevant activities. 4.8 To advise academic institutions involved in the training information workers in curriculum development. 4.9 To issue publications regarding the Association, its activities and information services in Namibia in general. 4.10 To promote study and research in the relevant fields and disseminate the results. 4.11 To promote the production of publications in the widest possible sense.	Constitution: http://www.unam.na/4320/niwa/const.htm
Persatuan Pustakawan Malaysia	R	Recognizing that libraries and information centres are strategic resources for national development, Persatuan Pustakawan Malaysia is committed to the creation of an information-rich knowledge-based civil society, through the promotion of information equity, lifelong and independent learning, and enhance-	http://www.pnm.my/ppm/

Organization	*Code Type*	*Mission Statement or Objectives*	*Mission Statement Source*
		ment of library and information professionals	
Norwegian Library Association	Code not found	The Norwegian Library Association (NLA) is a national independent organization with the main task to encourage and promote the development of all kinds of Norwegian library activities, including documentary and information activities.	http://www.norskbibliotekforening.no/NBF/nbf_english.htm

Conclusions

Codes of ethics for librarians and other information professionals are fairly recent phenomena. More than 80 percent of American and more than 90 percent of information association codes of ethics were created after 1980. Moreover, most professional information associations have yet to promulgate formal codes although some subsume ethical considerations in their constitutions and mission statements. If the trends manifested in the 1990s continue into the third millennium, it is likely that more organizations will, first, be created, and second, that these new organizations and those that pre-existed them will develop new ethics codes.

Information profession codes of ethics vary in content, as we have seen. Several different explanations have been offered. In some cases, professional associations regulate the profession, sometimes "informally" and sometimes as a consequence of legal mandate. Others emanate from large, general-purpose organizations with wide constituencies. Others represent very specific and narrowly defined constituencies. And finally, professional information organizations arise in a variety of social systems that place different expectations and demands on their professional organizations. These various factors help explain the wide range of different codes of ethics these groups promulgate.

That said, there has been an increase in the rate at which new and existing organizations produce new codes of ethics. It seems likely (based on a work in progress) that as a minimum, these new codes of ethics will be more detailed and perhaps more deontological, prescriptive and/or proscriptive than their aspirational ancestors. In sum, the story is not yet fully told. There will likely be further evolution in the creation of new associations in the information professions and new codes of ethics to reflect their needs and the changing needs of the societies they serve.

Notes

1. Peterson, Randall (2001). "Toward a More Deontological Approach to the Ethical Use of Social Influence" J.M. Darley, D.M. Messick, and T. R. Tyler, eds., Social Influences on Ethical Behavior in Organization. Lawrence Erlbaum Associates: Mahway, N.J.

2. Frankel, Mark (1989). "Professional Codes: Why, How, and What Impact" *Journal of Business Ethics 8*: 109–15.

3. Bentham, Jeremy. *An Introduction to the Principles of Morals and Legislation.* (1789) Printed in the year 1780, and now

first published, by Jeremy Bentham. London: Printed for T. Payne, and son, at the Mew gate.

4. Kant, Immanuel. (1998) *Groundwork of the Metaphysics of Morals.* (1998). Translated and edited by Mary Gregor; with an introduction by Christine M. Korsgaard. Cambridge, U.K.; New York: Cambridge University Press.

5. Mintzberg, Henry (1979). *The Structuring of Organizations.* Englewood Cliffs, N.J.: Prentice-Hall.

6. Koehler, Wallace and J. Michael Pemberton (2000) "A Search for Core Values: Towards a Model Code of Ethics for Information Professionals," *Journal of Information Ethics 9,* 1: 26–54.

10

Preserving a Secret Garden for the Mind: The Ethics of User Privacy in the Digital Library

Paul Sturges and *Ursula Iliffe*

The Library as a Secret Garden

The metaphor of the library as a secret garden alludes to Frances Hodgson Burnett's much loved novel for children.[1] She describes the personal development and self-realization of two neglected and misunderstood children, Mary Lennox and Colin Craven, through their access to a garden that they are able to cultivate without the knowledge of parents or other adults. A servant boy, Dickon, shares their activities and it is he who instructs them in gardening. Under his guidance they begin to understand the lives of plants and animals and learn to give order to that part of the natural environment that surrounds them. It is precisely their access to the garden as a protected space in which they are able to discover for themselves, with only the help of a wise and understanding companion, that enables Mary and Colin to emerge as complete and rounded individuals able to face a world which had seemed to present insurmountable dangers.

The analogy with the library, a space containing a wealth of resources under the unintrusive guardianship of the librarian, is compelling. The library, like the garden, is a venue for learning through personal exploration, in contrast to the authoritarian structures of the schoolroom or the disciplines of family or institutional life. Study is, in essence, an utterly private activity, and the protection that the library offers for privacy is of the highest importance. We need privacy to pursue thought processes that we find difficult without interruption or interference. We might also have genuine reason to avoid others' knowledge of the programme of study we are following. This might be because we are carrying on original research that could bring recognition in some community of ideas, or developing an invention that could lead to wealth and fame. Alternatively, we might be following a line of thought so unorthodox that there is reason to fear the attention of the agents of authority.

Yet in any of these cases, to be able to use the library without unwelcome attention from others, we have to give up some part of our secrecy. Just as Mary and Colin had to share their secret with Dickon, so as to obtain the help that he could give, so we must share some knowledge of our interests with the librarian in exchange for the access that the librarian provides. Total privacy has never been fully possible for library users and now that is even less so. There is a clear danger that the confidential relationship between librarian and user may be in the process of being undermined by technology. This, in turn, threatens the valuable peace and security of the reader's secret garden. Since it is the records of the reader's transactions with the library that open up the possibility of the violation of secrecy, first let us look at library records.

Library Record Keeping

Surveillance Potential of Library Records

It is obvious that files of personal data relating to users could have real surveillance potential both for the authorities, and others with less legitimate interest. The point is illustrated by experience from the British Museum Library in the nineteenth century by numbers of Russian revolutionary émigrés, including Herzen, Lenin, Kropotkin, Kravchinskii and others.[2] The lists of library ticket holders still survive and reveal the frequent use of pseudonyms by the émigrés so as to avoid the attentions of the okhranna, the Russian secret service, which they had reason to believe was being supplied with their addresses by a member of the library staff.

Even more interesting than membership lists, however, are records of the consultation and borrowing of specific documents. Closed-access libraries could accumulate ledgers and call slips containing a complete record of users' consultation and borrowing of library books. However, files of these seem seldom to have been kept on a long-term basis, and where they have survived they are too clumsy for easy consultation. Only in the libraries of the former Soviet countries was this used to monitor the reading of those who might have dissident tendencies with any effective. Library record-keeping functioned as an instrument of the Soviet system of state control.

However, libraries outside the Soviet system produced remarkably few lasting records of transactions with their users. With the very widely used Brown issue system, for instance, the loan files revealed which user had a particular book, or which books a particular reader had borrowed, only whilst the loan continued. Afterwards no record of the transaction remained. Enquiries for information were usually only counted, and telephone enquiries left no trace, though letters containing enquiries might be retained with other correspondence. Interlibrary loans were more likely to leave records because the partner libraries needed detail for accurate financial compensation and management of the systems. For the most part, the library in the pre-digital age was, quite simply, not an institution in which privacy was strongly threatened by the either the abundance or the searchability of records of user transactions.

Archiving Library Records

Nor were records preserved in good order for future use. Librarians, despite their reputation as hoarders and protectors of information materials, have actually tended to be surprisingly little concerned with the historical archives of their own services. Despite the implications of a survey of British public libraries twenty years ago, which showed that fewer than half of those that responded had coherent policies and practices,[3] archiving is still regarded as a problem in Britain today.[4] This lack of attention to archiving for historical purposes follows from confusion over the keeping of semi current records for immediate practical use. A major comparative study of state's records laws in the USA[5] revealed that many American public librarians were unaware that statutes on retention and disclosure of records created in the course of state business also applied to libraries.

Records in the Digital Library

Today all but the smallest and worst-funded libraries make use of some digital technology, and great numbers of libraries have a very large and growing digital aspect. The parameters of privacy in this new environment are not well established, and guidance of the rather basic kind provided by Chmara is still appropriate.[6] What is clear, is that in the digital library, privacy from the librarian, or those who have access to the librarian's files, is even less possible than it was in libraries of print. Records of transactions are increasingly created in digital form and these are so much more comprehensive and easy to access than the old paper records. Archiving of the reading records of library users is now a natural function of the computerized management systems that are in universal use. The ability to monitor e-mail activity and use of the World Wide Web on terminals provided for public use in libraries is also part of system facilities. The same is true of a range of information finding activities by users, and librarians acting on their behalf, that necessarily involves electronic resources, particularly the Internet. Librarians, whether they would have it so or not, are now guardians of considerable volumes of personal data relating to their users, and they have a responsibility to come to terms with this situation.

Ethics and Law

Codes of Ethics

The confidentiality of the transaction between the user and the library is explicitly protected in all the most prominent statements of the ethics of the librarian. To quote the most obvious example, the American Library Association (ALA)'s Code of Ethics states quite simply that:

> We protect each library user's right to privacy and confidentiality with respect to information sought or received and resources consulted, borrowed, acquired or transmitted.[7]

So strong is attachment to this principle, that there is reason to suspect that confidentiality between librarian and client may be a value insufficiently questioned by the library profession. In a particularly revealing study by Hauptman,[8] librarians' responses to a request for information on a topic that might produce an ethical dilemma were unobtrusively tested. He asked at library reference desks for information on explosives, whilst conveying the impression that his motives for the enquiry might be dangerous. He met with instant compliance on every occasion the test was made. The librarians seemed not to be considering the ethical implications of their actions, except insofar as it was part of a confidential transaction with a member of the public. Some professional debate did follow the publication of this research, but it was fairly low-key. More recent similar research in Slovenia suggests that the same passive acceptance of the privacy principle remains intact.[9] Codes of ethics are not intended to take ethical issues out of the arena of debate, but to provide practitioners with guidance on decision making. If professionals stand aside from making judgements, then the provisions of the law provide the only real framework.

Data Protection Law

The law in many countries protects personal data held by organisations of all kinds. The UK, for instance, has the Data Protection Acts of 1984 and 1998. These laws are designed to ensure that personal data is collected, processed, used and disclosed in a lawful and controlled manner. The legislation is probably more important as a statement of principle than as a real barrier to misuse of data. For instance, the laws forbid the transfer of personal data from the European economic area, unless the recipient country has adequate privacy protection. This is all very well, but the USA, which is at the heart of all networked communication worldwide, lacks data protection laws. To exclude the USA from the exchange of data resources would be almost inconceivable when more than 50 percent of the world's Web sites are hosted there, and it is at the forefront of the development of e-business. To deal with this problem, the EU has made a "Safe Harbour" agreement with the USA, which depends on self-regulation, provides little apparent scope for enforcement and does not offer individuals the right to compensation for infringements of privacy. Whatever the general virtues of data protection law, its weakness in an environment of global information exchange is obvious. What is more, at the same time as weaknesses in the law are being identified more clearly, there are new challenges to the security of data, both official and commercial.

The Challenges

Official Challenges

The state is naturally sensitive on matters of national security, and the terrorist destruction of the World Trade Centre and their attack on the Pentagon on September 11, 2001, show precisely why. This concern with security reaches as far as libraries. Take the US Library Awareness Program for example.[10] Under this FBI program, which seems to have begun in the 1980s, librarians could be required to reveal names and reading habits of users who could be considered hostile to the USA. Despite a campaign of opposition by the American Library Association, the programme seems to have continued after 1988, when it was originally exposed. Although such a programme of surveillance of the intellectual activity of suspected enemies of the state was notionally possible in libraries before that time, it was unlikely to be very effective, for the practical reasons suggested above. In the digital library the challenge is much more real because the data that contains the answers is there.

There is also a new dimension to the challenge, resulting from public access to the Internet in libraries. Internet content includes extremist political comment, and provides a means for the exchange of subversive messages and illegally acquired data. Greater control of Internet communication thus comes on to the agenda. The Echelon system, a project of the US, British and other governments, exploits the technical capacity that governments possess to intercept telecommunications signals. Using monitoring centres (notably that at Menwith Hill in the UK), this system filters international telecommunications traffic for the presence of words that might suggest messages with subversive or criminal content. This is in itself only of indirect interest to librarians. What is worrying is the tendency to reinforce this technical capacity with a shift of legal responsibility to reveal data on to those who handle it rather than those who originate it.

A very striking example of this tendency is the UK Regulation of Investigatory Powers Act, passed in July, 2000. Amongst its other provisions, it requires that Internet service providers include a "reasonable interception capability" in their networks. If officially intercepted communications are encrypted, suspects can be made to divulge the decryption keys on pain of imprisonment. Although this does not explicitly concern the providers of access (as opposed to "service providers") it brings responsibility for disclosure of potentially confidential data much closer to service organisations like libraries.

Commercial Challenges

The tendency of such laws is reinforced by the availability of software products to keep track of what happens on an office (or library) network. Products can record keystrokes, time and date, name of program executed and the specific workstation on which activities occur. As an aid to the management of Internet access, and as possible filtering devices to limit "unacceptable use" of information, many libraries are already installing the products of companies like Surfcontrol. The company provides content filtering software integrated with a range of systems and applications such as firewalls, proxy servers, search engines and ISP services, offering systems protection against security breaches and inappropriate internal usage.[11] This provides precisely the capacity to monitor, and indeed control, information use that the libraries of the past lacked.

At the same time it must be pointed out, that this offers positive opportunities for libraries. Estabrook persuasively argues the case exploiting user data for the better identification of what users want and the more accurate targeting of services.[12] It is also obvious that the data reveals a great deal about the tastes and preferences of the library's users as consumers. Recent users of library OPACs (Online Public Access Catalogues) will have noticed that in a number of cases a link is offered to an e-bookseller such as Amazon.com. The library user can click on this make a purchase order for a copy of a book (maybe a book that the library does not hold) and the retailer pays a small commission to the library for the service. The evidence of people's reading and research could also be used to identify possible consumers in other categories. This kind of infringement of privacy, would clearly transform user data into a commodity rather than a confidential trust between professional and client.

The Loughborough Research

Because the issue of user privacy issue in the digital library is new and little discussed, the Legal and Professional Research Group of Loughborough University's Department of Information Science set out to research professional and user responses. *Re*:source (the UK Council on Museums Libraries and Archives) provided funding to investigate the issue and develop guidelines for library management practice.[13] A survey of librarians' awareness of the issue, and of practice in academic and special libraries in Britain, was conducted at the end of 2000. This was followed in the spring of 2001 by a survey of user perceptions in academic libraries. Initial analysis of the results of the surveys suggests that there is a dangerous gap between the privacy protection that the public believes the library offers, and the preparedness of librarians for providing this protection.

Over 400 users of a diverse group of academic libraries were interviewed to test user opinion. General levels of anxiety about threats to privacy were low amongst those surveyed. Highest levels of concern were over intrusion or mishandling of personal data by commercial organisations, with almost exactly 60 percent either very, or somewhat, concerned about this. Fewer than half of the respondents (46 percent) were aware of press reports concerning breaches of security which had put privacy at risk, and only 18 percent claimed to have experienced some invasion of their privacy whilst using the Internet. Fewer than 10 percent were in any way concerned about threats to privacy whilst using resources in the library. This was clearly based on trust in the library rather than indifference, because over 90 percent objected to the idea that libraries might sell information about users to commercial organisations, whilst 75 percent accepted that the library should monitor the use of electronic services to prevent misuse.

This relates in an interesting way to data from the earlier survey of librarians' awareness of privacy issues, and of practice in academic and special libraries in Britain. Findings from over 300 questionnaire responses (out of 1000 sent) show that the majority of the surveyed libraries have introduced data protection policies in line with the 1984 and 1998 Acts. However the majority was only 64 percent strong, and a remarkable 30 percent reported that there was no policy. Where there was policy, it might be expected to indicate that discussion of issues regarding privacy had taken place within the organization, but it is evident from the survey results that discussion of privacy issues between management and staff was rare. Although 14 percent of respondents indicated that discussion had taken place at some level within the organization (normally at management meetings), 81 percent indicated that decisions regarding privacy issues were made at management meetings without further briefing. Nevertheless, 66 percent of respondents considered security of data and protecting individual privacy to be of the highest importance in policy terms.

When asked what procedures were in place so as to respond when users requested information held on themselves, the picture is even less satisfactory. It is evident from the results of this survey that procedures ranged from the formal (18 percent of respondents had designated, and trained, data protection officers in the library) to 35 percent of respondents who replied that they "did not know" where to direct users who requested information. In 43 percent of cases, the librarian would make a decision on whether information should be divulged. However, in some circumstances, the data protection officer of the parent organization would be consulted for further advice prior to divulging information.

In contrast to this somewhat confused position with regard to protecting the privacy of library users, responses on matters concerning possible restriction of user access to information were much less ambiguous. 82 percent of respondents had implemented an Acceptable Use Policy (AUP) for use of library facilities, with a further 3 percent indicating plans for implementing an AUP in the near future.

Conclusions

Whilst analysis of the responses to both surveys is not yet complete, it is clear from results so far that users' faith in libraries as protectors of their personal data is to a good extent matched by librarians' strong perception of the importance of the issue. Where there is a gap, is in libraries' less-than-perfect preparedness to deal with privacy problems. Policy is unclear in a substantial minority of institutions and only in very small numbers of institutions has policy been developed through a consultative process between management and staff. This is obviously an unsatisfactory situation, but the project is intended to lead to the development of a policy guidelines document. The content of the surveys and other supporting research already suggests areas of content for these guidelines including: the consultation processes that should be followed; devising procedures for response to cases; designation of responsible persons and reporting procedures; documenting policy and presenting it to users for maximum awareness; and procedures for periodic and case-related review of policy.

To return to the metaphor of the secret garden, it was the height of the walls, the strength of the gate, and the steadfastness of their helper that allowed Frances Hodgson Burnett's young characters the scope in which to learn and develop. There is no real equivalent in the library to the physical barriers that gave them the privacy they needed. In fact, the situation of the library is paradoxical in that it is a public space at the same time as it offers privacy to its users. The only way that this privacy can be guaranteed is through the ethical standards of the librarians who are their helpers. However, this does not just mean ethics as principles: it has to include ethical conduct. This, in turn, is not just principled conduct in response to problems or incidents, but a preparedness that is rooted in principles. The research suggests that this preparedness is not as strong as it should be. Whilst that continues to be the case, the trust that the research shows users place in their libraries is not fully repaid.

References

1. Burnett, Frances Hodgson. *The secret garden*. London: Heinemann. 1911. (1957 edition).

2. Henderson, Robert. Russian political emigrés and the British Museum Library. *Library History* 9 1991. 59–68.

3. Sturges, Paul. The future of the library's past: library administrative records preservation, policy and practice. *IFLA Journal* 9 1983. 28–33

4. Black, Alistair and Purcell, Mark. Corporate memory or corporate blunder? *Library History Newsletter* 3 2001. 7–9.

5. Wiegand, Shirley A. *Library records: a retention and confidentiality guide*. Westport, Conn: Greenwood Press, 1994.

6. Chmara, Theresa. Privacy and confidentiality issues in providing public access to the Internet. *Library Administration and Management* 15 2001. 20–22.

7. Code of Ethics (1995) of the American Library Association. http://www.ala.org/alaorg/oif/ethics.html Accessed 07.02.2001

8. Hauptman, Robert. Professionalism or culpability? An experiment in ethics. *Wilson Library Bulletin* 50 1976. 626–7.

9. Juznic, Primoz. Excuse me, how do I commit suicide? Access to ethically debatable items of information in public libraries. *Library Management* 22 2001. 75–79.

10. Foerstel, Herbert S. *Surveillance in the stacks: the FBI's Library Awareness Program*. Westport, Conn: Greenwood Press, 1991.

11. Surfcontrol (2000) Managing Responsible Internet Usage. http://www.srfcontrol.com/news/press-releases/content Accessed 14.03.2001.

12. Estabrook, Leigh. Sacred trust or competitive opportunity: using patron records. *Library Journal* 121 1996. 48–49.

13. Sturges, P., Teng, V. and Iliffe, U. User privacy in the digital library environment: a matter of concern for information professionals. *Library Management* 22 2001. 364–370.

11

Libraries in the World of E-Commerce: Technological Opportunities and Ethical Implications

J.B. Hill and *Eric W. Johnson*

Introduction

With the advent of the Internet, library resources have become increasingly commercialized. While advertising has always been present in libraries through subscriptions to popular magazines and newspapers, librarians are now finding that free commercial Web sites and even subscription-based databases are filling the screens of library users with advertising as never before. Libraries benefit indirectly from these advertisements, as advertising revenues help underwrite the providers' cost of collecting and disseminating information. Facing static budgets and escalating costs, some libraries have decided that they can more directly benefit from advertising and other e-commerce solutions.

Virtually all libraries have discovered the advantages of offering and promoting their services on the Internet. This presence provides greater opportunities for libraries to emulate e-commerce sites and partner with commercial entities in delivering and enhancing services as well as developing income streams. Companies seek to attract customers via the Web through the placement of banner ads, development of e-mail customer lists and creation of links for Web referrals. With the use of Web pages and the latest generation of OPAC software, libraries can emulate successful commercial sites by incorporating advertisements, linking to commercial sites and using push technology. Established information providers, such as *Encyclopedia Britannica* and Lexis Nexis, now incorporate advertising in the delivery of their products. Is it time for libraries to follow suit? This paper addresses recent developments and examines the ethical issues associated with libraries developing commercial relationships via e-commerce.

Commercialism in Libraries and the Public Sector

Since the 1980's, there has been a greater acceptance of the privatization of activities and services that have traditionally rested within the exclusive domain of the public sector. As a result, commercial interests in the public sphere have continued to grow, finding public institutions such as schools and libraries to be attractive and willing markets.

During the 1990's, public schools embraced commercialization and privatization. Commercial activities such as program sponsorship, exclusive agreements, appropriation of space, sponsored educational materials, electronic marketing and privatization all experienced significant growth during this period.[1] A U.S. General Accounting Office report chronicled the growth of commercial activities in public schools in the 1990's, "a period characterized by tightened school budgets."[2] The study found that without comprehensive state and federal laws and regulations, the degree of commercial activities varied greatly throughout the different localities and concluded that "new technologies, particularly involving the Internet, might increase opportunities for schools to earn money but raise concerns about student privacy."

The need for technology has driven many underfunded schools to make commercial arrangements with companies such as ChannelOne and ZapMe! While critics have called these arrangements "a Faustian bargain and yet another attempt by corporate America to buy the hearts, minds and spending habits of schoolchildren," these companies have been successful in providing technology to a large number of technology-hungry schools through the sale of advertising time.[3] In the ZapMe! Agreement, ZapMe! provides computers (and ads) in exchange for a promise that students will use the computers a minimum of 4 hours per day. School libraries and media centers have been the beneficiaries of ZapMe! computer labs.

Public libraries have also benefited from arrangements with the private sector. Most notably, the Gates Library Foundation's provision of Microsoft-based computers and Microsoft software has greatly increased the computer resources of small public libraries. While Bill Gates has been heralded as a great benefactor to libraries, Microsoft also benefits from the gift by creating greater future demand for Microsoft products. Critics suggest that this indicates a current willingness of libraries to embrace "corporatization" and "commercialization" that is counter to the traditional mission of libraries.[4]

In actuality, commercial interests have always been present in libraries and library organizations. Libraries have always accepted indirect advertising through magazine and newspaper advertisements. The placement of these ads supported the publication of these items, keeping these products viable in the market and affordable to libraries. In the electronic arena, established information providers such as Lexis Nexis have incorporated banner advertisements.

Recently, Britannica.com attempted unsuccessfully to support the availability of the entire *Encyclopædia Britannica* through ad revenue.[5] Other corporate-sponsored, advertising-supported information appears daily on the Internet screens in libraries.

The American Library Association (ALA) has long accepted corporate sponsorship and partnerships to further its initiatives. Weary librarians at ALA conferences have eagerly taken advantage of corporate sponsorship by riding shuttle buses, complaining more about the buses' running late than the commercialization of the organization.

Other library organizations have accepted corporate sponsorship to further their mission. Recently, Louisiana's statewide LOUIS Consortium negotiated with one of its database suppliers, the Gale Group, to sponsor billboard advertising for the consortium in an effort to raise public awareness of LOUIS and the services that the consortium provides to the citizens of the state. Once created, the billboards have continued to be made available as public service announcements on unused billboards throughout the state during 2001. The arrangement proved beneficial for the consortium as Web page hits increased as a result of the promotion. Other consortia are reportedly investigating similar promotional arrangements with other vendors.[6]

At first glance, these relationships seem to be a win-win situation for library organizations and corporate sponsors. The non-profit organization gains a service it can not afford or legally purchase for itself while the corporate sponsor gains publicity and the goodwill of its customers. Most librarians accept this as a reasonable practice. However, these relationships have their critics. In responding to ALA's acceptance of corporate sponsorship, Rosenzweig asks "by what right do we, in effect, sell our profession's reputation for impartiality to companies for promotional purposes?"[7]

With the advent of the Internet, additional opportunities for commercial arrangements will force librarians and library organizations to examine their role in the organizations and populations they serve, and ask themselves what professional price does commercialism exact.

Commercial Opportunities through E-Commerce

The Internet is changing the way that businesses do business so it is reasonable that the Internet will also have a significant effect on the way that non-profit organizations deliver goods and services. Although the Internet was developed for the non-profit research industry, the commercial potential of the Internet has driven Internet growth. While e-commerce is still in its infancy, Internet advertising revenues have increased from $40 million in 1995 to $8.2 billion in 2000, and in 2000 the 140 million Internet users generated $168 billion in business transactions.[8]

E-commerce offers libraries a variety of opportunities. Acquisitions departments have embraced e-commerce for faster, streamlined ordering of materials. Just as libraries have become e-commerce customers, libraries have begun to look to commercial models to direct them in the marketing of resources and services and become what Gerry McKiernan calls the "commercialized library."[9]

Toward this end, Steve Coffman suggests that libraries should look to Amazon.com for the future of library services.[10]

Some libraries are following this advice and beginning to view their Web pages as "portals" to information resources. Portals are "systems which gather a variety of useful information resources into a single, 'one stop' Web page, helping the user to avoid being overwhelmed by 'infoglut' or feeling lost on the Web."[11] Commercial portals have become commonplace on the Internet. Yahoo, with its customizable My Yahoo!, was one of the first Web sites to adopt the idea of a personalized interface. Today most of the major search engines and subject directories offer customizable portals.

A few large academic libraries have begun experimenting with the delivery of personalized services through library portals. North Carolina State University, California Polytechnic State University, Cornell University, New York University, the University of Utah, the University of Washington and Virginia Commonwealth University have been experimenting with personalized portals since the late 1990's. To date, the reaction at those campuses has been mixed.[12]

However, the demand for customized services, one of the tenets of e-commerce, will increasingly influence library services. While only a few libraries have adopted the portal approach, the latest generation of library OPAC software (e.g. Sirsi's iBistro) facilitates the incorporation of some of the same customization features that Amazon and Yahoo have popularized. With out-of-the-box features such as an Internet search engine interface, personal customization options, collaborative filters (e.g., "other customers have also selected..."), links to commercial and non-commercial sites and the opportunity for banner ads, the library catalog is now positioned to take advantage of e-commerce design features and commercial opportunities.

Banner Ads

A number of libraries have begun to use banner ads to advertise library databases and services. Gerry McKiernan at Iowa State University has created BANaRAMa(sm): A Registry of Library Promotional Banner Pages to monitor this trend. BANaRAMa(sm) is "a categorized listing of library or library-related Web sites that use banner 'ads' or scrawling or scrolling messages, to promote library collections, resources, or services."[13]

Library patrons are routinely bombarded by "the shrill, intrusive and unavoidable nature of corporate-based information and ads on the Web."[14] The library has no control over the ads that appear on the commercial Web sites and electronic services (e.g. Lexis Nexis) to which the library directly refers patrons or provides access; however, advertisements on the library's Web site are controllable. The library can theoretically select advertisers that are responsible and serve the mission of the library and institution.

For e-commerce advertisers, a library's Web site offers a potentially attractive market. The Web site is heavily visited and some components of the site, such as the online catalog, have a high degree of stickiness (i.e. the ability to retain users on the site for significant periods of time). The library is a trusted source for information, so the e-commerce site may inherit a bit of that trustworthiness. Library users have known demographics so marketing opportunities are easily identified.

While there has been some discussion of government advertising and library advertising, few libraries have yet to embrace the practice of advertising on their Web sites.[15] On the other hand, many libraries have shown a willingness to participate in e-commerce through "Associates" or "Affiliate" programs.

Associates Programs

Associates programs are e-commerce arrangements where referral fees are paid to owners of Web sites that refer customers. These referral fees may be fees for each referral or a percentage of the sales generated by the referrals. Amazon.com was one of the first e-commerce sites to establish an associates program. Currently, Amazon.com pays from 5 to 15 percent of each purchase as a referral fee to the owner of the page that refers the customer. BarnesandNoble.com has an affiliate program that pays a referral fee of up to 7 percent of each purchase. By 2001, Amazon.com had over 500,000 associate program members and BarnesandNoble.com had over 380,000 affiliate partners.[16] Virtually all other online booksellers have copied Amazon.com and developed associates programs.

For the e-commerce vendor, associates programs offer an easy, inexpensive method to generate business. The associate member is in effect advertising for the company and then forwarding the potential customers to e-commerce site. The e-commerce company only needs to pay the associate when a sale is made and income is received.

Alibris, an online out-of-print and hard-to-find book dealer, has targeted library acquisitions departments and library patrons by reaching agreements with two primary bibliographic databases, Bowker's booksinprint.com and OCLC's WorldCat.[17] The agreements will permit links from bibliographic records to the bookseller's site for purchase of materials.

Libraries have begun reaching agreements with booksellers through the booksellers' associates programs. Peter Scott has developed a list of some libraries that are members of associates programs.[18] A few of the public libraries that have joined associates programs are the Tacoma (Washington) Public Library, the Public Library of Charlotte & Mecklenburg County, North Carolina, the Pequea Valley (Pennsylvania) Public Library, the New York Public Library and the Winnipeg Millennium Library.

Many of the libraries that have joined the associates programs have touted the added value of links to booksellers. For example, Tacoma (Washington) Public Library's online catalog has a statement/hyperlink at the bottom of bibliographic records in the library's catalog that reads "Check the Amazon.com on-line bookstore for review and other information...." "'Amazon.com is more than an on-line bookstore. It is an electronic gathering place for people who love and value books,' said J. Abel Corpus, President of the Library's Board of Trustees explaining why a public library would partner with the on-line commercial Web site."[19]

Other libraries explain the financial incentives of their affiliation. For example, the Public Library of Charlotte & Mecklenburg County, North Carolina has a link from its Web page that states "Support PLCMC Buy Books Online." The page allows patrons to search Amazon from the Web page: "Use Amazon.com's search tool below to find and purchase a book by author, title or keyword and support the Public Library of Charlotte & Mecklenburg County. Not only do you save money by purchasing books at a discount, but Amazon.com will also donate a portion of your purchases to the library. Thank you for your support!"[20]

The St. Charles (Illinois) Public Library is not directly a member of an associates program; however, the library has a Friends group that sponsors fundraising activities, including a membership in an associates program. Currently, the Friends raise money for the library through sales by Amazon.com. "As an Amazon.com Associate, the Friends will receive up to 15 percent in referral fees for books ordered as a result of the direct link from the Library's Web site."[21]

The Pequea Valley Public Library in Pennsylvania has a "Support Us" link on its Web page with links to e-commerce sites such as Amazon.com, 1bookstreet.com, Allbooks4less.com, magazines.com and textbookx.com. The page states that "we have setup arrangements with the following companies to donate part of your purchase to the Library. If you are going to purchase a book, why not click through here? It will be the same price and you are supporting the library."[22]

The New York Public Library sells a wide variety of products online via "The Library Shop," an online gift shop hosted by Yahoo! Store. The New York Public Library Online Bookstore also sells books and gift certificates through links to BarnesandNoble.com. "A portion of each sale through BarnesandNoble.com when entered from NYPL's Online Bookstore contributes to the support of The New York Public Library."[23]

The Winnipeg Millennium Library has one of the most ambitious fund-raising e-commerce sites. In addition to requesting donations for the library, the library's Web site has an e-commerce shopping mall where library users can make purchases from 140 different merchants, including Amazon.com, L. L. Bean, Dell and 1-800-Flowers.[24]

Public libraries seem more inclined to link to online booksellers such as Amazon.com and BarnesandNoble.com. Most academic libraries that link to Amazon seem to do so as parts of Web links for patrons to find bibliographic information rather than to receive reimbursement. However some universities, such as CUNY, Duke and Valparaiso, have begun generating revenues by linking to online booksellers.

Valparaiso Law School Library provides a link to Amazon.com, suggesting that students "will pay Amazon's usual discounted price and Valparaiso Law School will receive a donation equal to 5 percent of this price."[25] The CUNY Graduate Center's Virtual Bookshop provides links to Amazon.com, BAMM.com and Alibris.com. The stated purpose of the Virtual Bookshop is "to help students purchase books for classes and help raise money for the Mina Rees Library in the process."[26] Duke University's Fuqua School of Business Library's "Virtual Book Store" highlights current business books and allows patrons to click a link to see the status and location in the library or link to Amazon for reviews or purchases. In a twist on the role of the library, the library suggests that the patrons "'try before you buy' by checking out a book from the Library before purchasing it!"[27]

Ethical Implications of E-Commerce

The ethical considerations connected to advertising, partnerships with commercial vendors, and the attraction of potential customers for these vendors are many and varied. On the one hand, an argument may be made for providing the library patron with a range of options in securing needed information or material; on the other, a reading of the American Library Association's *Code of Ethics* might put some of the latest partnerships between libraries and commercial vendors under ethical scrutiny.

Adopted by the ALA Council on June 28, 1995, the current *ALA Code of Ethics* has its origins from the "Suggested Code of Ethics" that appeared in the 1930 American Library Association Bulletin. The current code states:

> We provide the highest level of service to all library users through appropriate and usefully organized resources; equitable service policies; equitable access; and accurate, unbiased, and courteous responses to all requests.
>
> We uphold the principles of intellectual freedom and resist all efforts to censor library resources.
>
> We protect each library user's right to privacy and confidentiality with respect to information sought or received and resources consulted, borrowed, acquired or transmitted.
>
> We recognize and respect intellectual property rights.
>
> We treat co-workers and other colleagues with respect, fairness and good faith, and advocate conditions of employment that safeguard the rights and welfare of all employees of our institutions.
>
> We do not advance private interests at the expense of library users, colleagues, or our employing institutions.
>
> We distinguish between our personal convictions and professional duties and do not allow our personal beliefs to interfere with fair representation of the aims of our institutions or the provision of access to their information resources.
>
> We strive for excellence in the profession by maintaining and enhancing our own knowledge and skills, by encouraging the professional development of co-workers, and by fostering the aspirations of potential members of the profession.[28]

Three specific statements in the *Code* seem especially tied to this burgeoning and somewhat gray area. The first concerns the provision of "equitable access" to service and resources; the second provides for the protection of "each library user's right to privacy and confidentiality with respect to information sought or received"; the third states outright that "we do not advance private interests at the expense of library users." How do these tenets of library ethics hold up in this new era of e-commerce?

One of the long-standing controversies in the library world has been "fee vs. free," that is, providing information or service to a patron at a cost to that patron. Traditionally libraries were the temples of "free" knowledge for all, but realistically the books and other materials they offered were not entirely free, since taxpayers, private subscribers, state and city governments or tuition-paying students actually provided the funding to support the library. As the world has shifted from a print mode into an electronic one, the costs associated with information and its access have risen. With the advent of electronic searching, libraries began passing on the costs of searching databases and obtaining abstracts and later full-text articles to the patrons requesting them. The access to the information may be equal for all, but actually having it placed in your hands might come at a cost.

Links to commercial vendors such as Amazon.com or BarnesandNoble.com may continue to widen the gulf between the information haves and have-nots. A patron finds that his library does not carry a specific book he is seeking, but if he owns a credit card, and if there is a link to a vendor on the library's Web page or online catalog, he can have the desired title in his hands in a matter of days. The patron without the financial means to purchase his information must take the traditional and often more time-consuming routes of interlibrary loan (borrowing the material from another library), trying other libraries, or settling for alternate information. Income becomes a key factor in obtaining needed information.

A more insidious effect of such library-vendor links might be a replacement of free services by fee-based services and the reliance by the library on the patron to find (and pay for) his own material, thereby saving the library some dollars, and actually netting the library some dollars if it receives a percentage of sales. Without intending to do so, libraries could be encouraging users to bypass publicly supported services for pay services. Libraries must be careful not to relinquish their mission of information to and for the people nor turn over their purchasing role to their patrons, and make the effort to offer and promote free services as prominently as fee-based services.

Privacy and confidentiality of users also come into play when dealing with commercial vendors. It has become a standard in the electronic industry to collect data on computer users who visit specific Web sites, who respond to contests and giveaways, and who purchase goods via the Internet. In a monthly column in *Information Today*, Robin P. Peek reports that Sun Microsystems CEO Scott McNealy had stated, "Get over it, you have no privacy anyway." Peek goes on to wonder how many people are prepared to "surrender what shreds remain of their privacy" to allow various advertising schemes, in which a reward of some sort is dangled before them, to work.[29]

The average library user may not realize that in linking to a commercial site from the library's Web page he is providing personal and demographic information to the owners of that site. Heckart suggests that "enticements encourage customers to forget that they are being manipulated to reveal information about themselves and their preferences."[30] Privacy is increasingly being supplanted by informal consent. Internet users are agreeing to provide personal information as a trade off for personalized service.

For libraries, such portals present two potential problems. The collection of patron data will decrease the level of privacy that library users have historically enjoyed and the creation of specialized services based on this data will lead to inequitable levels of service. If libraries make a conscious effort to ensure patron privacy, then "digital libraries might be seen as a refuge where users could trust that personal information would not be abused."[31]

At the very least, a warning such as that offered by some Web mail providers might be in order to alert the patrons that they are leaving the library site, and that the library has no control over the content and practices of the new site. They might also consider stating the privacy issues involved in linking onto a commercial site; if they know, for example, that a service collects information on customers, they can state that in a disclaimer.

The third ethical point mentioned in the ALA *Code of Ethics*, advancing private interests at the expense of library users, connects directly to library-vendor partnerships. As previously stated, Alibris, Amazon.com and BarnesandNoble.com have similar associates programs. When OCLC, a global library cooperative with over 40,000 members, announced a link from its FirstSearch Web site to the Alibris Web site, a debate immediately ensued on the College Libraries listserv. One librarian called it "an unholy alliance with selected vast commercial conglomerates" that could ruin local booksellers "who are struggling to survive in hostile times."[32] Another felt that "librarians would be better off if they worried less about their purity and more about giving users what they want," noting that no one was forcing users of WorldCat to link to Alibris.[33] A third was fine with the idea, as long as OCLC listed other out-of-print suppliers as well and did not give Alibris a monopoly.[34]

A number of ethical issues arise from this practice. First and foremost, is the library advancing private interests (e.g., a commission for supplying customers to the vendor) at the expense of the library user? True, no one is forcing the patron to click on a link, much less make a purchase from the partnering vendor. But many are uncomfortable with the creeping commercialism that this practice seems to espouse. Yet this is only one example of such a partnership between the library and a vendor. Databases subscribed to by libraries and made widely available to their users have long had banner ads displayed on their pages. The library is certainly not endorsing these advertisers, nor benefiting from their appearance in the database, yet there they are, enticing users of the database to become new customers.

Vendors have also provided free advertising and publicity for libraries and library consortia and supported library conference activities and events. By doing so the vendors have advertised their own products and gotten their names out into the library world. Gale's sponsorship of an advertising campaign for the LOUIS Library Consortium in Louisiana has been noted; other vendors regularly use librarians in their full-page ads in the various professional library journals.

Little attention has been paid to the ethical concerns around such generous vendor support. Yet are libraries not tacitly showing support for these vendors with such initiatives? If a library accepts free mousepads with advertising on them and places them next to their public workstations, are they sending the message to their users that they should buy from these advertised companies? Or are they simply providing another service to their patrons, and letting the patrons decide for themselves whether they will take the bait?

A serious related issue to these partnerships spills over from the ethical arena to the legal one. State- or city-supported libraries, whether they be public or academic, must go through a competitive bidding process in order to purchase goods or services. The inclusion of a banner ad on a library's Web page and the subsequent receipt of money as a result of patron purchasing might very well be seen as an unfair advantage being given to one company over another if such as bidding process did not take place beforehand.

A further issue involves equal access by outside groups to the public library. Unless they establish specific guidelines, libraries as public organizations may not be able to reject anyone's advertising, unlike private organizations such as newspapers and radio and television stations, which can and do. Taking this to the extreme, any hate group could gain legitimacy by advertising on a library's Web page.[35] Libraries using such advertising must weigh these considerations carefully and examine existing state and local laws before entering into any partnerships with vendors which might later be construed as being somewhat shady or turn out to be detrimental, rather than beneficial, to these libraries.

Conclusion

Just as the advent of the computer radically changed the manner in which the world conducts business, it also brought monumental changes to the ways in which libraries provided information to their patrons. Now the lines between the commercial interests of Business and the traditionally gratis services of the Library are beginning to blur, as the two become partners in this new era of information. As with any such partnerships, ethical and legal concerns are bound to arise, and must be carefully considered if this partnership is to be successful to both sides.

Given the rapid development of the Electronic Age, such an alliance can be highly beneficial and mutually rewarding, as long as both parties take into account their missions and goals. The "fee vs. free" debate will take on an increased importance in the coming years, and libraries will need to take steps slowly when entering into agreements with commercial vendors. There is no reason that such agreements cannot bring to library users and information seekers new levels of service and resources, as long as ethics are not cast by the wayside in the development of this partnership. It is the patron, after all, for whom libraries exist, and that central and all-important *raison d'etre* cannot and must not be forgotten or ignored.

References

1. Alex Molnar, "The Commercial Transformation America's Schools," Paper presented at the John Dewey Memorial Lecture, Association for Supervision and Curriculum Development Conference, New Orleans, LA, 26 March 2000, <http://www.asu.edu/educ/epsl/Archives/cace-00-01.htm> (22 September 2001).

2. United States. General Accounting Office, *Public Education: Commercial Activities in Schools: Report to Congressional Requesters,* 2000, <http://purl.access.gpo.gov/GPO/LPS8561> (22 September 2001).

3. Michael Bazeley, "ZapMe! School Role Debated," *Silicon Valley News* 7, no. 6

(1999), <http://www0.mercurycenter.com/svtech/news/indepth/docs/zapme032299.htm> (22 September 2001).

4. Juris Dilevko, "Why Sally Tisdale is Really Upset About the State of Libraries: Socio-Political Implications of Internet Information Sources," *Journal of Information Ethics* 8, no. 1 (Spring 1999): 37–62.

5. Steven M. Zeitchik, "Looking for Cash and Answers, Britannica Restructures," *Publishers Weekly* 248, no. 21 (May 21 2001): 24.

6. Carolyn Coco, "LOUIS Public Relations Campaign in Full Swing," *Louisiana Libraries* 63, no. 2 (Fall 2000): 27.

7. Mark Rosenzweig, "Branded! Hucksterism @ Your Library," *American Libraries* 32, no.5 (May 2001): 46.

8. Marcus Chi-Hung Ling and Kevin Lawler, "Internet Advertising, Game Theory and Consumer Welfare," *Electronic Commerce Research* 1 (2001): 169–181; Interactive Advertising Bureau, "Interactive Advertising Bureau (IAB) Reports $8.2 Billion Online Ad Revenue in the United States for Year 2000 Fourth Quarter Totals $2.2 Billion," April 23, 2001, <http://www.iab.net/news/content/revenue.html> (22 September 2001).

9. Gerry McKiernan, "The 'Commercialized' Library," *Archive of the Web4Lib Electronic Discussion*, 7 Aug 2000, <http://sunsite.berkeley.edu/Web4Lib/archive/0008/0076.html> (22 September 2001).

10. Steve Coffman, "Building Earth's Largest Library: Driving into the Future," *Searcher* 7, no. 3 (March 1999), <http://www.infotoday.com/searcher/mar99/coffman.htm> (22 September 2001).

11. Michal Looney and Peter Lyman, "Portals in Higher Education," *EDUCAUSE Review* 35, no. 4 (July/Aug 2000): 30–33.

12. Eric Lease Morgan, ed., "Special Issue: User-Customizable Library Portals," *Information Technology and Libraries* 19, no. 4 (Dec 2000): 166–205.

13. Gerry McKiernan, "BANaRAMa(sm): A Registry of Library Promotional Banner Pages," July 3, 2000, <http://www.public.iastate.edu/~CYBERSTACKS/Banarama.htm> (22 September 2001).

14. See note 4 above.

15. Brian Kelly, "Beyond Design: Advertising on Your Web Site," Paper presented at the Internet Librarian International 2001 Conference, London, March 27, 2001, <http://www.ukoln.ac.uk/web-focus/events/conferences/ili-2001/advertising/> (22 September 2001); Brian Kelly, "Legal, Decent, Honest and Truthful?" *Electronic Public Information*, July 2001, <http://www.ukoln.ac.uk/web-focus/articles/spin-2001/word2000-html/> (22 September 2001); Jonathan G. S. Koppell, "Analysis: Government sites debate Web ads," CNN.com, February 8, 2001, <http://europe.cnn.com/2001/TECH/industry/02/08/gov.ads.idg/index.html> (22 September 2001); Skip Rudolph et.al., "Affiliating with Online Vendors; Productive Partnerships?" Paper presented at the ALCTS Acquisitions Section's Acquisitions Librarians/Vendors of Library Materials Discussion Group, ALA Midwinter Meeting, Washington, D.C., January 13, 2001; Peter Scott, "Making Money with the Internet," Paper presented at NetSpeed2000, Calgary, Manitoba, Canada, September 2000, <http://www.lights.com/~scott/netspeed2000> (22 September 2001).

16. Amazon.com, "Amazon.com Associates Program," 2001, <http://www.amazon.com/exec/obidos/subst/associates/join/associates.html/107-7232125-2261321> (22 September 2001). BarnesandNoble.com, "Barnes & Noble.com Affiliates Program," 2001, <http://www.barnesandnoble.com/affiliate/> (22 September 2001).

17. Alibris, "R. R. Bowker Joins Forces with Alibris to Enable Web-based Purchasing via booksinprint.com," June 15, 2001, <http://www.alibris.com/about/press_releases/06152001bowker.cfm > (22 September 2001); "Link to Alibris Available on OCLC FirstSearch Service," 20 September 2001, <FIRSTSEARCH-L@OCLC.ORG> (20 September 2001).

18. "Support a Library," <http://www.lights.com/webcats/support/libs.html> (22 September 2001).

19. Tacoma Public Library, "Tacoma Public Library Joins Amazon.com's Associates Program: Partnership Deepens Literary Resources for Library Patrons," <http://www.tpl.lib.wa.us/v2/News/Amazon.HTM> (22 September 2001).

20. Public Library of Charlotte & Mecklenburg County, "Support PLCMC Through Your Online Purchases," August 03, 2001, <http://www.plcmc.org/support/buyBooksOnline.htm> (22 September 2001).

21. St. Charles Public Library, "Amazon.com: A Friends of the Library Fund-Raiser," 2001, <http://www.st-charles.lib.il.us/low/amazon.htm> (22 September 2001).

22. Pequea Valley Public Library, "Buy New Books," <http://www.intercourse.lib.pa.us/main/buynewbooks.html> (22 September 2001).

23. New York Public Library, "The New York Public Library Online Bookstore," 1999, http://www.nypl.org/bookstore/ (22 September 2001).

24. Winnipeg Library, "Winnipeg's Millennium Library," <http://www.millenniumlibrary.com/flash.html> (22 September 2001).

25. Valparaiso University Law Library, "Valparaiso Law School Library," <http://www.valpo.edu/law/library/> (22 September 2001).

26. City University of New York, Graduate Center, "The CUNY Graduate Center's Virtual Bookshop," 2000, <http://www.gc.cuny.edu/bookshop/howto.html> (22 September 2001).

27. Duke University. The Ford Library at the Fuqua School of Business, "Library Bookstore FAQ," <http://www.lib.duke.edu/fsb/bookshopfaq.htm> (22 September 2001).

28. American Library Association, "American Library Association Code of Ethics," June 28, 1995, <http://www.ala.org/alaorg/oif/codeofethics.pdf> (22 September 2001).

29. Robin P. Peek, "New Web Advertising Venues Emerge Offering Rewards to the Viewer," *Information Today* 16, no. 10 (November 1999): 46.

30. Ronald J. Heckart, "Imagining the Digital Library in a Commercialized Internet," *The Journal of Academic Librarianship* 25, no. 4 (July 1999): 274–280.

31. See note 30 above.

32. Barbara Fister, "OCLC Bezoscat (oops, worldcat)," 21 September 2001, <COLLIB-L@acs.wooster.edu> (21 September 2001).

33. Carol Goodson, "Re: OCLC Bezoscat (oops, worldcat)," 21 September 2001, <COLLIB-L@acs.wooster.edu> (21 September 2001).

34. Barbara J. Morse, "Re: OCLC Bezoscat (oops, worldcat)," 21 September 2001, <COLLIB-L@acs.wooster.edu> (21 September 2001).

35. Bruce Pomerantz, "Advertising on Library Webpages," *Archive of the Web4Lib Electronic Discussion*, 25 Oct 1997, <http://sunsite.berkeley.edu/Web4Lib/archive/9710/0484.html> (22 September 2001).

12

INTRACULTURAL RECIPROCITY, INFORMATION ETHICS, AND THE SURVIVAL OF LIBRARIANSHIP IN THE 21ST CENTURY

Bill Crowley and *Deborah Ginsberg*

Abstract

This paper explores the operation of *intracultural reciprocity* in the ongoing valuation and long-term survival of America's 21st century librarians, as well as the nation's information or knowledge management specialists. Librarians and the staff of related information organizations are employed in a vast spectrum of work contexts. In consequence, the authors, who theorize from the perspective of *cultural pragmatism*, assert that no global predictions are possible regarding the future of such professionals. Instead, the effects of *intracultural reciprocity* on "librarian" survival in a number of arenas are explored. *Intracultural reciprocity* is defined by the authors to include both the changing, context-specific perceptions of mutual worth by participants in geographical, organizational, social, and other cultural arenas, as well as the willingness of arena participants to act on the basis of such perceptions. Interculturally reciprocal factors affecting the future of "librarianship" in various arenas are seen as including: perception of a collegial relationship of librarians, information specialists, or knowledge managers with other arena participants; degree of association with prevailing ethical ideals; customer valuation of services; extent of organizational autonomy and financial independence; for-profit, not-for-profit, corporate, academic, or governmental status; and ability to modify programs to meet changing demands.

Problem Statement

The authors believe that discussion of the very large and ill-defined problem addressed in this paper — the survival of librarianship in the 21st century—can best be introduced through a consideration of two suggestive cases. The first, Nancy Lemon's article, "Climbing the Value Chain: A Case Study in Rethinking the Corporate Library Function," deals with the conversion of the Owens Corning Corporate Library into an entity renamed *Knowledge Resource Services*. According to Lemon, this transformation was more than a simple alternation in name. It also included a number of significant personnel changes.

> We created a single new job title for each of our staff— Knowledge Resource Analyst. This job title covers all the previous job responsibilities, from Information Specialist to library support staff. Job responsibilities and compensation are ultimately defined by level of skill(s) achieved within a wide range of knowledge and skills required to work in the Center. Knowledge and skill are now the factors that determine career path and pay opportunity, rather than academic background and job title.[1]

For Lemon, this change process involved what appeared to be an acceptable level of human costs. "There were some casualties. Not everyone was personally suited for the transition to this vision for the future. The makeup of the staff changed during this time."[2]

The second case consists of a posting by Debbie Norley, employed with the Hillingdon Libraries, a United Kingdom (British) public library. In her e-mail, Norley asked for help from the PUBLIB maillist community with several issues resulting from widespread use of the Internet for reference assistance at her library. As recounted by Norley, the ease of use of the Internet and the availability of government funding led her employer to train "all library staff"— not just librarians— in using electronic resources to meet the information needs of "readers." Included in this transformation seems to be a job redefinition. To again quote Norley, "We have been told we are no longer librarians, but are 'Information Gateways.'" For Norley, these developments have left the "professional staff" feeling "very threatened." She concluded her posting with the declaration that "Soon librarians will be extinct!"[3]

In reviewing Lemon's article and Norley's posting, the authors discerned a number of commonalities shared by the American corporate and British public library examples. First, both employing organizations apparently equate the work of library, information, or knowledge staff solely with information provision and/or analysis. Second, the newly baptized "Knowledge Resource Analysts" and "Information Gateways" appear to be losing claims to professional status. This diminution is signified by the formal or informal elimination of the title of "librarian" and the submersion of "information specialist" into a job category lacking educational credentials as a condition of membership.

These case studies also seem to be near-textbook examples of process theories of professionalism. Such theories stress that professionalism is an ongoing activity. Unlike past formulations, process theories stress the tentative nature of such status. According to higher education researchers Shelia Slaughter and

Larry L. Leslie, "professionals are not automatically accorded respect, deference, and decent salaries when they acquire credentials, a code of ethics, of a body of knowledge, state licensure, or even theory."[4]

Professionals of all types must function in an emerging 21st century environment where they are far less protected from competition. *Globalization*, a process resulting from harnessing the dynamics of multinational corporations to new telecommunications infrastructures, produces a worldwide market capable of undermining national and local prestige systems. Applying concepts advanced by Slaughter and Leslie, it can be expected that librarians and other professionals will be spending much of their careers locked into ongoing "struggles to establish and defend" the salience of their degrees, value of their expertise, boundaries of their jurisdictions, and legal and economic arrangements that undergird their practice.[5]

The authors hold that the enormous growth in the number of potential competitors, coupled with the expansion of end-user electronic resources, will make it impossible for many librarians, information specialists, and knowledge managers to secure acknowledged rights to manage information provision and analysis on the basis of their educational credentials. That battle for exclusivity has been lost in corporate environments and is being contested in K-12, higher education, and public library contexts. 21st century librarianship in the United States of America may well live or die — not on the basis of superior information expertise — but on the grounds of its ability to combine such expertise with support of a spectrum of values prized by significant subcultures within the broader national culture. Arguably, both U.S. public law and social custom hold libraries, with the exception of corporate information or knowledge management centers, to be "educational, cultural, and entertainment organizations which happen to be very good at organizing, conveying, and using information."[6]

Further,

> Contemporary understandings of the educational responsibilities included in this definition can include anything from classes on how to maximize use of the Web, readers advisory services to encourage adults to maintain and/or expand their reading abilities, adult basic education classes, telecommunicated university courses, film programs followed by discussions, and evening story hours.... In a solely information world, librarians can easily be devalued. In a world which prizes the librarian as educator, a stronger case can be made for her [his] continued worth.[7]

As a template for discerning the ability of 21st century librarians to thrive in various American contexts, the authors will be advancing the concept of *intracultural reciprocity*. This concept is defined as including the changing, context-specific perceptions of mutual worth by participants in geographical, organizational, social, and other cultural arenas, as well as the willingness of arena participants to act on the basis of such perceptions. For purposes of discussion, to draw on the formulations of Slaughter and Leslie (above), *intracultural reciprocity* involving the profession of librarianship is deemed to be present when librarians are components of a group that accepts, in whole or in part, the claims of its members to the salience of their degrees, value of their expertise, boundaries of their jurisdictions, and the legal and economic arrangements undergirding their practice. By design the concept of *intracultural reciprocity* implies a dynamic and changing reality; it can be extended — or withdrawn — in response to alterations in societal, cultural, or market contexts.

American Cultural Values in the Pre-Globalization Era

The authors accept the definition of "values" offered by the political scientist and sociologist Seymour Martin Lipset. According to Lipset, "values" are "culturally determined sentiments produced by institutions or major historical events."[8] *Institutions* producing cultural values can be as diverse in their composition as superpower nations, world religions, and multinational corporations, as well as local elementary schools, volunteer civic organizations, and nuclear or extended families. *Major historical events* can be anything from the revelation of the *Qur'an* to the prophet Muhammad, the unfolding of the European Enlightenment, or the success of the American Revolution.

Robert K. Merton, in a now-classic essay examining values in "contemporary American culture," discerned that "in some large measure, money has been consecrated as a value in itself." In the United States, achieving financial success can be such a privileged *end* that members of the national culture will, on occasion, accept or even esteem the use of "illegitimate but technically efficient means."[9] In other words, in the broader American culture it is expected that one will succeed and the achievement of such success is deemed to be more important than the legitimacy of the means utilized.

Merton's assertion aside, to characterize America solely as a nation obsessed with financial success would be a gross oversimplification of reality. Other cultural values, at times equally or more important, are often in play. As a result of a professional career largely devoted to analyzing the United States of America in cross-national contexts, Seymour Martin Lipset is convinced that America is an "outlier" among advanced industrialized nations in

- being the "most religious, optimistic, patriotic, rights-oriented, and individualistic," as well as the having the most people in jail, the most lawyers per capita, the lowest percentage of eligible voters actually voting, and "the highest rate of participation in voluntary organizations."
- rejecting hereditary classes and demonstrating a commitment to upward mobility, equality of opportunity, and meritocracy, even as it privileges low taxes and the "least egalitarian" income distribution. [10]

In Lipset's analysis, the Protestant dissenter values on which the United States was founded, values emphasizing the perfectibility of human nature, a direct relationship with God, and a strict personal moral code, have historically influenced the American forms of the other major religious traditions that have become a part of national culture. The result of the complicated interaction is a particularly moralistic people and culture occasionally making public policy decisions for reasons transcending market values. On the whole, according to Lipset

> Americans are utopian moralists who press hard to institutionalize virtue, to destroy evil people, and eliminate wicked institutions and practices. A majority even tell [*sic*] pollsters that God is the moral guiding force of American democracy. They tend to view social and political dramas as morality plays, as battles between God and the Devil, so that compromise is virtually unthinkable. To this day, Americans, in harmony with their sectarian roots, have a stronger sense of moral absolutism than Europeans and even Canadians.[11]

For better or worse, this often-contradictory compilation of market, religious, and other values was and is representative of critical aspects of American national culture and its component subcultures. Inevitably, such values played — and continue to play — significant roles in developing and supporting a broad spectrum of academic, public, school, and special libraries, as well as the more recent entities known as information and knowledge management centers.[12] Before examining how such traditional standards are likely to impact 21st century librarianship, the authors believe a brief review of the influence of globalization, a phenomenon of the last two decades, is warranted.

American Values in a Globalized Context

In an extended analysis of the effects of global political economic change (globalization) on the national higher education and research policies of Australia, Canada, the United Kingdom and the United States, Shelia Slaughter and Larry L. Leslie discerned a number of trends with impact even beyond these crucial sectors. According to Slaughter and Leslie, a broad spectrum of economists, from the conservative Chicago School to post-Marxists, "all see the emergence, in traditional industrialized nations in the 1980s, of a global market creating conditions that mean less money for social welfare and education functions and more money for building corporate competitiveness."[13]

Slaughter and Leslie identified particularly strong benefits for areas identified with "technoscience," a concept defined to include such areas such as "computers, telecommunications, electronics, advanced materials, artificial intelligence, and biotechnology" which emphasize knowledge as a commodity. Technoscience areas gained in financial support while those "fields that were not close to the market, such as philosophy and religion, foreign languages, letters and performing arts, or fields that served the social welfare functions of the state, such as education and home economics, lost funds."[14] It should be noted that the national systems of higher education being transformed by the market include the American and Canadian American Library Association (ALA)-accredited programs that award professional credentials to many would-be librarians, information specialists, and knowledge managers. Here, it may be asserted that a parallel development is taking place *within* these ALA programs, the *internal* transformation from *library* to *information*-oriented instruction described by Daniel Callison and Carol L. Tilley as "the subjugation of librarianship."[15] Although a still controversial development, dropping "library" from program titles and privileging "information" education may be defended by the faculty and administrators involved as part of an effort to help insure program survival while helping graduates achieve *intracultural reciprocity* with other players in the for-profit arenas characteristic of globalized environments.

It must be stressed that fields losing support in a globalized market remain important sources of the values prized within the United States of America. Even in a market-influenced culture, aesthetic, humanistic, and moral activities cannot be fully contained in profit and loss models. For example, a recent *Chronicle of Higher Education* account of a Nebraska dispute over the use of fetal tissue in state university research noted how each side drew on religious traditions to justify its actions. Even in a globalized context, critical American concerns cannot be described solely in market terms.[16] The authors believe that the concept of the public library and public school as "public goods," to be supported through taxation for the common benefit, may also need to be viewed through similar moral lenses.

Nonetheless, the influence of the globalization in and on America's national culture and its constituent subcultures remains a potent and growing force, even as some who most enthusiastically embraced the market economy may now be suffering from its fluctuations. Anecdotal evidence in the Chicago area in the spring and summer of 2001 reveals that a number of corporate knowledge managers and information specialists, downsized in response to negative economic conditions, are applying for positions in local public libraries or school systems. It would be ironic indeed if this market-driven exodus of graduates of ALA-accredited programs from the corporate to the public sector helps to reduce growing professional shortages in more traditional library contexts.[17]

Yet, hiring ex-corporate knowledge managers in the public sector brings its own problems. The individuals thus employed are unlikely to have taken courses on youth literature and services or adult reading needs. They are even less likely to possess the certification required for employment as school library media specialists in a number of states. As such, they may have to be reeducated for work in the public sector.

The massive reallocation of university resources tracked by Slaughter and Leslie, where academic administrators have responded to globalization by redirecting money "to the natural sciences and engineering and away from the social sciences, the humanities, and most of the professional schools," has stripped "high enrollment units of resources needed to meet student demand."[18] Within the academic subsector of library and information education, a similar redirection of valuable resources, in this case, the working hours of the full-time faculty has been documented. It seems to be the case that the teaching of traditional "library" courses is now being shifted to part-time instructors in a number of ALA-accredited programs. To students of higher education, who understand that the academic prestige and level of resources directed of a course are often equated with it being taught by a full-time faculty member, this development reflects a diminished status for library concerns.[19]

Relevant Statistical Data

According to the latest data available online from the Association for Library and Information Science Education or ALISE, a total of 5,046 "ALA-accredited" master's degrees were awarded in academic year 1998–99. This figure compares with a figure of 5,024 such degrees awarded in academic year 1997–98 and 5,063 awarded in academic year 1996–97.[20] Associate, bachelor, and doctoral degrees were also granted by American Library Association-accredited programs.[21] However, the master's degree data are the most useful for pondering the future of librarians. Public libraries and school library media center employers tend to view the master's degree, preferably from an ALA-accredited program, as the optimum credential for professionals. It thus functions much like the MBA, MPA, or MSW degrees in conferring some level of professional status.[22] The dominance of the master's degree from an ALA-accredited program in the world of higher education is also evident. It has been retained as a criterion for hiring librarians even after the rest of the academic community, community colleges excepted, adopted the Ph.D. as the standard for employing faculty.[23]

Although suggestive, the data on ALA-accredited master's degrees have inherent limitations when speculating on the future of librarians. Among other restrictions, the numbers do not reflect the fact that the American Library Association, in an interesting example of *intracultural reciprocity*, officially affirms that certain master's degrees from programs accredited by the National Council for the Accreditation of Teacher Education (NCATE) and state education agencies are equally valid for employment as a school library media specialist.[24] The effects of such *intracultural reciprocity* in filling 21st century school library media positions are difficult to analyze. Unfortunately, reliable data on the number of such "alternative" degrees do not seem to be readily available (Personal communications August 2001).

Contested Library Futures — Private Sector

Further consideration of the future of 21st century librarianship must address a fact that American Library Association-accredited programs have been prone to gloss over in discussions of professional education. It is the reality that the term "information professional" is not always a satisfactory substitute for the word "librarian." As noted by Tim Wojcik,

> There are librarians in the public libraries in college/university libraries, in school/media center environments, and in the private sector with corporate libraries.... Information professionals typically work in the private sector. The titles of positions offered provide endless variety. Some include knowledge manager, information services specialist, knowledge management specialist, competitive intelligence analyst, etc.[25]

The authors believe that the "librarian" job title will largely disappear from the private sector in the 21st century. Graduates of ALA-accredited programs will undoubtedly find success in competing for corporate, government, and other "information," "knowledge," "competitive intelligence" positions. But the possession of a degree from an ALA-accredited program will not guarantee *intracultural reciprocity* with — and thus support from — other corporate players. The ALA-endorsed degree, although "hot" in the corporate sector during the growth era of the ".com world" may not even insure a competitive advantage for future job applicants.[26]

In the future, as electronic expertise is taught throughout the university world, those involved in corporate hiring decisions may have relevant credentials earned in business, computer science, or the other fields and disciplines educating students for a globalized market. When "information expertise" becomes more widespread, graduates of ALA-accredited programs are increasingly likely to be seen as merely one component of a larger application pool produced by an ever-wider spectrum of higher education programs. Under such circumstances, what researchers term *homophily*, or the tendency of individuals to associate with others who possess similar belief systems and educational experiences, will more and more be in play.[27] There will be a natural tendency for managers with management information systems (MIS) degrees or information-relevant MBA degrees to hire candidates with similar educational backgrounds.

The globalized market environment has encouraged new pathways to providing corporate personnel with information, knowledge management, or intelligence analysis skills. The results are contexts where numerous staff are expected to demonstrate "information" expertise as a condition of employment. In the for-profit sector, Merton's reminder of the enduring American emphasis on financial success is particularly applicable. To save costs, managers may be tempted to eliminate information or knowledge centers, or to follow the Owens Corning example and replace staff with degrees from ALA-accredited programs with less educated — and presumably less expensive — substitutes. Community colleges have developed substantial IT programs; the formerly unemployed who have become IT professionals via short courses of community college study may seem to be cost-effective alternatives to professional librarians with graduate educations.[28]

While generalizations are inevitably dangerous, it is fairly safe to assert that the leaders and other players in competitive private-sector environments are unlikely to accord *intracultural reciprocity* to holders of ALA-accredited master's degrees.[29] The authors thus believe that any meaningful discussion of the future of "librarians" in 21st century American society and its culture must be limited to the public sector and to the various academic environments— the ALA-accredited programs— that educate future librarians for employment in academic, public, and school library contexts.

Contested Library Futures — Public Sector

Academic Librarians

Several trends are now coming together to affect the long-term future of academic librarians. The first is the emerging belief that that decades of computerizing information, under the commendable leadership of academic librarians (or produced to meet their needs), are making all but the most esoteric information available in electronic formats for instructional purposes through academic Web pages. Negotiating access to ever-more-effective databases is now becoming a collaborative effort, carried out for their members by state or regional cooperatives. Second, cumulative decisions by traditional and emerging academic institutions to offer courses and entire degrees via the Web mean that there is less incentive for many students to visit the physical library.

Academic decision-makers are now facing increased demands to restrain costs by price-resistant consumers.[30] The recognition of new fiscal limits, if combined with a perception that library buildings and staff may be increasingly irrelevant, may encourage another round of library downsizing, comparable to that which decimated the ranks of catalogers after the rise of OCLC-assisted copy cataloging. In the near future, accreditation requirements for actual libraries and librarians may be eliminated to accommodate existing and emerging institutions offering degrees via the Internet.[31] If such changes in accreditation actually happen, even more traditional colleges and universities are likely to offer Web-based programs where instructors are expected to teach electronic information access as part of their courses. With diminishing use of on-campus library facilities, such institutions may seriously consider reducing the number of academic librarians to the levels required to maintain vendor contracts and handle the occasional and very specialized requests of faculty researchers.

In the higher-education component of the globalized economy discussed by Slaughter and Leslie (above), long-term survival for many academic librarians may involve adopting faculty requirements for *intracultural reciprocity* and enhancing their perceived value through earning doctorates and teaching information analysis and use in real and virtual classrooms to tuition-paying students.[32]

School Librarians

The 21st century prospects for school librarians, more often termed school library media specialists or, occasionally, information specialists, may be the most difficult to discern. Severe shortages do exist and a year-2000 survey has identified the existence of numerous position vacancies on a national level.[33] Depending on local contexts, these shortages of qualified personnel may contribute to removing educational requirements for appointment, as occurred in Pennsylvania in 1993.[34] They factor into the elimination of mandated school library media service, an action taken by Ohio's State Board of Education as recently as December 12, 2000.[35]

Initial analysis suggests that the elimination of educational requirements for school library media specialists and the removal of mandates for school library media centers will undermine *intracultural reciprocity* and contribute to school librarian deprofessionalization. Alternatively, in the globalized market economy described by Slaughter and Leslie, there is always the possibility that continuing shortages could lead to more positive developments. Numerous vacancies for school library media specialists could attract more students to ALA-accredited programs with school library components and/or their NCATE or state certified counterparts in colleges of education.

Public Libraries

The future of librarianship in American society as a whole may well be inextricably bound up with the fate of the nation's public libraries. In developing and delivering a broad range of programs, including pre-school and senior library services, public librarians and their support personnel are likely to offer both the first and the last library services used by most citizens. This extended interaction may even create mental templates through which the larger culture evaluates library services in any context. However, as with academic libraries and school libraries, success in this effort will require both the maintenance of *intracultural reciprocity* on the levels of local communities and the re-establishment of *intracultural reciprocity* between library practitioners and the faculty of programs accredited by the American Library Association.

For the most part, public libraries are locally-funded entities with a regularly demonstrated ability to adapt their service programs to meet changing community needs. In recent years, in addition to providing information, films, and books in multiple formats, public libraries have also added instruction on effective use of the Internet and evening storytelling hours to accommodate children whose parents or other caretakers are unable to bring them to the library during the working day. Resilience in responding to local demands, as such demands develop, is a strategy that is likely to prove effective over the long run. In fact, the public library's various publics will insist on such accommodations as a condition of continued funding and use.

Even in currently problematic areas, such as the dispute over the filtering of terminals to protect minors, it can be expected that the majority of the library using public will eventually impose a solution amenable to its wishes. Traditional American moral standards reacting to innovations in technology will virtually insure the filtering of children's terminals, combined with the active surveillance of children's use of such terminals by library staff, as an acceptable compromise in all but selected jurisdictions.[36]

Here, as might be discerned elsewhere in this paper, the authors are simply reporting possible futures and are not necessarily endorsing them. Lipset's moralized America may demand filtering children's terminals. However, it is equally likely to preserve a public library culture that otherwise advances its definitions of social good.

Fundamental to the arguments that public librarians will thrive throughout the 21st century is the reality that, in conjunction with library boards and local governments, it is the librarians themselves who determine employment qualifications. Through such efforts public librarians largely define their own conditions for *intracultural reciprocity* within their work cultures. This is a situation with rules far different from those operating in corporate, K-12, and academic contexts where administrators with MBAs, EdDs, and PhDs have the major responsibility for defining and acting upon the changing, context-specific perceptions of mutual worth.

Contested Library, Information, and Knowledge Educations

Despite the occasionally valid arguments advanced in its favor, the ongoing transformation of schools of library and information science into schools of information is viewed by many librarians in the public sector as a fundamental breach of faith with the practitioner communities that lobbied state legislatures and pressured higher education institutions to bring such programs into existence. Representative of this reaction is Michael Gorman who, in his recent work *Our Enduring Values: Librarianship in the 21st Century* asserts a number of severe ethical lapses regarding self-serving behavior on the part of information educators.[37] His bill of indictment declares that many information educators are

- Elbowing out many of the courses that would add to the education of librarians through emphasizing IS [information science] courses that have "little or no relevance to the real work of real librarians in real libraries."
- Pursuing "their own interests, grants, and promotion or tenure at the expense of useful library education."
- Not librarians and/or demonstrate "little interest in libraries and their mission-indeed, think that the library has no future."
- Subverting library education instead of founding schools of information. They thereby redirect, indeed misdirect, the educational aims of the traditional "suppliers of future librarians."
- Cumulatively, weakening and sickening the library profession, undermining its ability to preserve the knowledge of librarianship in order to safeguard the human record.[38]

Library practitioners know — and information educators choose to overlook — the reality that terming an academic department a library school, school of library and information science, or information school does not reflect a timeless intellectual distinction. In the universities of the middle ages, for example, everything but law, medicine, and theology tended to be subsumed under philosophy.

To adapt and extend a phrase of Roger Blumberg, transforming a school of library and information science into a school of information or informatics represents an *expedient partition of academic culture*, generally undertaken for the benefit of the faculty involved.[39] Nevertheless, there is a cost to such transformations. In the long run they will help undermine the professional status of numerous library practitioners in the public sector.

Library practitioners, who have struggled for decades to establish the validity of their graduate professional degrees, recognize a fundamental flaw in redefining librarians merely as information practitioners to be educated as "information intermediaries." This redefinition narrows the librarian's professional focus from culture, education, information, and entertainment to information alone. Information, however, is the very same area where millions of others, with considerable differences in academic preparation, are now asserting competence.[40]

By eliminating the educational, cultural, and recreational roles of librarians through an information-centric curriculum, faculty in ALA-accredited programs have laid the intellectual groundwork for city councils and library boards to extend *intracultural reciprocity* with librarians—and thus an implied acceptance of the right to work in librarian positions—to countless individuals with alternative information educations. These individuals may "know" information and Web design but are unlikely to have taken courses in children's literature, young adult services, literacy, adult services, or leisure reading needs. Local communities, it should be stressed, have long prized these services.

If librarians with master's degrees from ALA-accredited programs are only information intermediaries, then they are subject to replacement by other information intermediaries who may have lower educational credentials and, in a number of cases, cost less for the library to employ. More instances of the Owens Corning and UK's Hillingdon Libraries's cases of deprofessionalization may be expected.

As one of the authors wrote in another context, the battle over defining the nature of ALA-accredited programs in the 21st century may have reached the point where "aroused [library] professionals may use the accreditation process, or even the formal and informal political worlds that help support LIS [library and information studies] programs in state universities, to rein in a professorate which has pursued self-interest to the detriment of the 'library' component of the library and information professions."[41]

In a very real sense, defeat by librarians in this struggle may well result in the inability of the library community to uphold its hard-won professional standards.

Concluding Observations

The pragmatic philosopher Abraham Kaplan once asserted, "Ours is the age of the symbol. It is really quite extraordinary how many intellectual disciplines either have come into being around processes of symbolization or have begun to focus about the nature of language and symbolism."[42] In the opinion of the authors, the future of librarianship itself will depend on whether or not the *library*, as symbol, can retain and expand its multiple meanings.

Librarianship is either a separate field with identifiable educational, informational, and recreational components or it is a subset of information science. Where librarians control or influence *intracultural reciprocity* and thereby define the specific educational and general knowledge requirements for their institutions, they will continue to exist. If librarianship is seen only as a subsector of information and possessing skills which can be acquired through a spectrum of intellectual contexts, it will become merely a larger representation of the Owens Corning and Hillingdon Libraries' scenarios where others control the organizational culture and skill with specific databases, not in-depth knowledge, is prized.

The future struggle to defend librarianship, or to define it away, will be intense because the stakes, for all involved, are so high.

Notes

1. Nancy Lemon, "Climbing the Value Chain: A Case Study in Rethinking the Corporate Library Function," *Online* 20 (November/December 1996), 55.

2. Ibid., 57.

3. Debbie Norley, "[PUBLIB] Reference Services Using Internet." 26 June 2001. PUBLIB Archive. Accessed June 28, 2001.

4. Sheila Slaughter and Larry L. Leslie, *Academic Capitalism: Politics, Policies, and the Entrepreneurial University* (Baltimore: Johns Hopkins, 1997), 173.

5. Ibid, passim.

6. Bill Crowley, "'Soon Librarians Will be Extinct!'??" 28 June 2001. PUBLIB Archive. Accessed July 7, 2001.

7. Ibid.

8. Seymour Martin Lipset, *American Exceptionalism: A Double-Edged Sword* (New York: Norton, 1996), 25.

9. Robert K. Merton, *Social Theory and Social Structure*, enl. ed. (New York: Free Press, 1968), 189-190.

10. Lipset, *American Exceptionalism*, 26.

11. Ibid., 63.

12. An excellent summary of the development of the American library and information environment can be found in Richard E. Rubin, *Foundations of Library and Information Science*, updated ed. (New York: Neal-Schuman, 2000).

13. Slaughter and Leslie, *Academic Capitalism*, 14.

14. Ibid., 38, 61.

15. Daniel Callison and Carol L. Tilley, "Descriptive Impressions of the Library and Information Education Evolution of 1988-1998 as Reflected in Job Announcements, ALISE Descriptors, and New Course Titles," *Journal of Education for Library and Information Science* 42 (Summer 2001), 199.

16. Peter Schmidt, "A Clash of Values in the Heartland: Scientific Promise and Abortion Politics are at Odds Over Fetal-Tissue Research," *Chronicle of Higher Education*, 6 April 2001. http://chronicle.com/weekly/v47/i30/30a02501.htm. Accessed July 21, 2001.

17. John W. Fountain, "Librarians Adjust Image in an Effort to Fill Jobs," *New York Times On the Web*, 23 August 2001. http://www.nytimes.com. Accessed August 25, 2001.

18. Slaughter and Leslie, *Academic Capitalism*, 240.

19. See the analyses in Suzanne Hildenbrand, "The Information Age vs. Gender Equity," *Library Journal*, (15 April 1999), 44-47 and Callison and Tilley, "Descriptive Impressions."

20. Association for Library and Information Science Education, *Library and Information Statistical Reports* http://ils.unc.edu/ALISE/. Accessed August 9, 2001.

21. Ibid.

22. For a classic account of the value of the professional MBA from two elite universities, see John Van Maanen, "Golden Passports: Managerial Socialization and Graduate Education," *Review of Higher Education* 6 (Summer 1983), 435-455.

23. Association of College & Research Libraries, American Library Association, "Statement on the Terminal Professional Degree for Academic Librarians." http://www.ala.org/acrl/guides/termdegr.html. Accessed February 19, 2001. For a cross-disciplinary overview of the value of the Ph.D., see Council of Graduate Schools, *A Policy Statement: The Doctor of Philosophy Degree* (Washington, DC: 1990).

24. American Association of School Librarians, American Library Association, "Position Statement on the Preparation of School Library Media Specialists" http://www.ala.org/aasl/positions/ps_prepschool.html. Accessed August 6, 2001.

25. Tim Wojcik, "Advantage: Information Profession." *About: The Human Internet: Librarians and Information Science*, 26 November 1999. http://librarians.about.com/library/weekly/aa112699.htm?once=true&. Accessed July 24, 2001.

26. Marissa Melton, "The Modern M.L.S. Degree-Library Schools Today are

Turning Out Webmasters," usnews.com http://www.usnews.com/usnews/edu/beyond/grad/gbmls.htm. Accessed June 28, 2001.

27. Everett M. Rogers, *Diffusion of Innovations*, 4th ed. (New York: Free Press, 1995), 18-19.

28. For an informative report on unemployed adults retrained for "information technology" careers in a wide spectrum of industries, see Washington State Board for Community and Technological Colleges, "Worker Retraining: Fifth Accountability Report for Worker Retraining Programs" (Olympia, WA: 1998), EDRS, ED 430633, microfiche.

29. See, for example, the recent account of how "competitive intelligence agents" are concerned about being mislabeled as "glorified librarians" in Ian Smith, "Competitive Analysis: Beware of Becoming a Glorified Librarian." http://www.powerhomebiz.com/vol36/librarian.htm. Accessed June 6, 2001.

30. See George Ritzer, *The McDonaldization Thesis* (London: Sage, 1998), particularly Chapter 11 "McUniversity in the Postmodern Consumer Society," 151-162.

31. Bill Crowley, "Tacit Knowledge, Tacit Ignorance, and the Future of Academic Librarianship," *College & Research Libraries*, forthcoming.

32. Ibid.

33. Nancy Everhart, "School Staffing Survey 2000: Looking for a Few Good Librarians," *SLJ Online: Articles* (September 1, 2000). http://www.slj.com/articles/articles/20000901_8998.asp. Accessed August 9, 2001.

34. Ibid.

35. Roxane E. Oakley, "New Standards for Ohio Schools and School Libraries," *State Library of Ohio News* 258 (Nov/Dec 2000), [2].

36. See both Lipset, *American Exceptionalism* for its discussion of the American focus on "black and white" morality and the commonsense approach to filtering terminals advocated in Leonard Kniffel, "Editorial: Ceaseless Filtering Flap Calls for One Assertion," *American Libraries* (October 1999), 40.

37. Michael Gorman, *Our Enduring Values: Librarianship in the 21st Century* (Chicago: American Library Association, 2000), 69.

38. Ibid.

39. Roger B. Blumberg, "Ex Libris," *The Sciences* 35(September/October 1995), 16.

40. See the discussion the information "labor market" in Rubin, *Foundations of Library and Information Science*, 340.

41. Bill Crowley, "The Control and Direction of Professional Education," *Journal of the American Society for Information Science* 50 (October 1999), 1128.

42. Abraham Kaplan, "The Age of the Symbol — A Philosophy of Library Education," in *The Intellectual Foundations of Library Education*, Ed. Don R. Swanson (Chicago: University of Chicago Press, 1965), 8.

13

Universal Bibliographic Control—A Contradiction in Terms? A Reflection on the Ethical Problems and Dilemmas of Universal Bibliographic Control

J.J. Britz and *Retha Snyman*

Introduction

Ethics in the field of information science has in the past ten years become a hot topic of discussion. Numerous ethical issues are being debated, for example the privacy of users, the right of access to information, copyright, the relationship between quality of information and the responsibility of the information worker, censorship and the social responsibility of information workers (e.g. bridging the gap between the information rich and the information poor).

However, it is interesting to note that very little literature has recently been devoted to the ethical issues pertaining to universal bibliographic control. Yet this topic has increased in importance because it underscores the most important ethical challenge of the digital era, namely *access to information.*[1]

This paper therefore deals with the main ethical issues with regard to universal bibliographic control. The focus will be specifically on the ethical dilemmas created by the tools (language and information technology) used to constitute universal bibliographic control. It will be argued that the notion of universal bibliographic control is unachievable.

The content is structured as follows: In the first part a brief overview is given of universal bibliographic control. This overview provides the background to the main ethical issues which comprise the second part of the paper. The ethical dilemmas of universal bibliographic control are discussed in the third part.

What Is Universal Bibliographic Control?

Behrens[2] stated "There is far too much information available — and in so many different forms—for any one person to be aware of all of it." To be able to make use of the information we have to be able to find it. We also need to ensure that as new information is generated it can be found by both present and future generations. Bibliographic control enables us to do this. Lor[3] applies the metaphor of a net, as in a fishing net or a butterfly net, in order to explain bibliographic control. He pictures bibliographic control as creating a finely-meshed net of bibliographies and bibliographic databases which is so comprehensive that nothing that is published can escape being recorded, located and made available for use. The aim of bibliographic control is therefore to list information sources in a systematic manner to enable people to become aware of what information is available, and where it can be located. The main bibliographic activities involve acquiring information sources; compiling bibliographic descriptions for these sources; assigning bibliographic access points to the descriptions; subject cataloguing (which includes classification, assigning verbal subject headings, indexing and abstracting); and authority control.

Various levels of bibliographic control can be identified, namely universal, national, regional and local bibliographic control. The focus of this paper will be on universal bibliographic control (UBC). Universal bibliographic control is a long-term programme and as such has been adopted by Unesco and the International Federation of Library Associations and Institutions (IFLA) as a major policy objective: to develop a worldwide system for the control and exchange of bibliographic information, in order to make universally and promptly available, in a form which is internationally acceptable, bibliographic information on publications issued in all countries. Through universal bibliographic control it may be feasible to establish an international bibliographic network made up of "component national parts, all integrated at the international level to form the total system".[4] Universal bibliographic control has at its basis two assumptions, namely:

- The recognition that each country is best qualified to identify and record the publications of its national authors.
- The acceptance by all countries of international bibliographic standards in making bibliographic records.

From the above it is clear that an interrelationship exists between national and universal bibliographic control. Bibliographic control on a national level provides a system which makes the identification and location of information sources within the country's borders possible. Apart from the identification, recovery, collection and preservation of the physical items which originate in the country, the creation of bibliographic records which describe and identify the publications is very important. The publication on its own is of no value to the information community without the records indicating its existence and giving access to the content.

When looking at national bibliographic control in relation to universal bibliographic control it is important, in addition to the collection of items, for the national bibliographic agency to also be responsible for the creation of authority and bibliographic records for every new publication issued in accordance with accepted international standards. If all countries try to apply bibliographic control on the national level, a degree of universal bibliographic control could be possible.

The Main Ethical Issues Pertaining to Universal Bibliographic Control

Based on the above outline of universal bibliographic control it can be argued that it is in essence a utilitarian ethic and its maxim is to locate and provide equal access to information for all. It is therefore the social and moral responsibility of institutions and the information profession involved in universal bibliographic control, to ensure that people are made aware of what information is available on a subject or by a certain author and where it can be located. This responsibility is closely linked to the notion of power because, as it is put by Maggio[5] "...power belongs to those who do the naming, which is why naming is one of the most critical issues for fairness and accurate language."

Thus, the following core values form the basis for ethical thinking in the field of universal bibliographic control:

- Respect for human dignity and freedom.
- The guarantee of the democratic right of access to information and by implication the right to a minimum standard of living.
- The guarantee of equal opportunities for access to information.
- The acknowledgement of the right to be represented in a rightful manner.
- The right to freedom of expression.
- The protection of ownership of information.

Based on these core values the following ethical challenges can be identified:

- How can the right of access to information as well as the establishment of equal opportunities for access to information be ensured?
- How can the right to be presented in a rightful manner be ensured and protected? This ethical issue pertains not only to authors but also, and even more specifically, to the using of incorrect and wrong descriptions of peoples and objects in meta-language to create universal control. Buchanan[6] in her discussion on information inequity, reminds us also about the problem of third world scientists which are not always quoted in the Science Citation Index, because of language and the perception that their work is less valuable.
- How can the quality, integrity and sustainability of the documented information be guaranteed? Which

standards must be used and to what extent must a cataloger bear moral responsibility for the work that has been done by someone else and what must be the minimum level of cataloguing?[7]

- Must there be any censorship in universal bibliographic control? Will an ethical paradox, with regard to freedom of expression, be created if censorship is applied? Would it be morally acceptable to exclude material that for example denies the Holocaust? How can it be ensured that there is no conscious bias in the choosing of concepts and that bibliographers have a tolerance for a wide variety of viewpoints?
- Acknowledgement of the ownership of information. As one of the core values it is important to recognise information as a product of intellectual work which has an economic value that must be protected. Capurro [8] rightfully indicates that it is one of the most important and difficult moral and legal questions in the information field. What contributes to this problem is the fact that there are different legal and moral traditions. Europe emphasizes moral rights, the Anglo-American tradition focuses on economic rights. In some countries in Africa intellectual property is an unknown concept. Universal bibliographic control is not only confronted with this variety of traditions, but also with the ethical challenge of whether intellectual property might inhibit the right of access to information. Related to intellectual property is the fact that "bad" cataloging can make the work of authors inaccessible.
- The question of how to locate and access information has also an ethical bearing. For example: should the choice of concepts (pointers) be determined by users or by catalogers? What is the moral responsibility of information professionals towards user education to enable people to locate and access information effectively? These ethical questions relate closely to the core value of equal opportunities for access to information.

The Ethical Dilemmas of Universal Bibliographic Control

However, the notion of a universal bibliographic control, with the main aim of ensuring the location of information as well as its universal accessibility is unachievable. The main reason for this "unachievability" of universal bibliographic control lies in the tools, namely language and information technology, that are used to constitute universal bibliographic control. Based on the core value of access to information it can be seen as a moral dilemma. In this part of the paper this moral dilemma will be elaborated upon.

The Dilemma of Language and Universal Bibliographic Control

Language is one of the tools used by humans to classify reality (for example to distinguish between a car and a ship) and to give meaning to things that exist. As such it would not be controversial to argue that language is one of the most important instruments that might create a common meaning across cultures and between people with regard to the organising, finding and use of information — in other words: to achieve universal bibliographic control. Olson [9] even argues that the idea of a universal language to represent subjects (reality) was already inherent in Cutter's rules for bibliographic control.

As a fundamental tool, language is therefore used in bibliographic control to represent and retrieve documented information at a universal level. To be able to achieve these aims a dual function is assigned to language. The first is a descriptive function and the second a control function.[10] As a descriptive function language is used as "pointers" or metadata (a representational use of language) and also as descriptor to do subject analysis. The control function of language, on the other hand, pertains to the establishment of a standard structure and terminology to enable the controlled retrieval of information. Miller,[11] in his article on control and cataloging, rightly warns against an uncontrolled language environment because it might end up in chaos with regard to the retrieval of information.

However, the use of language to achieve universal bibliographic control is problematic. When one examines the literature on language and bibliographic control it seems that there are critical questions regarding the use of biased language towards, for example, minorities implying either their marginalisation or exclusion.[12,13,14,15,16] To try to solve these issues Marshall[17] published a book in 1977 with the title *On equal terms: A thesaurus for non-sexist indexing and cataloging*, to advise the Library of Congress in the choice of less biased concepts regarding groups such as women, religious minorities, race and ethnicity.

Of more fundamental importance is the problematic relationship between language and reality. This relationship has been debated by philosophers and linguistics over centuries (e.g. Nietzsche, Wittgenstein, de Saussure, Pierce, Eco, Barthes and Derrida). It is a dilemma — in the words of Tarnas[18] — that nobody can escape from. This dilemma is of specific relevance to the way in which language is used for universal bibliographic control (descriptive and control use), because there is no direct, universal relationship between the signifier (in terms of bibliographic control: "pointers") and the signified (the text to which the pointers refer as well as the objects in reality).

No one language and no word have a privileged connection to the "truth" and no word or text can claim decisive authority. This explains why there are different uses and variations of the same word in different contexts and situations (polysemy); or why many words represent the same concept (synonymy); and why ambiguity exists, where one has to take into consideration the context to understand the meaning of a specific word, and where words can change their meaning in new eras. Therefore, it can be argued that there cannot be a single universal language that is all-inclusive in coverage and in perspective and in interpretation.

This argument can be strengthened by the fact that language is seen as a form of social interaction within specific contexts rather than as mere objective symbols that mirror a relationship between these symbols and the facts they symbolize.[19,20] This, which can be called "the deeper cultural meaning of language" is referred to by Barthes[21] as the *mythologies* behind words which have a socially unifying effect. He uses the meaning of the word "steak" in France to illustrate the cultural mythologies behind words. According to Barthes[22] the eating of steak in France represents powerful and hearty eating. This deeper cultural meaning of language makes the attempts to universal bibliographic control, and by implication universal interaction by means of language, unachievable.

Based on this problematic relationship between language and reality one has therefore to agree with Olson[23] that there cannot be one universal language that can be used to construct universal bibliographic control. Universal bibliographic control is nothing else than the "...use of limited, standardised systems for representation of information."[24]

The nearest that one can get to a universal identifying language might be mathematics or the use of proper names such as Peter Smith, which refers most probably to a male person. Logical atomists and logical positivists tend to regard proper names as the ideal form of language.[25] However, variations occur in the presentation of proper names, for example Tchaikovsky, Tschaikovsky, Chaykovsky, etc.

Another possibility is the use of an author number to represent an author. The notion of a standard author number has been suggested at various occasions. Pocet (cited in Taylor[26]), Malinconico (cited in Taylor[27]) as well as Snyman and Jansen van Rensburg[28] pleaded for such a number. However, the question remains whether local and international communities will be prepared to accept the use of an author number to represent authors.

Furthermore, bibliographic control does not work with only proper names—it also works with full texts and the objects/subjects to which these texts refer. For example, a text might be about American Indians. The question then comes into play—which meta-concepts must be assigned that will reflect them truly?—Indians, American Indians, American aborigines, Ameridians, Amerinds, Native Americans, etc?

Are there then any solutions to this dilemma of language and univeral bibliographic control? If one works with the assumption that universal bibliographic control is based on the notion that there is one universal meta-language that can be used to achieve this, then the answer is most certainly no. Language does not have the ability to create a universal body of control and access. In this sense the concept "universal bibliographic control" is a contradiction in terms. Rather, one has to accept the limitations of language as a tool to create universal bibliographic control and focus on the correct usage of concepts, bearing in mind the fact that such a universal meta-language will always exclude and/or marginalise people.

The most effective way in which a catalog (bibliographic control) might work is when people share a situated language. This ideal situation implies a shared social interface between the creators of the catalog, the creators of the knowledge and the users thereof. This is most probably only possible within a shared culture or a shared profession, for example the medical profession, which has a shared scientific language.

The Dilemma of Information Technology and Universal Bibliographic Control

One of the biggest changes that information technology brought about, and which introduces us into the new economy of information, is the unbundling of information from its traditional physical carriers (paper and other print media). In the electronic world information is no longer bound to a linear flow, but it can "travel by itself," making the traditional channels unnecessary or uneconomical.[29] It furthermore implies that documents no longer exist on their own. They have become interlinked with other sources. As Lindquist[30] remarks: "With electronic information it is usually more convenient to let the different parts reside in their respective technologies and link them together when presented." With this new economy of information more people can be reached at the same time, be exposed to more information in an interactive way (e-mail, interactive TV, etc.) and information itself can be customized, changed, altered, copied and destroyed, and this can be done at essentially zero cost. The unbundling of information introduces us with a new kind of information flexibility and a move away from "textuality to multimediality."[31]

Apart from all the positive outcomes and trade-offs that this new economics of information offers, it also has some limitations and restrictions—of which some have serious implications for universal bibliographic control. One of the main problems is the unstableness of the infostrucure (Internet). This does not only refer to power failures and a lack of bandwidth, but is much more applicable to issues such as unstable pointers to information (e.g. the ongoing changes of URLs), the lack of quality control, ineffective search engines and the incompatibility of hardware and software.

What is of relevance for catalogers is that ineffective search engines on the Web retrieve too much irrelevant information. Searches on the Internet frequently produce extensive lists of search results and searchers have to spend most of their time going through them in an effort to find the useful information. This is mainly due to a lack of standardized terminology and authority control. The standard and traditional pointers like issue, publisher, pages and date are no longer applicable in the electronic environment and possible new pointers such as URLs are not reliable.[32]

Another related issue that impacts on universal bibliographic control, is the idea that the introduction of modern information and communication technologies will bring about the transparent communication of knowledge reflecting the ideal situation of information everywhere at all times. It is rather the opposite — as was illustrated by postmodernist thinkers such as Foucault, Baudrillard, and Barthes. Digital information loses more meaning and there is more corruption of text.[33] Digital information actually "unbundles" meaning because time and space — the tradition boundaries for understanding — have vanished. An inverse relationship between distance and meaning is being created and this makes the universal control of information by means of universal standardized pointers virtually impossible.

What exacerbates this problem is

that the traditional tools of bibliographic control were not developed for and are therefore not suited to control and centralize the Internet, which is in essence a diversified system. It was developed for a different information environment—focusing on a single object description and linear access.[34] This poses a serious threat to the whole philosophy that underlies bibliographic control, namely the control and regulation of information in the paradigm of a written culture. Bibliographic control bodies all over the world are therefore confronted with the same question: can the Internet be catalogued?[35] Can we use traditional tools for the new paradigm of a culture of electronic mediated exchange? Is it possible to control unbundled information that "wants to be free?"[36]

For catalogers, these questions have become a moral dilemma: the unsolvable problem of controlling of the uncontrollable. New tools and software were developed in an effort to find a pathway to information in the digitized world. One of these tools is the introduction of a new concept called "metadata"—which is defined as "...data associated with objects which relieves their potential users of having to have full advance knowledge of existence and characteristics."[37] Metadata systems, for example Dublin Core, therefore focus on the standardization of bibliographic information, summaries, indexing terms and abstracts—all surrogates for original digital information.

However, this was and still is to a large extent an uncoordinated initiative involving a variety of roleplayers within and outside the library world—most of them with their own agendas. As such, it did not contribute to efforts to establish some form of standardization in cataloging tools. Catalogers were therefore not only confronted with a new, seemingly uncontrollable information environment, but also the question of how to control the controlling processes. Who will set the standards and which software will be used? Will the Library of Congress become the *de facto* leader in the library world? Will Dublin Core become the *lingua franca* for metadata—a suggestion that is made by Milstead and Feldman.[38] Which software systems for OPAC catalogs will be used and how compatible will they be? Vellucci[39] reflects that: "...it is unrealistic to believe that the organizational system of any one group will adopted by all players in the electronic arena." Milstread and Feldman[40] also take a view: "...with no governing body, and no central profession, as well as splinter groups with large investments in having their proposals becoming widespread ... the outlook for a single structure and thesaurus of meta data seems dim." This inability to control controlled vocabularies has created a chaotic atmosphere of clashing standards contributing to the moral dilemma of the search for a universal bibliographic control.

Conclusion

Despite Unesco and IFLA's efforts to develop a worldwide system for the control and exchange of bibliographic information, the notion of universal bibliographic control is unachievable. The main reason for this unachievability lies in the ethical dilemmas created by language and technology, two of the tools of bibliographic control. Therefore, universal bibliographic control will remain a contradiction in terms.

References

1. R. Capurro, "Ethics and information in the digital age," in LIDA 2001: *Annual Course and Conference Libraries in the Digital Age*, Dubrovnik, Croatia, 23–27 May (2001), 1–6.

2. S.J. Behrens, *Bibliographic control and information sources*, 3rd ed (Pretoria: University of South Africa, 2000), 60.

3. P.J. Lor, "Bibliographic standards in context: current challenges in bibliographic control," in *Seminar on Bibliographic Standards for the Promotion of Co-operation, Pretoria, 1–2 February 1996*, ed. H.S. Coetzee (Pretoria: University of Pretoria, 1996), 3.

4. International Federation of Library Associations and Institutions. International Office for UBC. *Guidelines for the national bibliographic agency and the national bibliography* (Paris: Unesco, 1979), 1.

5. R. Maggio, *The bias free word finder: a dictionary of non-discriminatory language* (Boston: Beacon, 1991), 15.

6. E. A. Buchanan, "An overview of information ethics in a world-wide context," *Ethics and Information Technology*, 1(3) (1999):195.

7. S.S. Intner, "Ethics in cataloguing," *Technicalities*, 13(11) (1993):5.

8. Capurro, 4.

9. H.A. Olson, "Between control and chaos: an ethical perspective on authority control" (3 August 2001). <http://www.oclc.org/oclc/man/authconf/olson.htm.>.

10. J. Milstead and F. Feldman, "Metadata: cataloguing by any other name" (3 August 2001) <http://www.onlineinc.com/onlinemag/OL1999/milstead1.html>.

11. P. Miller, "I say what I mean, but I do not mean what I say?" Ariadne 23 (2000):1–13 <http://www.ariadne.ac.uk/issue23/metadata/>b.

12. S. Berman, *Prejudices and antipathies: a tract on the LC subject headings concerning people* (Metuchen, N.J.: Scarecrow, 1971).

13. S.S. Intner.

14. P. Miller.

15. Olson.

16. M.N. Rogers, "Are we on equal terms yet? Subject headings concerning women in LCSH, 1975–1991," *Library Resources & Technical Services*, 37 (1993):181–196.

17. J.K. Marshall, *On equal terms: a thesaurus for non-sexist indexing and cataloguing* (New York: Neal-Schumann, 1977).

18. R. Tarnas, *The passion of the western mind: understanding the ideas that have shaped our world view* (New York: Ballantine Books, 1993), 398.

19. L. Introna, *Cooperation, coordination and interpretation in virtual environments: some thoughts on working together* (2001) (Unpublished).

20. N. Luhman, *Social systems* (California: Stanford University Press, 1995).

21. R. Barthes, *Mythologies* (St Albans: Paladin, 1973).

22. Barthes, 62–64.

23. Olson, 1.

24. Ibid.

25. R. Hartland, *Superstructuralism: the philosophy of structuralism and post structuralism* (New York: Routledge, 1994), 17.

26. AG Taylor, "Research and theoretical considerations in authority control," in *Authority control in the online environment: considerations and practices*, edited by B.B. Tillet (New York: Haworth, 1989):29–56.

27. Ibid.

28. Retha Snyman and M. Jansen van Rensburg, "Reengineering authority control," *The Electronic Library*, 17(5) (1999): 313–321.

29. P.B. Evans and T.S. Wurster, "Strategy and the new economics of information," *Harvard Business Review*, September–October 1997, 71–82.

30. M.G. Lindquist, "Citations in the digital space", *The Journal of Electronic Publishing*, (3 August 2001). <http://www.press.umich.edu/jep/04-03/linquist.html>.

31. Linquist, 6.
32. Linquist, 3.
33. M. Poster, *The mode of information: poststructionalism and social context*, (Oxford: Polity Press, 1990).
34. S.L. Vellucci,
35. Milstead &Veldman, 4.
36. P. Himanen, *The hacker ethic and the spirit of the Information Age*, (London: Secker & Warburg, 2001), 12.
37. Milstead and Feldman, 2.
38. Milstead and Feldman, 11.
39. Vellucci, 1.
40. Milstread and Feldman, 8.

Bibliography

Barthes, R. *Mythologies*. St Albans: Paladin, 1973.

Behrens, S.J. *Bibliographic control and information source*. 3rd ed. Pretoria: University of South Africa, 2000.

Berman, S. *Prejudices and antipathies: a tract on the LC subject headings concerning people*. Metuchen, N.J.: Scarecrow, 1984.

Buchanan, E.A. "An overview of information ethical issues in a world-wide context." *Ethics and Information Technology*, 1 (3) (1999): 193–201.

Capurro, R. "Ethics and information in the digital age." In: *LIDA 2001. Annual course and conference Libraries in the digital age*, Dubrovnik, Croatia, 23–27 May 2001: 1–6.

Evans, P.B., and Wurster, T.S. "Strategy and the new economics of information. *Harvard Business Review*. September–October (1997):71–82.

Hartland, R. *Superstructuralism: the philosophy of structuralism and post structuralism*. New York: Routledge, 1994.

Himanen, P. *The hacker ethic and the spirit of the Information Age*. London: Secker & Warburg, 2001.

International Federation of Library Asociations and Institutions. International Office for UBC. *Guidelines for the national bibliographic agency and the national bibliography*. Paris: Unesco, 1979.

Intner, S.S. "Ethics in cataloguing." *Technicalities*, 13 (11) (1993): 5–8.

Introna, L. *Cooperation, coordination and interpretation in virtual environments: Some thoughts on working-together*. (2001) (Unpublished).

Lindquist, M.G. 1998. "Citations in the digital space." *The Journal of Elecronic Publishing*. <http://www.press.umich.edu/jep/04-03/lindquist.html>.

Lor, P.J. "Bibliographic standards in context: current challenges in bibliographic control." In *Seminar on Bibliographic Standards for the Promotion of Co-operation, Pretoria, 1–2 February 1996* edited by H.S. Coetzee. Pretoria: University of Pretoria, 1996: 1–23.

Luhman, N. *Social systems*. Stanford University Press: California, 1995.

Maggio, R. *The bias free word finder: a dictionary of nondiscrimentory language*. Boston: Beacon, 1991.

Marshall, J.K. *On equal terms: a thesaurus for nonsexist indexing and cataloging*. New York: Neal-Schumann, 1977.

Miller, P. "I say what I mean, but do I mean what I say?" *Ariadne*, 23 (3 August 2001). <http://www.ariadne.ac.uk/issue23/metadata/>.

Milstead, J., and Feldman, F. "Metadata: cataloging by any other name." (5 August 2001). <http://www.onlineinc.com/onlinemag/OL1999/milstead1.html>.

Olson, H.A. "Between control and chaos: an ethical perspective on authority control." (3 August 2001). <http://www.oclc.org/oclc/man/authconf/holson.htm>.

Poster, M. *The mode of information: Poststructionalism and social context*. Oxford: Polity Press, 1990.

Rogers, M.N. "Are we on equal terms yet? Subject headings concerning women in LCSH, 1975–1991," *Library Resources & Technical Services*, 37 (1993): 181–196.

Snyman, Retha, and Jansen van Rensburg, M. "Reengineering name authority control." *The Electronic Library* 17(5) (1999): 313–321.

Tarnas, R. *The passion of the western mind:*

understanding the ideas that have shaped our world view. New York: Ballantine Books, 1993.

Taylor, A.G. "Research and theoretical considerations in authority control," in *Authority control in the online environment: considerations and practices*, edited by B.B. Tillet. New York: Haworth, 1989: 29–56.

Vellucci, S.L. "Options for organizing electronic resources: the coexistence of metadata. (1997). <http://www.asis.org/Bulletin/Oct-97/vellucci.htm>.

14

It Is Not Just a Matter of Ethics II: An Examination of Issues Related to the Ethical Provision of Consumer Health Services in Public Libraries

Nancy Zimmerman and *Feili Tu*

Introduction

In today's world of technology, with exponentially-expanding amounts of medical data available to the public at the click of a mouse, the roles and responsibilities of the reference librarian and the ethical issues concerning the provision of medical and consumer health information (CHI) in public libraries require examination. What is the role of the public reference librarian in today's information-rich world: intermediary, teacher, or objective provider of information?

Since CHI is a primary information need identified by public library users,[1] what special awareness and knowledge should public reference librarians have concerning its ethical delivery? Are reference librarians being educated for ethical awareness? This paper is the second in a series of investigations by the authors that examine the complexities surrounding the provision of CHI in public libraries.[2] The goal of this research is to improve the effectiveness of CHI services when the consequences of ineffective or unethical service are not "just a matter of ethics," but may, quite literally, influence life and death decision-making.

Educational Services Role of the Public Librarian

In the opening chapter of their text on reference services that is widely used in reference courses in LIS programs, Bopp and Smith pay tribute to the work of Samuel Rothstein:

> Reference librarianship—the professional specialty that has reference service as its focus—had its origins in the second half of the nineteenth century, particularly in response to one of that era's most important accomplishments: the spread of education.... As the educational level of the general population rose, more people came to their local public libraries to use the collections there. Because these individuals were not skilled in library use, the need for an intermediary between library users and library collections was recognized. That intermediary was a librarian.[3]

The librarian was no longer the gatekeeper of information but the mediator, the human interface, the guide to the information that met the users' information need. This established a trust between the user and the reference librarian, trust that the information retrieved and interpreted was accurate and confidential.

Reference librarianship in public libraries today is experiencing rapid growth and change due to access to information in electronic formats.[4] The availability of vast amounts of information through the Internet has erased the boundaries of the "reference collection," changed the trust relationship between user and librarian, and created new challenges for the reference librarian in public libraries.

In a recent article, David Majka wrote eloquently of these challenges:

> We are encountering a population unable to effectively analyze the quality, quantity, and source of the information they retrieve. The pernicious problem, along with its associated consequences, is spreading rapidly, affecting people at all levels of society.... It arises from a pervasive misperception regarding the worth of electronic information resources. Many library users—past, present, and potential—think, wrongly, that they have been freed from their need for us.... Everyone with a PC and an Internet account now thinks that those acquisitions enlist them as a superior searcher and articles in the mass media reinforce this delusion.... We [librarians] are the primary intermediaries for information retrieval.[5]

The Internet and other electronic databases have changed library collections from resources selected by professional librarians, with a commitment to accuracy and currency of information, to a large, uncontrolled and unregulated universe of information. Trust in the library and librarian as the true, accurate keeper and mediator of information has also changed. That trust has shifted to the Internet as 'Omnipotent Provider of Information.' Majka humorously, but with sad reality, provides us with the definition of a new breed of information user, "the inforamus [*sic*], immured in a state of surfdumb [*sic*], doing bad searches with inadequate search engines in a morass of disorganized, incomplete and sometimes inaccurate information, who is perfectly happy with the results."[6] As it was for the librarian of the 19th century, it is now the responsibility of the contemporary reference librarian to help the 'inforamus.' The librarian must assume the educator role, must become the mediator, the human interface, the guide to the information for the user.

Librarians must equip their users to face the variety of information sources available to them. This is particularly critical for CHI. While this move to a more active role in information education seems a natural outcome of our historical precedents, the perceived power of the Internet makes this more difficult. The need to eliminate the 'inforamus' mentality, particularly for health related information, makes the provision of educational services and the need to reestablish the trust relationship between user and librarian an imperative. Awareness of the ethical implications of CHI services by the reference librarian is essential.

Ethics in Reference Service

The ethical considerations that underlie the reference activities of librarians receive little attention in the professional literature nor are the ethics of reference well covered in the education of librarians. Scholars such as Rothstein, Hauptman, and Dowd[7] deplore the fact that reference librarians lack interest in the subject of ethics and give little thought to or reflection on the ethical dilemmas of reference services. Reference courses are crammed with covering rapidly increasing reference sources and information retrieval and searching techniques. The topic of ethics is covered only briefly, if at all, and usually only in the context of confidentiality and access equity. A review of the major textbooks[8] used by reference classes in graduate schools of library and information science (LIS) education found little coverage of ethics beyond references to professional codes or a few case studies. Few LIS schools offer a course in information ethics.[9] It appears that little attention is paid to ethical issues and reflection in LIS curricula. Newly-minted reference librarians are ill-prepared, as Almagno, Hauptman, and Dowd[10] suggest, to deal with the hard questions and decisions of information ethics that arise in practice.

Guidelines for Information Services prepared by The Reference and Users Association (RUSA) of the American Library Association (ALA) is an attempt to offer some guidance for reference and information services. The document is directed toward the library and what it should do rather than toward the information professionals themselves; the guidelines are institutional rather than personal/professional. The ethics section falls to last in the document and is dispensed with by a one-sentence section stating, "*The American Library Association's Code of Ethics* governs the conduct of all staff members providing information services."[11] Unfortunately, ALA's ethics code is basically passive and "toothless."[12]

Consumer Health Services in Public Libraries

While the results of bad, incomplete, and/or inaccurate searching and information retrieval may not produce life-threatening situations in the context of a student term paper or assignment, these same results can precipitate "pernicious" consequences when the topic is health related. Today's consumers tend to take more control of their own health care. Current trends in health promotion, disease prevention, and health consumerism promote this. According to a recent article in the *Wall Street Journal*,[13] consumers with access to carefully vetted medical information visit emergency rooms and doctors' offices less frequently. Research shows that the provision of CHI to the general public is effective in two ways: it improves quality of life within families, and it promotes public health to a variety of people. Although CHI is not meant to provide therapy for specific conditions, it is a powerful mechanism for shaping people's ideas on health promotion and disease prevention, thereby modifying outlooks and insights regarding achievement of a good quality of life and reasonable health care costs.

According to a survey conducted by the National Health Council,[14] three-quarters of Americans pay a moderate amount or a great deal of attention to medical and health news. A study conducted by D'Elia and Zimmerman for the New York State Regents Commission on Library Services for the 21st Century found that when asked how important it was for them to have, on a day to day basis, information about various topics, 41.5 percent of the survey respondents ranked the topic of "personal health information" very important. Of the 18 topics presented for consideration in the survey, "personal health information" was the number-one information requirement for New York State residents.[15] Increasingly, the general public is accessing CHI in both print and electronic formats through resources in public libraries.

The professional literature provides guidance for the provision of medical reference services in health-related institutions by librarians with specialization in medical reference,[16] but there is little published guidance to help the general reference librarian in public libraries. Only two studies (in Ontario, 1989, and in Michigan, 1997),[17] have investigated the provision of CHI services in public libraries. No nationwide study has been done to examine the current status of the provision of CHI services in public libraries.

No standards for CHI services in public libraries have been released by the Medical Library Association (MLA), the Public Library Association (PLA), or any state library. The only guidelines for this type of service are the *Guidelines for Medical, Legal, and Business Information Service Responses*, prepared by RUSA.[18] As with many such statements recommending best practice, the guidelines are stated as 'vague absolutes,' implying that the expectations placed upon librarians are simple and straightforward, but little real guidance is provided addressing the complex ethical context of health-related reference service. For example, the RUSA guidelines state, "A library's service staff must have the knowledge and preparation appropriate to meet the routine legal, medical, or business information needs of their clientele,"[19] but the document does not define the degree or level of knowledge or "routine." While librarians are experts in identifying and providing information, they are not practicing health professionals. Librarians are taught to verify the source and authenticity of information, but they lack the health sciences background necessary to be held responsible for the scientific accuracy of the information. The RUSA guidelines go on to say that, "questions beyond [the librarians'] level of competency should be referred ... to individuals as well as to published sources in a variety of formats,"[20] but do not address the associated issues of privacy and confidentiality. But the RUSA guidelines are helpful in *categorizing* the complex ethical issues underlying CHI services in public libraries to include the role of the information service staff concerning advice, confidentiality, tact, and information accuracy and currency.

Consumer Health Information: The Internet and Libraries

Many adult users rely on public libraries for accessing Internet resources. The Internet has silently revolutionized public access to CHI and profoundly influenced public health promotion. An MSNBC broadcast of April 24, 1998, reported that consumers see the Internet as a main channel for seeking health information. In 1995, an astonishing 15.6 million adults (approximately 43 percent of all Internet users) searched for online health information. The number of Internet users seeking CHI was projected to be 27.1 million in 1998.[21] Increasingly, users access health-related information directly using the Internet rather than obtaining the information from health care providers.[22]

Unfortunately, research has found that health-related information on the Internet can be overwhelming, incomplete, and/or inaccurate and lacks health disclaimers, caveats, and other health-related alerts to notify users that the information provided is not intended nor implied to be a replacement or an alternative for professional health-related advice.[23] Public librarians are aware of the increasing demands for health-related information and libraries must reconcile their mission of providing medical information along with the rest of their responsibilities to the community. This presents a unique opportunity for reference librarians to become the human interface for users seeking CHI. By preparing themselves to accept these challenges and by working directly with library users, the reference librarian can deal responsibly with the complex processes of obtaining accurate, ethically delivered CHI.

Issues Relating to Ethical Delivery of CHI in Public Libraries

Issues relating to the ethical delivery of CHI in public libraries include the role of the reference librarian concerning information accuracy and currency, advice, confidentiality and privacy, and tact and bias as suggested by the RUSA guidelines. Completeness is a necessary addition to this list. Concern for quality of information is a mark of professionalism. While public reference librarians are taught to verify the source and authenticity of information, they often lack the health sciences background necessary to be held responsible for the scientific accuracy. If the consistency of research findings that have lead to acceptance of the "55 percent rule" of how well reference librarians find the correct answer to factual questions,[24] there should be much concern regarding the quality and accuracy of health-related information response. Rothstein offers explanation and additional clarification of this concern:

> The reference librarian must serve anonymous clients whose needs and capabilities they cannot really know; they must be prepared to give instant answers to questions covering almost every conceivable subject; they must operate in full public view and under harassing requirements for speed.... Add in the fact that many of the ... questioners themselves may be ignorant or rude, and is it any wonder that reference librarians may be tempted to take the self-exculpatory view of the imperfections in their relationships with clients?[25]

Research shows that the resources on the Internet also lack health disclaimers, caveats, currency dates, and other health-related alert messages to notify users that the information provided is not intended nor implied to be a replacement or an alternative for professional health-related advice. These messages also serve as indicators to show that information providers take ethical responsibility for quality control in terms of providing valid and reliable consumer health information,[26] but their absence makes the task of verification of the quality of CHI even more difficult for the reference librarian. Still, librarians have an ethical responsibility to provide accurate and current information utilizing all the professional skills and resources available to them or by referring the user to additional information sources. One factor often overlooked is completeness. Information may be accurate, as far as what is actually provided, and timely, but not necessarily complete. In health-related matters, incomplete information may prove to be as dangerous as misinformation. Without sufficient background knowledge, omissions of information are the most difficult information fault to recognize. Consulting multiple, current resources and a commitment to quality is the best way to minimize omissions and impact quality.

Reference librarians need to be careful not to cross over from provision to advice and they need to be aware of the perceptions of users concerning identification and interpretation of information. While advice may be given regarding the relative merits of sources, reference librarians must be mindful not to give opinions or the impression to users that provision of information means endorsement of the information as medically accurate or that it constitutes medical advice. Eakin and colleagues have differentiated between health information and health education. As an information provider, the librarian should disseminate the information "without interpretation, without opinion or counseling, and with no attempt to influence the actions or decision making of the individual."[27] In their educational services role, they may teach users how to judge the merits of the information sources accessed, but they must refrain from interpreting the information. For clarification and understanding of health-related information, multiple sources should be provided to the user for content comparison. Librarians must also develop and articulate for users their policies and roles in health information provision and should supply the same sort of disclaimers, caveats, and alert messages for their work as should appear on Internet resources.

As part of the trust relationship, and in some states, the law, guarding the privacy and confidentiality of the user must be considered an ethical responsibility. Confidentiality and privacy are values accepted in library circles and have been discussed in multiple publications.[28] Librarians are usually aware that information requests, searches, log books, and patron records are confidential and they do need to understand the laws of each state and local policies. In many libraries, they are beginning to adopt information technologies, such as "cookie washers" that automatically clean the computer's browser's cache, cookies, and history, to help assure user confidentiality and privacy of CHI queries. But it is the hard issues, such as when a user asks for health-related information on potentially harmful topics, such as suicide, euthanasia, or as in the Dowd study,[29] the use of cocaine, that require ethical reflection and decision-making skills within the reference context.

Trust in the library as a sanctuary where users can feel unconstrained by the materials they use or the queries they pose is critical to the public library mission, but as Hauptman points out, as librarians strive to avoid censorship and bias and to protect confidentiality, they may well be abjuring other responsibilities to society.[30]

Reference librarians are often faced with helping users find CHI on topics that may be sensitive, uncomfortable to discuss, controversial, and/or personally offensive. There is, in deciding what sources to consult or how much time to allocate to the inquiry, the potential for bias, lack of objectivity, or insensitivity. When values of the institution, the provider, and the user conflict, the librarian will need to make an ethical decision. However, whatever the inquiry, the librarian has a duty to use discretion, tact, and be responsive to the user during the reference process.

The Education of Reference Librarians for Delivery of CHI in Public Libraries

ALA-accredited library and information science (LIS) programs are the primary providers of education for reference librarianship. The curricula of these LIS education programs have a direct and crucial impact on the professional development of public librarians nationwide. Currently, of all the courses offered in all the ALA-accredited and Association for Library and Information Science Education (ALISE)-affiliated library and information science education programs, only one deals specifically with CHI services.[31] Other courses on medical information services are directed toward those who will work in medical libraries.

The Medical Library Association has acknowledged the need for increased competency among practicing librarians for CHI services by offering a continuing education credential program, the Consumer Health Information Specialist Program.[32] One of the target audiences for this program is public librarians, but this does not address the dearth of coverage of CHI and ethical issues in the masters level curricular of LIS programs.

As discussed previously, there is little mention of ethics in LIS reference courses or textbooks. Review of the reference textbooks also found little on health-related issues or sources. Students in the masters degree programs accredited by ALA have little access to preparation for provision of CHI services unless they enroll in electives designed specifically for those wishing to become medical librarians. As the next investigation in this series, the authors plan to undertake a formal study of course syllabi and survey of course instructors to assess the coverage of CHI services included in the reference curricula of ALA-accredited and ALISE-affiliated LIS programs. It is important that a thorough investigation of the current status of LIS health reference service education be undertaken to inform the improvement of that education. This is an ethical responsibility of the profession . The qualifications of the service personnel influence the service quality.

An understanding of current consumer health information services in public libraries is also critical. Assessments of current consumer health information services provided in public libraries are crucial to helping those libraries improve the effectiveness of services and develop appropriate service policies. It is necessary to assess current CHI services provided in public libraries nation-wide, to clarify the current support needs from the National Library of Medicine (NLM), to identify the use of NLM resources in public libraries, and to analyze from the employing libraries' and the librarians' perspectives the competencies and ethical preparation needed in LIS education to prepare reference librarians to deliver CHI. The authors plan to submit proposals for funding to conduct this study and look forward to continuing their investigation of the issues related to the education of information professionals for ethical provision of CHI services in public libraries.

Notes

1. New York State Regents Commission on Library Services for the 21st Century, *A Telephone Survey of Residents of New York State Concerning Library Services: Executive Summary*. By George D'Elia and Nancy P. Zimmerman (Albany: The New York Board of Regents, 1999), 24.

2. Feili Tu and Nancy P. Zimmerman, "It Is Not Just a Matter of Ethics: A Survey of the Provision of Health Disclaimers, Caveats, and Other Health-related Alerts in Consumer Health Information on Eating Disorders on the Internet," *International Information and Library Review* 32 (2000): 325–339.

3. Samuel Rothstein, "The Development of the Concept of Reference Service in American Libraries, 1850–1900," *The Library Quarterly* 23 (January 1953): 7–8 quoted in Richard E. Bopp and Linda C. Smith, *Reference and Information Services: An Introduction*, 2d ed. (Englewood, CO: Libraries Unlimited, 1995), 4.

4. Richard E. Bopp and Linda C. Smith, *Reference and Information Services: An Introduction*, 2d ed.(Englewood, CO: Libraries Unlimited, 1995), 4.

5. David Majka, "The Conqueror Bookworm: Solid Research and Good Scholarship vs. Surfdumb and Inforamus," *American Libraries* 32 (June/July 2001): 61–62.

6. Ibid., 62.

7. Studies of this type include: Robert C. Dowd, "I Want to Find out How to Freebase Cocaine or Yet Another Unobtrusive Test of Reference Performance," *The Reference Librarian* 25/25 (1989): 483–493; Robert Hauptman, "Professionalism or Culpability? An Experiment in Ethics," *Wilson Library Bulletin* 50 (April 1976), 626–627; Samuel Rothstein, "Where Does It Hurt? Identifying the Real Concerns in the Ethics of Reference Service," *Reference Librarian* 4 (Summer 1982): 1–12.

8. Richard E. Bopp and Linda C. Smith, *Reference and Information Services: An Introduction*, 2d ed.(Englewood, CO: Libraries Unlimited, 1995); Richard E. Bopp and Linda C. Smith, *Reference and Information Services: An Introduction*, 3d ed.(Englewood, CO: Libraries Unlimited, 2001); William A. Katz,

Introduction to Reference Work, 7th ed., 2 vols. (Columbus, OH: McGraw-Hill Higher Education, 1996).

9. Ethics courses are offered at Kent State University, School of Library and Information Science; Long Island University, Palmer School of Library and Information Science; and University of Pittsburgh, School of Information Sciences.

10. Stephen Almagno as quoted in Barbara Rockenbach, "Information Ethics at the University of Pittsburgh," *Journal of Information Ethics* 7 (Fall 1998), 13–18; Robert C. Dowd, "I Want to Find out How to Freebase Cocaine or Yet Another Unobtrusive Test of Reference Performance," *The Reference Librarian* 25/25 (1989): 483–493; Robert Hauptman, "Professionalism or Culpability? An Experiment in Ethics," *Wilson Library Bulletin* 50 (April 1976), 626–627.

11. Available: http://www.ala.org/rusa/standard.html. Last accessed 23 September 2001.

12. Samuel Rothstein, "Where Does It Hurt? Identifying the Real Concerns in the Ethics of Reference Service," *Reference Librarian* 4 (Summer 1982): 2.

13. L. Landro, " Health Groups Push 'Information Therapy' to Help Treat Patients," *Wall Street Journal* (New York), 2 February 2001, sec. B1.

14. National Health Council, *Americans Talk About Science and Medical News* (Washington, DC: Author, 1997).

15. New York State Regents Commission on Library Services for the 21st Century, 24.

16. Articles of this type include: John A. Gray, "The Health Sciences Librarian's Exposure to Malpractice Liability Because of Negligent Provision of Information," *Bulletin of the Medical Library Association* 77 (January 1989), 33–37; Julie A. Rothstein, "Ethics and the Role of the Medical Librarian: Health Care Information and the New Consumer," *Bulletin of the Medical Library Association* 81 (July 1993), 253–258; M. Sandra Wood, "Public Service Ethics in Health Sciences," *Library Trends* 40 (Fall 1991), 244–257.

17. L.M. Baker, L. Spang, C. Gogolowski, and M.R. Vizzaccaro, *The Provision of Consumer Health Information by Public Librarians in Michigan: Final Report of a Research Project* (Detroit, MI: Wayne State University, 1997), ERIC EDRS, ED 415860; J.G. Marshall, C. Stewards, and E.L. Dilworth, "Health Information Services in Ontario Public Libraries," *Canadian Library Journal* 48 (1991), 37–44.

18. Available: http://www.ala.org/rusa/standard.html. Last accessed 23 September 2001.

19. Ibid.

20. Ibid.

21. National Health Council.

22. Tu and Zimmerman, 327.

23. Ibid., 329.

24. Peter Hernon and Charles R. McClure, "Library Reference Service: An Unrecognized Crisis—A Symposium," *Journal of Academic Librarianship* 13 (May 1987): 69–80.

25. Rothstein, 1982, 4.

26. Tu and Zimmerman, 329.

27. D. Eakin, S.L. Jackson, and G.G. Hannigan, "Consumer Health Information: Libraries as Partners," *Bulletin of the Medical Library Association* 68 (1980), 223.

28. Studies include: Rhoda Garoogian, "Librarian/Patron Confidentiality: An Ethical Challenge," *Library Trends* 40 (Fall 1991), 216–233; Mark Stover, "Confidentiality and Privacy in Reference Service," *RQ* (Winter 1987), 240–244.

29. Robert C. Dowd, "I Want to Find out How to Freebase Cocaine or Yet Another Unobtrusive Test of Reference Performance," *The Reference Librarian* 25/25 (1989): 483–493.

30. Robert Hauptman, "Professionalism or Culpability? An Experiment in Ethics," *Wilson Library Bulletin* 50 (April 1976), 626–627.

31. This course is taught at the University of North Carolina at Chapel Hill, School of Library and Information Science.

32. Information available: http://www.nlm.nih.gov/news/press_releases/ehip.html. Last accessed 23 September 2001.

Topical Issues

15

The Internet: Plagiarism's Newest Accomplice?

J. Wayne King and *A. Dale King*

Abstract

College students are writing a report for a strategic management class and the professor notices that no resources are from hard copies; all sources have been from "hits," or searches, on the Internet. One is left to ponder if the credibility of the report has been compromised in any way or if there was the possibility that the report may actually be better because all business research now tends to be computer driven. And one of the main issues centers on the concern for plagiarism and the ability of the academic to verify the uniqueness of the report and the identification of the author.

As students are required to research, analyze, and report in the business field, it is becoming more and more prevalent that many students are looking for the quick and easy way to research secondary data and report on their findings. But the panacea for information-gathering is not the Internet and all it has to offer. Many times students are looking for something that will allow them to research items, especially in the business arena, with statistics and number interpretation. The Internet and the World Wide Web (WWW), in fact, can be a great source of information for this purpose. It does not, however, offer everything because the credibility of many sources listed on the Internet and through the World Wide Web does not have veracity.

Also, the ability of students to utilize others' works and have them credited to themselves is very easy. Sites and their "pages" change with great regularity and the ability to cover plagiarism is relatively easy. There is virtually no paper trail for ascertaining listings on the Internet and the WWW if the posting no longer exists, or has significantly changed.

This report will identify instances where students have knowingly or unknowingly misused the WWW and the Internet in their business reports. Specific examples will be demonstrated to show what these irregularities are and possible alternatives for their modification.

In the ever-changing world of business academia, it is a growing challenge to encourage business students to creatively write unique, distinctively different reports. Report-writing assignments on assessing organizations and their effectiveness are a necessary project to training the business professionals of the future. One of the most challenging aspects of this educational process, however, is encouraging students to write clear, concise, and complete reports that are original works, or when they aren't original, that the students give adequate and appropriate credit for others' works.

The computer is a man-made tool that has greatly helped in the dissemination of information and the storage of information. As students are required to research, analyze, and report in the business field, it is becoming more and more prevalent that many students are looking for the quick and easy way to research secondary data and report their findings. But the panacea for information gathering is not the Internet and the search engines it provides. There are many responsibilities surrounding the use of this complex tool in academic settings and one of the areas of most concern ethically is in the area of plagiarism. Many zealous, and yet somewhat lazy, students view the computer, and other information technology advancements, as being a panacea for all their secondary research woes. Students want easy and fast ways to conduct the research for their business assignments. They want this information fast — now — and they may not be overly concerned about the integrity of the work and giving credit where credit is due. While the computer and search engines are very useful tools, in many instances, the computer may actually serve as an accomplice to plagiarism in academic writing.

Many times, students may be looking for something that allows them to research items, especially in the business arena, with statistics and number interpretation. They may feel uncomfortable and/or inadequate in translating the statistics into meaningful narrative or graphs. So, they may be looking for someone else's work to fill this void.

If looking at recent assignments received from senior-level business students is any example, you may find that there are major concerns facing instructors receiving original, unique reports from business students. "Wendy's has a total of 5,792 restaurants — 5,095 in five operating regions of the United States, 324 in Canada, and 373 restaurants outside of North America."[1] In actuality, in looking at the 2000 Summary Annual Report to Shareholders, one could find the same statement on page 6. Thus, this statement was not an original statement formulated by XYZ Student, but in fact, was secondary research gleaned from a widely distributed Annual Report.[2]

In another student's report, also on Wendy's, one could read, "For the third quarter, which ended on September 30, 2001, system wide sales grew 7 percent to a record $2.2 billion."[3] After further research, however, it is found that again, this information is not original information by Student 2, but in fact is contained on the Wendy's Investor Web Page.[4]

As technology is exponentially increasing, so is the incidence of plagiarism in academic settings. In computer information searches, students and the tools they use have become much more sophisticated, and more alarmingly, much more difficult to trace. Recent occurrences of computer plagiarism are not exclusively concerns of business professors. On a recent episode of *The Education of Max Bickford*, a professor challenged students she suspected of plagiarism by assigning failing grades. The students countered with excuses much like what are offered in the actual classroom. Time, workload, unfamiliarity with subject matter, as well as others were offered as reasons for using others' work and not giving proper credit. All of these excuses are offered in the actual college classrooms today as well.[5]

Walter Maner stated that he "coined the phrase 'computer ethics' in 1976,"[6] and yet, found that it was an oxymoron because academia tended to discredit the notion of computer ethics. But what was first though of as "operational" ethics, can now have an even more pervasive concern in the learning process as well. At that time, academics did not want to use the study of computer ethics in their curriculum and did not consider computer ethics scholarly. Maner indicated that the push for computer ethics training was kept alive due to the concern of a small group of members of the American Association of Philosophy Teachers.[7]

The Internet and other aspects of the World Wide Web can be a great source of information for the purpose of research and in-depth analysis after research. It does not, however, offer everything because the credibility of many sources listed on the Internet and through the World Wide Web cannot be ascertained.

As technology is exponentially increasing, so is the incidence of cyberplagiarism. Much of the fault can be placed on unsuspecting or unfamiliar users who have the ability to use the computer as a tool, but lack the skills to know how to protect the information their computers contain. There are others, however, who knowingly use others' information and do not properly give credit for the work they have "lifted."

An introductory-level physics professor at the University of Virginia began an electronic database of reports submitted by students to assist in grading. After a recent disgruntled student complained about her grade and the higher grades received by some students, students who she alleged to have used others' work without citing the work as such, the professor found that 148 student reports had possible plagiarism concerns. Some of the reports matched verbatim other reports, while additional reports matched sentences or key phrases. The University of Virginia is known for its very strict Honor Code, and he challenged these students by filing Honor-Code charges. Subsequently, some students have left the University, while other students' charges are pending. It was found that some were unknowingly copied and others knowingly used the work of someone else without giving proper credit.[8] The scandal has wreaked havoc on the prestigious campus long known for honesty and integrity. The UVA professor, Professor Louis Bloomfield, has developed a software package that he distributes free to professors so that others may be able to ascertain that students' reports are in fact original and unique.[9]

Academic plagiarism is on the rise at both colleges and high school levels, according to author Don McCabe of

Rutgers University. "In fall 1999, one in 20 students surveyed ... at colleges, said they had turned in a paper taken in whole or in large part from the Internet. One in 10 had done *cut-and-paste plagiarism*."[10] Among high school students, however, the numbers were even more alarming. "One in seven took a paper in whole or large part, and one in two acknowledged cut-and-paste plagiarism."[11] Thus, the pipeline from high schools to colleges and universities indicates that the plagiarism problem can be leading to greater concerns for professors in the future. Professor McCabe asserts, "...if colleges and universities don't start doing more to lay out expectations for students to help them understand appropriate uses of the Internet, we're going to have a problem."[12]

Businesses must have information, especially accurate, relevant information regarding their internal and external environments. Naturally, other knowledge is important, such as the product's performance to specifications or ideals, but it is the information relating to what the competition is doing and what the marketplace wants that could mean success or failure for a firm. Having this data is crucial and, therefore, sets the stage for ethical struggles for companies and employees in its data gathering and information use, which can be preceded by the struggle for ethical report writing techniques of promising businesspeople.

Our evolving emphasis on reliable, realistic, and fast business decision-making skills, has called for a need for more exhaustive computer searches. Alternatives for organizations centered on realistic information encourage the researcher and writer to secure all the facts in as timely a manner as possible. But, sometimes this information is incorporated into reports that are, in fact, secondary research as opposed to primary writing. Improprieties can cause the integrity of a report to come into question, since the report is mainly a CPA (cut, paste, and assemble) report as opposed to an original report. There is an increasing push on academia to explain what the social responsibilities are in the electronic information age, just as there was prior to the WWW and the Internet.

Richard Severson, in *The Principles of Information Ethics*, indicates that there are Four Principles of Information Ethics. These are "1) Respect for Intellectual Property; 2) Respect for Privacy; 3) Fair Representations; and 4) Nonmaleficence (or 'doing no harm')."[13] In comparing these principles to the UVA situation, we see that many would assert that the students had very little respect for others' work and did not act fairly when presenting the reports as their own. Also, there was obvious harm caused by the students' actions, due to the university and professor's responses to the questionable reports. Colleges go to great extent to protect their images and goodwill with the public, but this can be shattered in a short time if the integrity of the academic program is questioned, much as has been witnessed in the UVA situation.

Severson's Four Principles follow the same ethical challenge, which Kenneth Blanchard and Norman Vincent Peale simplistically proposed in *The Power of Ethical Management*. This book was a discussion of business ethics, not just information ethics, which focused on an "Ethics Check" centered on three relatively simple, thought-provoking questions: "Is It Legal?; Is It Balanced?; and How Will It Make Me Feel About Myself?"[14] Both Blanchard and Peale's book and Severson's book treat ethics as a concern for self-esteem and the individual involvement in the ethical dilemma. One wonders how the physics students at UVA and the business students previously mentioned felt after it became public knowledge that they had allegedly compromised their integrity by submitting others' work as their own.

Following another assertion by the Kings in "Hacking 101: Does It Appear We are Training the Cyberspace Criminals of the Future?"[15], the authors indicate there are examples of plagiarism that are on the rise, because students may not be applying the simple Ethics Check as suggested above. Assessing these cases, situations, and principles suggests an educational approach to applying ethics in business report writing and decision-making. Though simplistic, Blanchard's and Peale's "Ethics Check" is easy to understand and easy to apply. All ethical dilemmas could be assessed using the three easy questions and would be relatively straightforward to incorporate into any classroom discussion on ethical report writing:

1. Is It Legal? What does the law have to say about the action or inaction? There is an element of subjectivity in applying laws, but the laws do exist which can help guide ethical decision making in information technology.

2. Is It Balanced? Can it be fairly applied to all involved? Are there areas of inequity? Are there areas of equity? Can equity be assured in all situations?

3. How Will It Make Me Feel? Once the decision is made, can the decision-makers face themselves, their peers, and their families? Can decision-makers live with themselves and their decisions? This aspect follows the self-esteem concern presented earlier in this report. It also has an element of subjectivity, but relies upon individuals' values and morals, as well as organizational values and morals, of right and wrong assessments.[16]

A call for greater awareness of proper report-writing techniques recognizes the credibility and integrity issues that plagiarism may bring to the student, the business program, and the college. In today's colleges and universities, expectations should exist within the school that whomever writes a report, has been trained to follow appropriate procedures that are fair, legal, and livable. But that is not always the case, and the professor should be ready to react to ethical dilemmas caused by improper writing techniques, much like Professor Bloomfield responded.

The premise of fairness, a subjective and sometimes disparate ideal, can cause great concern for universities and colleges today. It has been said, though unable to give credit for the quote, "Character is how you act when no one is watching." Likewise, character is what you would want reported to your superiors, your family, and your peers. Is it unethical only if it is reported? This quote directly addresses the livable aspect of the principles proposed by Blanchard and Peale.

The focus of this report relies upon the continuing concern about plagiarism, though now there is a relatively new accomplice in the mechanics of plagiarism. Addressing these issues is not confined to just business programs. If college students applied the three simple principles suggested by Blanchard's and Peale's Ethics Check to their actions, they would have failed on most aspects. This gives more credence to a call for a heightened exploration of the need of ethical training in computer searches and citings in schools and colleges. There would be no guarantee that this training would eliminate plagiarism and its impropriety, but the training would call for more awareness of the ramifications of such unethical behavior within college communities.

Technological computer searches do not leave the paper trail that manual searches have from the past. It is much easier to "cover your tracks," though not completely, as illustrated by the previously mentioned cases, utilizing electronic technology than in using a hard copy search. Technological listings can be traced, but not as easily as the old paper trails. Some relatively new and innovative programs are available on the Internet and WWW to assist the professor in such searches. These programs include www.turnitin.com, www.findsame.com, www.integriguard.com, and www.plagiarism.com. These are only a few of the many programs that are being developed to help the professor in ascertaining whether the report is original. This is especially true with the burgeoning industry of complete reports available for sale on the Internet. Students can buy reports of varying lengths and levels of difficulties on assigned topics from commercial term paper vendors such as www.schoolsucks.com and www.fastpapers.com. There would be no question as to these "complete" reports being subject to plagiarism concerns since there is no original work by the submitting student in the report.

As we move even deeper into the next millennium, computer ethics training in high schools, colleges, and universities, must make greater strides, which haven't been made in the relatively short life of the computer as a business tool. When considering the level of the computer operator, it is interesting to note the varying degrees of acceptance of Blanchard and Peale's principles. Training may have a direct impact on the degree of ethical computer secondary research techniques at American and international business programs.

Colleges and universities are discovering that "implicit codes" may not be enough; there must be more "explicit codes" employed to better combat these growing cyber integrity breaches. But are "explicit codes" truly going to be enough; are we finding that cyber integrity breaches are on the upswing to the point that guarding the Internet and cyberspace may be nearly impossible. Are we finding that young folks, as well as those older, are more concerned with the grade and what they can "get away with" than what is right? It takes applications of explicit Honor Codes, written in times pre-Internet and WWW, to the new information-technology field, to further combat plagiarism.

An ethics component in the writing curriculum in schools and colleges is warranted and necessary. It could better prepare the business professionals of the future to develop and follow an established code of conduct, ethics chain of command, and ethics accountability in their writing. If the budding technology protégés follow the Ethics Check, it will demonstrate a social and corporate conscience, which will lead them to successful careers in the business arena.

Endnotes

1. Student, XYZ. "Wendy's Corporate Analysis." (October 18, 2001) 5.
2. "2000 Summary Annual Report," Wendy's International, Dublin, Ohio. 6.
3. Student2, XYZ, "Wendy's Executive Analysis." (October 18, 2001) 10.
4. www.wendys-ubvest.com/ne/wen31.htm.
5. *The Education of Max Bickford*, CBS, November 11, 2001.
6. Maner, Walter. "Unique Ethical Problems in Information Technology." *Science and Engineering Ethics, no. 2* (April 1996): 137–154.
7. Parker, Donn. *Crime by Computer*. New York: Scribner's, 1976.
8. Felps, Paula. "Plagiarism plagues Web World," *The Roanoke Times, (June 28, 2001): 3D.*
9. Bloomfield, Louis. *The Today Show*, NBC, November 2001.
10. "At colleges and high schools, Internet plagiarism is on the rise," *The Roanoke Times*, (April 29, 2001): A18.
11. Ibid..
12. Ibid.
13. Severson, Richard W. *The Principles of Information Ethics*. New York: M.E. Sharpe, 1997: 39.
14. Blanchard, K., and Peale, N.V. *The Power of Ethical Management*. Ballantine Books, 1988.
15. King, J.W., and King, A.D. Hacking 101: Does It Appear We Are Training the Cyberspace Criminals of the Future. *International Information and Library Review 32,* (2000) 467.
16. Ibid.

16

WATERMARKING: FROM ETHICS TO PRAXIS

Spyridoula M. Armeni, Sofia F. Lioli,
and *Dimitrios Christodoulakis*

Abstract

The widespread use of the Internet led to the transfer of huge numbers of digital objects throughout the world's networks. And it is no surprise that illegal copies of digital objects (e.g. music, images and video) are also distributed over the very same media. Digital copies, however, are of a different nature than other kinds of copies, such as paper copies. A digital copy is identical to the original digital object and there is no obvious way to separate them (the original from the copied one) by inspection. But according to Kant "*a copy is a work of the author's (opus).*"[1] The owner of a copy should not publish it without the consent of the author or generally the creator.

New technologies provide to users easy access to digital objects. Preventing access to them is not the solution. The philosophy of the Internet is based on *open source projects*, where one may use the project or the source code, but should definitely cite the creators; see for example the GNU Project.[2] Under this umbrella, access to digital objects cannot be forbidden. Nevertheless, there still should be a way to prove ownership of the objects.

In order to secure Intellectual Property Rights, watermarking techniques have been developed. Watermarking techniques are techniques that embed a mark (a watermark) into the digital object. A lot of research has been done to investigate how the watermark can certify the creator of the digital object or the authenticity of the digital object. This paper examines such issues as the ethics of using the watermarking concept.

Introduction

The term *philosophy*, according to the Ancient Greeks, refers to the way of human beings' existence. Thus, ethics as science of philosophy is mainly interested in defining the ethical meaning of human life and the criteria which establish an act as ethical from any point of view. As Kant says, "*what should I do?*"[3]

Ethics, as a scientific discipline, defines the rules and the principles that regulate human acts. In addition to that, ethics philosophers strive to find out the causes and the contact point between acts and motives. Consequently, the scope of ethical philosophy is *the act* and its diverse specifications. When an action is characterized as ethical it shapes or modifies the inter-personal relationships and this is the reason why it acquires an ethical value.

Everything that a human being creates, s/he *accomplishes it* and thus the term "*act*" from just a simple word obtains a social content. This is justifiable, since the acts take place by human beings who are members of a broader society. Therefore, the result of a person's act affects all the members of the society. It is important at this point to note that a person feels obliged to abide by unwritten ethical rules. Although one may argue that there are people that do not do so, it is a fact that all persons at least obey their internal ethical rules, if not the general ones.

From antiquity onward, apart from the unwritten ethical rules there was also the need for legal rules. The legal rules are those that lead to the punishment of an act while the unwritten ethical rules are governed by our conscience. Consequently, the law punishes a non-acceptable act while it could simply have been disapproved or criticized by people simply from its ethical content. Generally, we could say that the ethical part of the result of an act relegates to the initial intention only.[4]

In the broad scientific society, we could say that many scientists/researchers nowadays do not want to combine their research subject with philosophy. Nevertheless, philosophy is tightly intertwined with science. Philosophy gives the scientists the ability to question the methodology of a scientist's own research.

The connection point between philosophy and science is the *experiment* and the *observation* that are used as a means of expression and recording of the association of these two. So, experiment and observation connect philosophy to science in order to initiate research.

Considering research as a starting point, we came to different identification methods of authentication for digital objects and their owners. Models of research that were based on trial and error led us to the development of watermarking methods. Watermarking is referred to techniques, which protect the Intellectual Property Rights (IPRs) of the owners.

The need for such identification is not a new issue. At the beginning watermarking techniques were applied to paper material, while nowadays with the rapid and broad distribution of information through the Internet, the old-type watermarking techniques have evolved to digital watermarking techniques.

In conclusion, the knowledge that is produced both by philosophy and science blooms in civilization, making their appearance as a result of this "*evolution.*" Human beings evolve as entities who are defined by the personal, local, national, ethical, religious and universal values.

IPRs and Copyright Issues

The Internet and generally online communication have met with an unprecedented rate of growth. Its evolution has surprisingly changed our daily behavior. The Internet brings to our homes trends in many diverse fields that travel around the world the net. Virtual environments and visions that promise unexpected experiences appear endlessly.

In the effort to diffuse information over the network, new software has been implemented, images are transported daily all over the world, icons expand their meaning providing well-understood metaphors of the virtual environment. Words that never existed before have been created, such as "cybercrime," "cybernauts," "cybersheriffs," etc. In this entire medley, claims of intellectual property and intellectual property rights (IPRs) arise. According to Lehman and Brown[5]:

> Intellectual property is a subtle and esoteric area of the law that evolves in response to technological change.

Intellectual property issues spring up from the physical world, where physical objects encapsulate the concept of property. So, copyright issues are more than requisite in order to protect these rights. In analogy, intellectual work such as literary, computer programs, artistic work and so on must have the right to be copyrighted, safeguarding the IPRs of their creators.

The World Intellectual Property Organization (WIPO) is responsible for the administration of the international intellectual property treaties. According to the WIPO[6]:

> Copyright is the legal protection extended to the owner of the rights in an original work that he has created. It comprises two main sets of rights: the economic rights and the moral rights.

Intellectual property, which could be characterized as the fruit of human creativity and invention, is divided into two categories.[7] The first is *industrial property*, which includes inventions, trademarks, industrial design, and geographic pointers to source. The second category is *copyright and related rights*, which includes a broad array of literary and artistic works.

Although laws have been created to protect the IPRs, it is difficult for intellectual property law to keep pace with technology. New technology has diminished distances. One may copy digital material from one country to another in minimal time. If the infringer and the infringement are in same country, then the laws are clear. But if the infringer is in a country where a certain action is not considered copyright infringement and the work is located on a server in another country, where such an action is illegal, then the conflict of laws is not an easily resolvable situation. It is very complicated to determine what country's laws should be applied. An example of conflicting laws is the case that "Diamond" Joe Gutnick has taken Dow Jones' *Barron's* magazine to an *Australian* court, because he believes that he was defamed in an article. Particularly, the magazine is published in the US *but* it is available through the Net and Gutnick argues that he has therefore been defamed in Australia and can seek a judgment, and possibly damages. The publishers want the case to be heard in America, which has laxer laws on defamation.[8]

The general confusion is obvious. Thus, there are many people who support universal laws for the new technology regardless of geography. The institution of global laws would solve many disagreements and problems. It seems that something like this would have many difficulties and thus it will take a lot of time. In the meantime the situation remains the same, if not already worse.

The Internet

From the very beginning, the cardinal feature of the Internet was the free exchange of ideas, messages, pictures and, generally, digital objects. At that time, it was not easy to foresee the Internet's potential for rapid growth as well as its numerous and diverse uses. However, this evolution is a reality, and there is positive indication that it will continue to evolve for many years to come. Beyond the initial design and ideas, illegal acts within the limits of the Internet create many problems. Disturbing and disruptive behavior range from unauthorized access, theft of electronic property, launching of destructive worms and viruses, racism, defamation, and harassment to an incident involving a form of online rape.[9] Hence, on this side there are the new technologies and the Internet with their cardinal feature of free exchange that allows breaches, and on the other side there are the illegal actions, the law and its consequences.

In particular, there are two main trends on the Internet: 1) one must pay to get and use what s/he seeks and, 2) one can get what s/he wants for free. The former is a usual situation, as it happens in the real world. In that case the Internet is used as an advertisement place, where one promotes a product in order to increase the number of customers-clients. On the other hand, the latter is based on another philosophy, one in which the Internet is a new place where there are no differences among people and everybody contributes to its development. As Rapaport says "*nobody is small on the Web.*"[10] This is more manifest in the software industry. There is software that one can buy, which is usually sold by big companies, and there is software that is given free on the net. The latter trend is strongly supported by GNU. GNU is a recursive acronym for "GNU's Not Unix"; it is pronounced "guh-NEW." The GNU Project was launched in 1984 to develop a complete Unix-like operating system, which is free software: the GNU system.[11] *Free software* does not just mean that the user has the freedom to run an executable file. It means that the user is totally free to copy, distribute, study, change and improve the software. It is a matter of liberty.

A program is free software, referred as open-source project, if users have all of the freedoms mentioned above. Thus, the user should be free to redistribute copies, either with or without modifications, either *gratis* or charging a fee for distribution, to anyone anywhere, without having to ask or pay for permission.[12] If the user does publish her/his changes, s/he is not required to notify anyone in particular, or in any particular way. The freedom to use a program means the freedom for any kind of person or organization to use it on any kind of computer system, for any kind of job, and without being required to communicate subsequently with the developer or any other specific agent.

In spite of this, the reference or the mention that a new program depends on GNU software could, in no case, be considered as restriction. If someone uses a GNU program as a building block of a new software program, then the new software is also characterized as GNU. The philosophy is to get helped and also to help others.

This dominant perception of free software can be extended to other digital objects, such as images and music, coming into contradiction with copyright issues that protect these objects.

In order to prevent breaches and infringements there could be a suggestion to control every aspect of the Internet against actions and operations that are generally unacceptable. Nevertheless, such a suggestion could only be characterized as pure utopia. It is enough to see what happened in Australia, for someone to understand how impractical such a thing would be. When the Australian government decided that they wanted to moderate the naming convention used for domain names in Australia, the practical measures that were employed to make sure that this was enforced were taken to the extreme.[13] For instance any word that was considered offensive would not be granted ".au" extension to the domain name. This approach was fatally flawed, as many people simply used their credit cards and purchased domain names overseas instead of in Australia. They use a ".com" extension instead.

If such a thing as the naming of the URLs was difficult to be taken under control, then the control of the transmission of every digital object, such as images, video or software is totally unfeasible. Under this scope, one may consider that since it is impossible to control the Internet, it should be left the way it is. But is that correct? What about the copyright issues of digital objects? Are copyright protection and free exchange two contradictory issues?

The fact is that the Internet is not immune from copyright, regardless of what some people might like to think.[14] However the solution would not be to prevent the distribution of digital objects. The existence of a way to verify the authenticity of the watermarked object or its legal owner, could lend wings to the philosophy of the Internet.

This should be accomplished, as it is done for many things, by *educating* people, and by shaping their social behavior in order to react with respect to Copyright issues. It is known that shaping social behavior online takes more than new laws and modified edicts.[15] As Immanuel Kant claims in his work, "Grundlegung der Metaphysik der Sitten"[16]:

> Then, that the moral is good, it is not enough; for the ethical laws worth observing, they should also be driven by esoteric will. (Denn bei dem, was moralisch gut sein soll, ist es nicht genug, daß es dem sittlichen Gesetze gemäß sei, sondern es muß auch um desselben willen geschehen.)

But it is also known that if the users are aware of the consequences, they shape their actions accordingly. As Kreie and Cronan claim: "*Perhaps the most useful information this study offers managers is the fact that both men and women indicated that an awareness of consequences for a behavior could alter how people behave.*"[17] For this reason, the users must become aware of the meaning and consequences of their actions.[18]

A possible solution could be to place the digital objects on the Internet, and for those that are copyrighted, a watermark could be embedded into them. From time to time an authorized team could perform tests, in order to verify the authenticity or the owner of the digital objects, and of course the infringers would be punished. It is up to the users, if they want to exhibit their work as copyrighted or not. This cannot be reprimanded. But they are the same users that may want to use a digital object that may be copyrighted. In any case the copyright should also be respected. If we let the Internet system run with rules like these, then the system itself will find the most effective way for its continuation.

Watermarking Issues

Watermarking techniques are not new. One of the oldest watermark findings at the Cambridge area (c. 1550) has depicted the monograms TGE RG, which was an abbreviation of the paper-maker name and the place; Thomas Goodrich Eliensis— Remy/Remigius Guedon.[19] At that time, watermarks were mainly used to identify the mill producing the paper; a means of guaranteeing quality. The principle of watermarking is also well known from bank notes.

In this information age, the pervasive nature of digitized data invades into most of the classic techniques. As a consequence, from watermarking techniques, we slipped into digital watermarking techniques. Digital watermarking may be described as a technique that is used to convey information imperceptibly or not, firstly by embedding it into the cover data and secondly by retrieving it. Different watermarking techniques have been developed for diverse types of digital objects, such as text, audio, image and video.

Text Watermarking

Watermarking techniques that are applied to texts are among the most difficult ones. Software watermarking could also be characterized as a type of text watermarking.

Briefly, we will refer to the different techniques that are used for Text Watermarking. Firstly there are the open-space methods, where the spacing is the key of authenticating the documents, depending on the spacing between the sentences or the words. Methods applying format modifications on the text are similar to the open space methods, where the appearance of the texts proves its authentication. An example of such modifications could be the word or line shifting in a text. Hereafter, there are the syntactic and the semantic methods, where the authentication of the texts is based on the syntactic and the semantic analysis of the text, respective. Finally, there are also methods with which texts and generally documents are manipulated as images.

Unfortunately, it is extremely simple to remove completely such watermarks, when they are embedded by methods based on line-shift code, word-shift code, font code altering of the word fonts, and generally methods that alter a little bit the appearance of the text. On the contrary, the semantic and the syntactic analysis offer a more robust way for embedding the watermark.

Audio Watermarking

Audio Watermarking techniques have drawn a great deal of commercial interest, since music and generally sounds are widely spread all over the Internet. Audio Watermarking is the process of secretly embedding sideband data within a host signal. Its usefulness is more than justified if someone considers the controversy regarding piracy of CD-quality music across the Internet in MPEG Layer III (MP3) format.

The audio watermarking techniques that have been proposed aim to develop an effective mechanism for watermarking audio works, and some of them also may offer a monitoring system for tracking musical performances in TV and radio markets, as well as on the Internet.

Image Watermarking

Digital Watermarking techniques for images are also of great importance, since digital images can be produced from many sources, such as scanners, digital photographs, computer graphics, digital cameras, or even by satellites. These can be differentiated as visible watermarking techniques and as invisible ones.

In the visible watermarking techniques the watermark is superimposed into the image and thus it becomes visible. Notwithstanding the visible watermarking techniques, the invisible ones have an advantage over the former. In fact, the former aim to inhibit the illegal use of the images just on sight, while the latter still embed the watermark and thus provide protection by no visible alteration of the image. Such techniques typically modify pixel intensities (spatial domain techniques) or modify the transform coefficients (frequency domain techniques).

Video Watermarking

Such Digital Image Watermarking techniques are divided into visible and invisible techniques; Digital Video Watermarking techniques can also have proportionately the same categorization. The TV station's graphical logo that is included in any video the station transmits, could be considered as a typical example of visible video watermark. Invisible video watermarking techniques are also very attractive, since there can be an ascertainment if the video is watermarked without affecting the video visibly.

Why Watermarking?

It is obvious that there is no *general* watermarking method. There are different types of digital objects, and for each type of digital object there are a plenty of watermarking methods. In addition to that, the watermarking methods are also purpose dependent. There are various general scenarios to which watermarking could be applied; and in each of them the requirements, that watermarking systems have to comply with, are somehow different.

The role of the watermark is multifarious. It can be used for authentication of digital objects, for authorship identification, for protection against copyright violations, for verifying the legal holders and for preventing pirates from coping the protected objects.

Authentication

A common application of watermarking systems is the one in which digital objects are required to verify their authenticity. In authentication applications any modifications of the original data should be detected. For this purpose, *fragile* watermarks are used. These don't have to be resistant to any modifications, such as geometric transformations or compression. They exploit the attributes of the digital objects, such as edge characteristics in still images, in order to check the integrity of the host data and to detect possible modifications. Of course, watermarks that are not fragile can also be used for authentication of the digital objects. When fragile watermarks are used, their absence from the digital objects is strong evidence that the particular digital object has been modified, while by using robust watermarks, the comparison between the recovered watermark and the original one provides information about data integrity.

Copyright Protection

Copyright protection is the most prominent application of watermarking today. Publishing of digital objects on the WWW contributes to their wide spread, often leaving the creators unprotected from unauthorized use of their creations. The IPRs of the creators can be ensured by embedding information about the source or the copyright owner of the data, thus preventing others from claiming ownership.

For such applications the watermarks should remain robust with any modification of the host data. The extracted watermark should be unambiguous and able to resolve rightful ownership.

Fingerprinting

Fingerprinting is a method that is used to verify the legal recipients.[20] In fingerprinting a different watermark is embedded in each distributed copy of the digital objects. Fingerprinting techniques are used for identifying the last distributor of the digital object. Therefore, when illegal copies are found, the miscreant can be tracked.

The existence of the watermark in fingerprinting techniques is of vital importance. Consequently, the watermarks should withstand any attacks and be unambiguous at the recovery process, as well as in copyright protection techniques.

Copy Protection

Copy protection techniques follow a *more strict policy* in comparison with the previous techniques. The role of the watermark here is not to identify the owner or the legal recipients, but to activate the protecting process, to disallow unauthorized users from copying the digital objects.

Watermarking can also be used to encode copy-control information retrievable from both digital and analog signals. Usually, the copy-protection system provides the capability for one-time copying.

Copy protection has been applied on DVD systems where a watermark, which includes copy information, is embedded in the data. Until now, copy protection techniques have been used in closed systems, while in open systems like WWW, they are technically complex to apply.

Conclusions

The Internet is governed by two main trends: the first is the free exchange of any kind of digital object, while the other one is the transaction that is based on money—an evolution of traditional commerce. Both trends are respectable and the decision whether a digital object should be copyright protected is up to the authors-creators. Nonetheless, the rapidly expanding use of the Internet provides ample opportunities for deceivers to apply their skills.

There is a lot that must be done in order to prevent unauthorized use of digital objects. First of all the user's behavior should be altered in such a way to comply with the IPRs. The most natural way would be if the users' acts were the impacts of their internal intention. By educating people and by shaping their social behavior they could react in compliance with copyright issues. The law should definitely help towards this direction. People aware of the consequences, shape accordingly their actions. The ownership of digital objects could be certified by the existence of a watermark within them.

Many problems arise though. First, there are no international laws that cover *Internet territory*, and this is very difficult since countries differ with respect to their laws and penalties. Moreover, there is no standardization of the watermarking methods, and thus there is no official watermarking technique legally in place. Consequently, the most complex part is that different scientific disciplines and all countries must collaborate with each other, meeting always at a lowest common denominator.

In this paper we attempted to present the problem of intellectual property rights over the Internet. We discussed possible solutions and their problems. Letting criticism replace condemnation and putting theory into praxis clearly requires awareness of the problem, willingness to solve it, practical and easily used tools, and both courage and responsibility to face the consequences of the outcome. Concern over IPRs, Internet reality notwithstanding, probably does as much as anything to foster the new wind of realism.

References

1. Kant, I. 1785. *Essay Three {8.77–87} of the Injustice of Counterfeiting Books* [online – cited 18 October 2001]. Available from World Wide Web: (http://www.hkbu.edu.hk/~ppp/fne/essay3.html).

2. GNU 2001. *GNU's Not Unix!* [online—cited 18 October 2001]. Available from World Wide Web: (http://www.gnu.org).

3. Kant, I. 1781. *Kritik der Reinen Vernunft* [online—cited 18 October 2001]. Available from World Wide Web: (http://www.netzhaus.ch/kantcd/).

4. Katsimani, Kyriakou S. 1982. *History of Philosophy.* Athens: Second edition, Educational Institute of National Bank. Greek Translation of *Histoire de la Philosophie — La Revolution Kantienne.* Encyclopédie de la Pléiade, Paris: Editions Gallimard, 1973.

5. Lehman, B., and Brown, R. 1995. *Intellectual Property and the National Information Infrastructure — The Report of the Working Group on Intellectual Property Rights — Information Infrastructure Task Force.*

6. WIPO. 1996. *World Intellectual Property Organization Copyright Treaty* [online — cited 16 October 2001]. Available from World Wide Web: (http://www.wipo.int).

7. WIPO, 1996.

8. Allison, L. 2001. *Law, Ethics, the Media and the InterNet* [online]. Available from World Wide Web: (http://www.csse.monash.edu.au/~lloyd/tilde/InterNet/Law/index.html).

9. Johnson, D.G. January 1997. "Ethics

Online." *Communication of the ACM* 40(1): 60–65.

10. Rapaport, R. 1997. "PR finds a New Cool Tool." Forbes 1997, Oct. 6: 101–108.

11. GNU 2001. GNU's Not Unix! [online—cited 18 October 2001]. Available from World Wide Web: (http://www.gnu.org).

12. GNU, 2001.

13. Blackman, D., and Leake, M. 2001. Towards a Universal World of Computer Ethics [online]. 2nd Australian Institute of Computer Ethics Conference, 2000 [cited October 2001]. Available from World Wide Web: (http://www.aice.swin.edu.au/events/AICE2000/papersindex.html).

14. Allison, 2001.

15. Johnson, 1997.

16. Koenig, C. 2001. Über den apriorischen Ursprung der Sittlichkeit in der Vernunft, Hausarbeit zum Hauptseminar "Kants Vernunftssittlichkeit" [online – cited 18 October 2001]. Available from World Wide Web: (http://www.uni-koeln.de/phil-fak/fs-philo/).

17. Kreie, J., and Cronan, T.P. September 1998. "How Men and Women View Ethics." Communications of the ACM 41(9): 70–76

18. Johnson, 1997.

19. Petitcolas, F., Anderson, R., and Kuhn, M. July 1999. "Information Hiding—Survey." Proc. of the IEEE, Special Issue on Protection of Multimedia Content 87(7): 1062–1078.

20. Kutter, M., and Hartung, F. 2000. "Introduction to Watermarking Techniques." In Katzenbeisser, S., Petitcolas, F.A.P. (Eds.), *Information Hiding Techniques for Steganography and Digital Watermarking*, Boston and London: Artech House, Inc.

17

Ethical Hacking: The Security Justification

Bryan Smith, William Yurcik, and *David Doss*

Abstract

The state of security on the Internet is poor and progress toward increased protection is slow. This has given rise to a class of action referred to as "ethical hacking." Companies are releasing software with little or no testing and no formal verification and expecting consumers to debug their product for them. For dot-com companies time-to-market is vital, security is not perceived as a marketing advantage, and implementing a secure design process an expensive sunk expense such that there is no economic incentive to produce bug-free software. There are even legislative initiatives to release software manufacturers from legal responsibility to their defective software.

Ethical hackers find bugs and fix bugs. In the process they beta test software for companies in exchange for access and information. They scan networks for bugs and share information about software bugs over the Internet. Alerting a software company to a bug, there is an expectation that they are helping but sometimes software companies do not respond in-kind. Thus Ethical Hackers often take it upon themselves to disclose sensitive information they have themselves discovered in a form of blackmail to motivate software vendors into action. There is an incredible ambiguity in that sometimes the ethical hacker is a respected university professor who is perceived as doing a service to the Internet community and sometimes the ethical hacker is suspicious foreign student who is perceived as a malicious cracker. It is not clear that without ethical hackers the Internet would be a more dangerous place.

Introduction

Hacking has come to have many different and often conflicting definitions. Hackers do not require certification, anyone can say they are a hacker.

For the purposes of this paper we define "hacking" as the software methodology to achieve a particular goal using self-taught programming experimentation "to make rough cuts."[1] Celebrated incidents of unauthorized computer intrusions into computer systems have been attributed to hackers due to the extensive programming experimentation needed to achieve success.

Computer intrusions are considered to be unethical and laws have been passed to prosecute such behavior. Spafford clearly states that computer intrusions are ethical only in life-saving circumstances.[2] Once hacking ability is used to commit a crime, the hacker becomes a criminal. However, a new class of "ethical hackers" has arisen who believe that probing for computer intrusions, a legal activity that provides sensitive information, provides a altruistic service to increase both local and global Internet security by exposing and fixing security flaws.

The debate between "ethical hacking" and criminal intrusion dates back to the very first widespread Internet virus, the Internet Worm of 1988. Robert Morris was convicted for intrusion damage caused by the Internet Worm but his defense lawyers argued that he had provided a service in exposing security flaws.[3]

Ethical hackers use their knowledge to help improve system security. Upon discovering a security flaw, they do not exploit the flaw; they fully disclose all relevant information to the affected users of the systems, software companies, mailing lists, trade press, or popular media. In contrast, unethical hackers (crackers) gain unauthorized access to subvert systems. Statistics show that the motivation of unethical hackers has changed from the pursuit of knowledge and the desire for challenge to the new lures of money, power, or political purposes (hactivism).[4] They privately share their knowledge of security flaws, maintain unauthorized access, and do damage to systems.[5]

The Problem

If history is any indication, the information-technology community is incapable of constructing networked information systems that can consistently prevent successful attacks.[6] The natural escalation of offensive threats versus defensive countermeasures has demonstrated time and again that no practical system can be built that is invulnerable to attack. Even an organization where network and computer security is paramount such as the U.S. Department of Defense has continuously demonstrated how susceptible it is to attack.

We posit that the main factor contributing to the poor state of security on the Internet is the lack of quality software testing. The intellectual complexity associated with software design, coding, and testing virtually ensures the presence of "bugs" in software that can be exploited by attackers. Most software today is tested for bugs by the penetrate-and-patch approach — when someone finds an exploitable security "hole" the software manufacturer issues a patch.

This approach has proved inadequate since after-the-fact security leaves bug vulnerabilities open until they are exploited. However, software manufacturers find this approach economically attractive — why invest time and money in assurance testing if consumers are not willing to pay a premium for secure software. Time-to-market survival dictates that software is released as early as possible, often with serious undetected security flaws.[7]

The problem presented by lack of quality testing is also acerbated by automated attacks, operating system homogeneity, and poor practices. Devastating attacks appear in executable scripts that can be downloaded to anonymously target systems anywhere in the world. The homogeneity of operating system software from the same manufacturer (i.e., Microsoft Windows) makes it possible for a single-attack strategy to have a wide-ranging and devastating impact. Poor system administration practices result in a system remaining susceptible to vulnerabilities even after corresponding patches have been issued from software manufacturers. It has been estimated that over 90 percent of all Internet attacks would have been deterred if system administrators had implemented the most current versions of their system software.[8]

The Scanning Solution?

Testing for security flaws appears to be a natural attraction many for hackers—it is both challenging and contributes to the public good by exposing and patching vulnerabilities. Manual testing has evolved into automated programs scanning a network of computers for known weaknesses.[9] Scanning is not a one-time fix—new software versions bring new bugs and new security flaws that can be exploited are discovered. The frequency of the scan will depend on the software lifecycle of the systems involved and the ability to cleanup vulnerabilities—it makes no sense to discover weaknesses if they are simply ignored.

In 1995 Dan Farmer introduced a scanner called SATAN (Security Administrator for Analyzing Networks).[10,11] Unlike previous automated scanners that ran on the particular system being analyzed, SATAN could analyze any system accessible over the Internet. The dual nature of SATAN was quickly understood even in the mass media- Newsweek published a brief article "SATAN: Friend or Foe?" (April 3, 1995). Proponents of SATAN view it as a system administration tool to find bugs to prevent intrusions. Opponents of SATAN view it as an easy-to-use tool an inexperienced hacker can use to bring down systems all over the Internet.

Hypocrisy—Beta Testing, Penetration Testing, and Hacking Contests

As a whole, the hacker community represents a testing environment far more effective than any one corporation could ever construct. Ethical hacking has become institutionalized by most major software companies in the form of beta testing new software with select groups of customers who will stress test and report back information about defects (e.g. extensive beta testing of Microsoft's Windows XP). Often the only reward for the beta testers is privileged access to the software. This may work well for testing software performance but security bugs do not often show up in beta testing unless the testing is done by security experts or a security bug is stumbled upon.[12] In the rare cases where a security flaw is discovered by beta testers, fixing the bug may not be a high priority for the software vendor and "ethical hackers" have sometimes had to resort to a form of blackmail (threaten release of bug information to mass media) to motivate action.

Some firms offer penetration testing or "ethical hacking" services.[13] For a fee ($15K to $200K), a red team will launch a controlled simulated attack to test known vulnerabilities and report back corrective patches that need to be installed.[14] An overall evaluation of a system's security will focus on there three questions:[15]

(A) What can an intruder see on the target system?

(B) What can an intruder do with the information from (A)

(C) Does anyone at the target system notice the intruder's attempts or successful attacks?

The hypocrisy in penetration testing is that organizations are paying hackers to attack with the same behavior that they would legally prosecute if under any other circumstances. The irony of penetration testing is that it is only superficial, real attacks will exploit unpublicized vulnerabilities, and the most attractive red team employee may be a "reformed" cracker-for-hire — who better to test your system than the kind of people who may break in?[16,17,18] If outsourcing penetration testing, trusting contractors becomes important because real things can be damaged and sensitive security details will be revealed. Public perception in the integrity of an organization's information assets may be more important than an objective technical security assessment. Lastly, quantitative system security assessments need to be mapped to an organization's subjective risk profile — all vulnerabilities do not have equal risks and there are different probabilities for exploitation:[19]

(A) What are you trying to protect?

(B) What are you trying to protect against?

(C) How much time, effort, and money is the organization willing to expend to obtain adequate protection?

Hacking contests are promoted by organizations for two reasons: to publicize the supposed security of a product against sustained hacking and to use the hacking community to harden software that has not been adequately tested. These contests are generally unfair and the prize money not scaled to the level of effort required but they still remain very popular — even causing network congestion.[20,21,22] The hypocrisy in contests is that organizations are paying (prize money) and thus encouraging the same expertise they would legally prosecute against if under any other circumstances.

Conclusions

Security on the Internet is broken and "ethical hacking" has evolved as part of the potential solution. Ethical hacking is fixing a system by compromising it — destructive testing in other domains — which has a long history of achievement but it is not clear that this technique is applicable for Internet security.

A security hole on one computer is not just an isolated problem as demonstrated by recent distributed denial-of-service attacks—processes on compromised computers can be used to attack other systems worldwide. At present, the Internet has poor security and "ethical hacking" may be one of the most effective ways to proactively plug rampant security holes. "Ethical hackers" see themselves as a necessary part of a larger vanguard protecting freedom and privacy in addition to security.

On the other hand, "ethical hacking" tools (such as scanners) have also been notorious tools of malicious attackers. A fine line exists between hacking for the public good and releasing scanning tools that enable malicious attacks. Trying to fix the Internet security problem with automated tools over a wide scale may have actually made the Internet less secure taken as a whole.

We have focused in this paper on technical aspects of what may intrinsically be a non-technical problem. If human intent does indeed dominate then technical solutions will not suffice and instead solutions will need to focus on behavioral modification. Internet security is a complex problem and while altruistic behavior such as "ethical hacking" may make a difference (not sure in which direction), there needs to be stronger incentives to software vendors, system administrators, and users to do the right thing.

References

1. William Hugh Murray. July 26 2000. *personal communications* (Email).

2. Eugene Spafford. 1992. Are Computer Hacker Break-ins Ethical? *Journal of Systems Software* 17:41–47.

3. Ted Eisenberg, 1995. The Computer Worm: A Report to the Provost of Cornell. within *Computer Ethics & Social Values.* by Deborah G. Johnson and Helen Nissenbaum, Prentice Hall, 60–89.

4. Charles C. Palmer, 2001. Ethical Hacking. *IBM Systems Journal.* 3: 769–780.

5. Martin D. Goslar, August 2001. Is There Such a Thing as "Ethical Hacking?" *Information Security.*

6. Bob Evans, June 4 2001. The Sorry State of Software. *InformationWeek* 112.

7. Christine Zimmerman, March 26 2001. Race to Deploy May Magnify Software Bugs. *InternetWeek* 13.

8. Bruce Schneier. 2000. *Secrets and Lies: Digital Security in a Networked World.* John Wiley & Sons.

9. Marco de Vivo, Eddy Carrasco, Germinal Isern, and Gabriela O. de Vivo. April 1999. A Review of Port Scanning Techniques. *ACM SIGCOMM Computer Communications Review* 2: 41–48.

10. Martin Freiss, 1997. *Protecting Networks with Satan.* O'Reilly Press.

11. Dan Farmer and Weitse Venema. 1993. *Improving the Security of Your Site By Breaking Into It.* <http://www.fish.com/security/admin-guide-to-cracking.html>.

12. Schneier 2000.

13. "Ethical Hacker" 1999. *IBMConsulting e-business advertisement, trademark, service mark & logo.*

14. Bradley J. Wood and Ruth A. Duggan. Red Teaming of Advanced Information Assurbnce Concepts. *DARPA Information Survivability Conference and Fxposition (DISCEX)* 112–118.

15. Palmer 2001.

16. Lewis Z. Koch, June 29 2000. Hacking for the Common Good? *Inter@ctive Week.*

17. Ira Winkler, July 2000. The "Ethical Hacker" Debate. *Information Security* 82.

18. Steph Marr, October 1999. Ethical Hackers: Latest IT Craze or Real Deterrent? *SC Magazine* 17.

19. Charles C. Palmer, 2001.

20. Henry Baltazar, June 26 2000. Hacker Attacks Welcomed. *eWeek* 30, 34.

21. Schneier 2000.

22. Mark Solomons, September 13 2000. Hackers Offered $10,000 Bait. *Financial Times.*

Bibliography

Baltazar, Henry. June 26, 2000. Hacker Attacks Welcomed. *eWeek* 30, 34.

de Vivo, Marco, Eddy Carrasco, Germinal Isern, and Gabriela O. de Vivo. April 1999. A Review of Port Scanning Techniques. ACM SIGCOMM *Computer Communications Review* 2: 41–48.

Eisenberg, Ted., et al., 1995. The Computer Worm: A Report to the Provost of Cornell. In *Computer Ethics & Social Values.* by Deborah G. Johnson and Helen Nissenbaum, Prentice Hall, 60–89.

"Ethical Hacker" 1999. *IBMConsulting e-business advertisement, trademark, service mark & logo.*

Evans, Bob. June 4, 2001. The Sorry State of Software. *InformationWeek* 112.

Farmer, Dan, and Weitse Venema. 1993. *Improving the Security of Your Site By Breaking Into It.* <http://www.fish.com/security/admin-guide-to-cracking.html>.

Freiss, Martin. 1997. *Protecting Networks with Satan.* O'Reilly Press.

Goslar, Martin D. August 2001. Is There Such a Thing as "Ethical Hacking"? *Information Security.*

Koch, Lewis Z. June 29, 2000. Hacking for the Common Good? *Inter@ctive Week.*

Marr, Steph. October 1999. Ethical Hackers: Latest IT Craze or Real Deterrent? *SC Magazine* 17–18.

Murray, William Hugh. July 26, 2000. *personal communications* (Email).

Palmer, Charles C. 2001. Ethical Hacking. *IBM Systems Journal.* 3: 769–780.

Schneier, Bruce. 2000. *Secrets and Lies: Digital Security in a Networked World.* John Wiley & Sons.

Solomons, Mark. September 13, 2000. Hackers Offered $10,000 Bait. *Financial Times.*

Spafford, Eugene H. 1992. Are Computer Hacker Break-ins Ethical? *Journal of Systems Software* 17:41–47.

Winkler, Ira. July 2000. The "Ethical Hacker" Debate. *Information Security* 82.

Wood, Bradley J., and Ruth A. Duggan. Red Teaming of Advanced Information Assurance Concepts. *DARPA Information Survivability Conference and Exposition (DISCEX)* 112–118.

Zimmerman, Christine. March 26, 2001. Race to Deploy May Magnify Software Bugs. *InternetWeek* 13.

18

Social Democracy and Information Media Policy

Alistair S. Duff

Introduction

It is widely believed that Western and semi-Western nations have become or are becoming "information societies." We are told that the economy is knowledge-based,[1] that we inhabit a post-industrial era,[2] that information flows are the vectors of modernisation,[3] that information and communication technologies hold the key to social progress,[4] that a new "virtual" culture is being engendered[5] and that the scale of all these changes is global.[6] Not everyone accepts all of these propositions, of course, especially when stated in a radically "transformationist" or deterministic form. Nevertheless, a vast range of theorists now embrace at least strands of the "information society thesis," and it is comparatively rare today to encounter a commentator flatly denying that information is playing a greater formative role in society than before.

The ongoing, multifaceted informatisation of society is the point of departure of the present essay.[7] Information has always been central to the functioning of societies and every society in the world is to a significant extent an information society, including those of the near and distant past (would anyone be able to substantiate the negative proposition that ancient Babylon or medieval Europe, say, were *not* dependent on information flows and primitive communication technologies?). But nowadays, as a result of palpable breakthroughs in the field of high technology, information has become especially salient in advanced societies and such societies have a particularly strong right to be denominated information societies. We should accept that we — i.e. the privileged citizens of Western nations— are in the midst of what Trevor Haywood calls a new "information moment."[8] That does not, to emphasise, entail that anyone is under any obligation to endorse the information society thesis in its unqualified sense; but it does certainly mean that information can no longer be ignored as a major category in the description of society, whatever branch of social science is being used. Logically, my argument below actually requires only the much weaker thesis that information is of *some* importance. It is like environmental policy: the justification of state interference in the environment requires not an endorsement of a strong environmentalist philosophy or even the view that the environment is more important than ever before, but only the proposition that the environment is sufficiently important to be a subject of governmental policy. Surely we can assume that much.

Now a distinction needs to be drawn between the *de facto* and the *de jure* information society thesis, or in other words between empirical and normative propositions about the trajectories and objectives of informatisation. The goal of the present paper is to develop a normative approach to the information society, and particularly to information media policy (a term I will spend time defining below), an approach grounded in a substantive social morality. This reflects my growing conviction that the information society thesis has lacked a sound ethical footing. While the articulation of a *de jure* theory of the information society would be needful in any case, it is particularly relevant under current conditions as a constructive alternative to the prevailing neo-liberal world order. It is surely becoming a matter of urgency to contest a state of affairs where information media policy is largely decided by unelected actors and lobbyists in the commercial sector, by crude technological determinism, and by the mysterious forces of "globalisation." This essentially libertarian orthodoxy, with roots in the politics of Ronald Reagan and Margaret Thatcher and their ideological mentors, privileges inordinately the social value of liberty and has resulted world-wide in more or less unfettered capitalism. I wish here to posit a more just ethic, namely social democracy, a moderate form of democratic socialism which legitimises an interventionist role for the state in several spheres, including those covered by information media policy.

The Principles of Social Democracy

The understanding of social democracy has always been poor. It has often been confused with, or misrepresented as, a disingenuous mode of communism. More recently it has also been wrongly equated with social liberalism, as in the present British doctrine of the Third Way.[9] Even within the ranks of social democracy, among those who would unreservedly sign themselves as democratic socialists, there has been disagreement over its essential nature. I wish, therefore, to attempt in this section to sketch a rough outline of social democracy. Space will not allow the articulation of a watertight position; some assertions will have to be left undefended, although I hope that elsewhere I may have opportunity to fill out the necessary details of a fully-fledged normative theory of the information society.

Speaking from within a now largely defunct tradition of European religious socialist thought, Paul Tillich once defined socialism as a resistance movement against the destruction of love in social reality.[10] The slogan captures beautifully the spirit of socialism, and seems particularly appropriate to the humane expression of socialism that is social democracy. The compassionate crusade for redress was the spring-board not only of socialism but also of the civil rights movement and indeed of all progressive political action. But socialism must be more than a resistance movement, an oppositional politics, an unthinking "anti-capitalism": it must also supply a picture of how social reality should be remoulded, a conception, that is, not so much of love (although compassion should always be the main motive) as of social justice. For social democracy, in a nutshell, is a liberal and egalitarian conception of justice in society. And it is, I propose, in the formulation of a feasible theory of the just society that social democracy at its best has shown itself to be infinitely superior not merely to raw capitalism but to Marxism-Leninism and all other versions and corruptions of the socialist ideal. Here, then, such a formulation is broached.

I have already cited liberty and equality, but that is little more than a rhetorical gambit. Practically every well-intentioned person in the West believes in "liberty, equality and fraternity," and it is only in the *interpretation* of such values that the characteristic divisions between socialist, liberal, and conservative emerge. What we really need is an axiology, a formal statement of a value system. Explicating these values, say by turning them into formulae or ordered sets of principles, is thus the chief task for the theory of social justice. Now, unquestionably, the most important and influential social philosopher with whom one could associate the ideal of social democracy is Harvard's John Rawls. Rawls's main contribution remains *A Theory of Justice*,[11] the seminal work which is credited not only with having breathed new life and sophistication into egalitarian thought, but also with having succeeded more or less single-handedly in reinventing the entire Anglo-American tradition of normative political philosophy. Here I wish to plot the main coordinates of Rawls's position and also to show where it needs to be modified. I will be relying mainly on a recently published edition of Rawls's lectures, *Justice as Fairness: A Restatement.*[12]

Rawls's aim is to articulate a theory of social justice which will commend itself as widely as possible among reasonable and well-intentioned observers in what he calls a state of "reflective equilibrium." A person is in such a state when he or she "has considered the leading conceptions of political justice found in our philosophical tradition (including views critical of the concept of justice itself [some think Marx's view is an example]), and has weighed the force of the different philosophical and other arguments for them."[13] Armed with this faith in the power of reason, Rawls sets out a formidably persuasive rational case for a doctrine he calls "justice as fairness." Presented as an alternative to utilitarianism, perfectionism and other competitor conceptions, justice as fairness is expressed in two principles:

(a) Each person has the same indefeasible claim to a fully adequate scheme of equal basic liberties, which scheme is compatible with the same scheme of liberties for all; and

(b) Social and economic inequalities are to satisfy two conditions: first, they are to be attached to offices and positions open to all under conditions of fair equality of opportunity; and second, they are to be to the greatest benefit of the least-advantaged members of society (the difference principle).[14]

The liberties required by the first principle are liberty of conscience and speech, freedom of religion, the right to vote, the right to own private (although not necessarily productive) property, and the like — in other words the usual list of civil and political freedoms cherished in liberal democracies. Rawls stipulates that the first principle, known as the liberty principle, has priority over the second, and that the first half of the second principle (equality of opportunity) has priority over the second half (the difference principle). These priority rules are absolute. "The priority of liberty," he tells us, "means that a basic liberty can be limited or denied only for the sake of one or more other basic liberties, and never for a greater public good understood as a greater net sum of social and economic advantages for society as a whole."[15] Or as Rawls originally put the matter in *A Theory of Justice*, "each person possesses an inviolability founded on justice that even the welfare of society as a whole cannot override."[16] The liberties of citizenship are therefore paramount, and cannot be compromised, after the manner of much Marxist and teleological thought, as part of some calculus of supposed future economic or social collective benefits. The first principle thus immediately rules out state socialism with a command economy[17] and also, I would have to add, most instances of Islamic socialism the world has seen so far.

This priority of the right over the good is the cornerstone of Rawls's normative position, as it arguably must be of any theorist soliciting widespread assent within a culture shaped by the Judaeo-Christian deontological tradition of respect for the rights of the individual. And we must, I think, go along with Rawls when he says that the basic liberties should be off the agenda of democratic societies, since to treat them otherwise "subjects them to the shifting circumstances of time and place, and by greatly raising the stakes of political controversy, dangerously increases the insecurity and hostility of public life."[18] However, while we should be unmistakably clear that social democracy is nothing if not a mode of liberal democracy, I would argue that social democracy can and should be rather more teleological than Rawls allows. It accepts the priority of the right over the good in general terms; it also endorses the priority of liberty in broad brush strokes; but it need not insist upon absolute priority for all of Rawls's specific liberties, where these stand unavoidably in the way of major goals of economic and social justice. The codification of the deontological-teleological balance is a delicate and complex philosophical task for social democratic thought. Here I would only suggest, by way of illustration, that while freedom of conscience and religion are nonnegotiable absolutes, freedom of expression should normally be limited in various ways in order to protect other persons and classes of persons. In this sense, the common good trumps specific individual rights without, arguably, violating any legitimate claims of justice.

The second principle, as can be seen, has two parts. First, it requires equality of opportunity, that is, the setting up of arrangements to give everyone a fair start in the game of life. This goes far beyond formal equal opportunities, as in laws against racial or sexual discrimination (such are assumed in even a minimally civilised society), to include the shaping of those background conditions and institutions which, Rawls rightly thinks, determine the individual's chance to make the most of his or her opportunities. As he puts it, "in all parts of society there are to be roughly the same prospects of culture and achievement for those similarly motivated and endowed."[19] The other half of the second principle reaches even further into the socio-economic structure and mandates, much to the horror of conservatives and libertarians, the politics of income redistribution. The difference principle, however, is much more subtle than most egalitarian schemes, and has been recognised as one of Rawls's most original contributions to political thought. As its name suggests, it is a principle which, while making socio-economic equality the benchmark or default distribution, goes on to sanction a degree of conditional inequality. Rawls's argument is that differential shares of the cake are morally justified and socially desirable under one specific condition, namely where the worst-off are better off than they would be under any alternative arrangement. The guiding intuition here, and it is surely one which must be taken seriously, is that an equality of misery is hardly the normative goal of politics. If an inegalitarian economic system, by embracing a measure of competition, incentives, or whatever, can generate a significantly larger gross national product than strict egalitarianism, then, so long as the least-advantaged are better off under such a regime, social justice is satisfied.

Now while the second principle, like the first, is essentially correct, and should be used as the normative framework for social democratic politics, it needs to be construed in a particular way. The difference principle, specifically, has been attacked from the right for being too egalitarian and from the left for allowing too much inequality, and Rawls's response has always been frustratingly noncommittal. I would wish, however, to impose an unequivocal left-wing interpretation. It cannot be the case, at least for an engaged social democrat, that small gains for the least-advantaged can justify huge gains for the rich, because a true socialist, while being primarily moved by compassion for those sunk in poverty, is also concerned about excessive wealth. For as R.H. Tawney, author of the earlier classic *Equality*, said, "the extremes both of riches and poverty are degrading and anti-social," and so it is necessary to "make war" on "privilege" as well as "destitution."[20] This is not to say that we should retreat from the difference principle into an espousal of crude arithmetic equality. Rather, as Tawney explained, it is a question of confounding the natural tendencies towards class division:

"What is repulsive is not that one man should earn more than others, for where community of environment, and a common education and habit of life, have bred a common tradition of respect and consideration, these details of the counting-house are forgotten or ignored. It is that some classes should be excluded from the heritage of civilization which others enjoy, and that the fact of human fellowship, which is ultimate and profound, should be obscured by economic contrasts, which are trivial and superficial."[21]

Such was the authentic voice of British egalitarianism, a voice which has a right to be heard again today, and not only in Britain. It is this "ultimate and profound fact of human fellowship," in other words the conception of society as a *community* as opposed to a mere association of (or tacit contract among) individuals, that is lacking in Rawls's account. To prove the good of brotherhood is not easy, but I think that any such argumentation, expressed with sufficient eloquence, would have a strong intuitive appeal in many cultures, not least those imbued with the values of the Judaeo-Christian tradition. Calibrated in these kinds of ways, by a more rather less stringent reading of the difference principle and by a richer vision of community, Rawlsian social democracy can, I believe, show the way forward for normative politics in the information age.

The Nature of Information Media Policy

The first part of this essay outlined a conception of social democracy, one rooted in an axiology. There was nothing particularly new in what was said, not surprisingly given that social democracy is a mature tradition going back at least one hundred and fifty years. All I can hope to have achieved so far is to have shown the desirability of social democracy as a political philosophy, in general terms. Now, in the second half of the paper, I wish to explore how social democracy impinges on the information society. For those of us who believe both in social democracy and in the importance of informational developments the application of the principles of the former to the latter has become an obligation. More concretely, we need to show how information media policy should look when social democratic norms have been factored into policy arguments. For unlike historicist views like Marxism, social democracy, being grounded not in grand narratives but in ethical values to which practical reason has access, is able to respond satisfactorily to changing realities in the world of economics and society.

The term "information media policy" in the paper's title may already have struck a discordant note. It is admittedly an unfamiliar term, one which runs together keywords normally kept apart. I wish to change that and to try to bring "information media policy" into more common use. This rubric symbolises a deliberate fusion of two policy fields whose historic separation no longer makes much sense, the fields being information policy and the hitherto *sui generis* specialism called media policy studies. I will say a little about each and then explain why a single overarching approach is now appropriate. After that we can move on directly to the application of social democratic norms.

The definition of information policy has always—in its relatively short conscious life — been problematic, as its more lucid commentators have acknowledged.[22] The seminal statement can be found in Marc Porat's *The Information Economy*, where information policy is defined as the area of government policy which "attends to the issues raised by the combined effects of information technologies (computers and telecommunications) on market and nonmarket events."[23] Setting information policy firmly within the context of the rising information economy which his report documented in painstaking detail, Porat wrote:

"In a rudimentary fashion, we begin to define the elements of 'information policy.' The major implication is that as information technologies 'invade' various sectors of the economy, old arrangements may come into conflict with the new. Applications of the new technologies may raise either economic issues or value conflicts that previously lay dormant. The seeds of tomorrow's opportunities and difficulties are sown today. And therein lies the presumption that information policy should adopt a prospective look at future applications of information technology."[24]

By way of illustration, Porat cited as a sign of impending informatisation the "edgy and uncomfortable feeling in the US Postal Service as electronic mail approaches."[25] We can look back and smile, but at the time they were penned his comments were radical and prescient. "Telecommunications policy is an appropriate starting place," he goes on to say, "but it is not enough. A telecommunication policy that ignores the computer is as barren as the reverse case."[26] The crucial point Porat was making, and an entirely valid one, was that government policymakers needed to begin seeing computers and telecommunications as an integrating process whose effects on society were no longer discrete. It was in pursuit of a coordinated approach to the social, economic, cultural, and political issues evoked by the *synergy* of compunications (computer-telecommunications) that the field of information policy came into being.

Now it was suggested about ten years ago[27] that little progress had been made since Porat in the typology of information policy. However, a new technological stage has most definitely been reached over the past decade, one which surely requires a new typology bringing all electronic media together into a single conceptual and policy framework. For now that the technological barriers between compunications and the older electronic mass media have more or less broken down, an information policy in the twenty-first century which ignores television and radio will be as "barren," to echo Porat's word, as a telecommunications policy in the 1980s which ignored information technology.

This has unsettling implications for old-fashioned media policy and media regulation studies. Radio, film, and television were, and to a large extent still are,[28] the subject matter of much media policy discourse — rarely telephones or computers. Against such closure, I propose that a new integrated field of information media policy should be developed as a synthesis of information policy and media policy, specialisms whose distinct identities have all but collapsed in the face of technological convergence. The titular priority of information over media may cause disquiet in some media policy circles, especially since a strong case can be made for the proposition that media policy studies has a more distinguished scholarly pedigree than information policy studies. Nevertheless, information is the more inclusive, more topical, and more important of the two keywords: we live, after all, as was agreed at the start, in some form of information society.

The scope of information media policy is thus very wide indeed, inheriting everything from the kingdoms of both information policy and media policy. It is helpful to recall here Robert Burger's list of topics for information policy, which comprised STI (scientific and technical information) policy, privacy issues, literacy, freedom of speech, libraries and archives, state and commercial secrecy, and access to government information, alongside the whole of what he called communication policy, i.e. broadcasting, telecommunications, spectrum allocation, cable systems, and transnational data flows.[29] That would seem a reasonable rough-and-ready portfolio for what I am calling information media policy, although I should like to add that information media policy also deals with the *quantity* of information flows through particular media and across society as a totality—a point long recognised by Japanese information policymakers.[30] Information media policy should seek to influence how much information exists in society, as well as the *quality* of the messages being conveyed. It should be noted also that information media policy ranges across various sectors of society, the socio-economic structure, the polity, and the culture; it is not largely confined, as was old-fashioned media policy, to culture. Many, therefore, of the most interesting ethical problems and most significant policy challenges confronting modern democracies fall within the domain of information media policy. In the final section, some initial thoughts are offered on what might be a distinctively social-democratic approach to some of these issues.

A Social Democratic Approach to Information Media Policy

The historic focus of social democracy on the socio-economic realm — the goals of egalitarian struggle were perforce concentrated in material improvements and handovers of the means of physical as opposed to cultural or intellectual production — has inevitably led to a comparative neglect of issues falling under information media policy. Where doctrine has been employed it has, curiously, tended to be stridently anti-interventionist, in stark contrast to its positive doctrine of state involvement in the economy and social structure. It is indeed one of the more amusing spectacles of civilised politics to see social democrats characteristically criticising conservatives for being *laissez-faire* about the market and intrusive apropos of social mores, while they themselves are *laissez-faire* about social mores and intrusive about the economy. A more morally consistent approach is now required, one which broadens out the agenda of social democracy to include an interventionist information media policy. A social democratic approach, therefore, should certainly support the proposition that information media policy belongs in the *mainstream* of public policy, that it is much more than a mere side-show to more important debates about the economy or full employment. It should also, arguably, conceptualise information media policy as a subset specifically of that branch of government policy known as social policy: as such it could adopt the commitments of what Tony Fitzpatrick calls "critical cyberpolicy" to both the autonomy of the subject *and* the avoidance of harm,[31] both liberalism and paternalism. A normative dual-track approach like that would seem to be faithful to the two principles of social justice defended earlier. But these are preliminary points only. I now turn to a major area where a social democratic approach can be clearly seen to result in concrete policy recommendations. The following remarks are merely exploratory and do not claim to constitute exhaustive statements: they are intended simply to illustrate the kinds of vital political issues upon which social democratic information media policy could be brought to bear.

Nick Moore stated recently that the choice for information policy is between "neo-liberal" and "dirigiste" approaches.[32] Social democracy, being a substantive position on the centre-left of the political spectrum, will directly answer this question in favour of dirigiste—collectivist, or perhaps, where adequate, Keynesian—principles in the area of information media policy. At the heart of the whole issue of the "digital divide" is the system of ownership of the means of information. Just as the pioneering socialists of the industrial age fought a hard battle for public ownership of the means of production, so socially-aware thinkers at the edge of the information age should be arguing for public rights in the ownership of the means of information (without, I should add, neglecting the former: there are serious flaws in the strong post-industrialist position according to which manufacturing industry is no longer of much importance in advanced societies). The matter, however, is not as simple as some socialists might have us believe. The goal is not state ownership of everything remotely connected to the production and distribution of knowledge or information, since to pursue such a rigorous end would be to repeat the costly errors of Marxism-Leninism all over again. Returning then to Rawls, the *Restatement* says that while the second principle rules out both laissez-faire capitalism and welfare-state capitalism, it is neutral between popular capitalism, or what Rawls calls "property-owning democracy," and "liberal (democratic) socialism."[33] The choice between these two economic systems, according to Rawls, comes down to context and expedience rather than being a matter of justice.

Here it is necessary to depart from Rawls, again not so much by going against what he says as by imposing a definite interpretation upon his principles. It is surely not a straight either/or alternative between a publicly owned economy and a privately owned economy. To suggest that is to forget the greater part of debate on economic politics since the Second World War. For, of course, it is the *mixed* economy that has been the benchmark since the post-war settlement, and the arguments between right and left have centred around the makeup of the mixed economy, especially as regards which industries should be in public ownership and which are better left to the market. Instead of rehearsing that whole debate, I would quickly retrieve one of the most important of the policy mantras, namely that the "commanding heights" of the economy should be publicly owned. And, applying that venerable social democratic norm to the information age, I would argue that the deregulation of the telecommunications infrastructure—or more colloquially the phone network—has been one of the most serious and widespread information media policy errors of the last twenty years. Further, I contend that the mistake can and should be reversed: that the renationalisation of the telecommunications infrastructure should be at the top of the information-media policy agenda. The full argument cannot be given here. But in essentials what is being suggested is that if, as most commentators agree, the telecommunications network is the nervous system of the information society, then the case for it being a public utility is as strong as ever was the case for nationalisation of mines or central banks or any other section of the industrial infrastructure. Moreover, the argument runs globally: the GII (global information infrastructure) should, with all due respect to North American feeling on this issue, be brought as much as possible within the fold of democratically-accountable public ownership.

However, to argue that the commanding heights of the network society should be in public ownership does not necessitate, under the moderate democratic socialist position I am advocating, a negative attitude to free enterprise — or even to "capitalism," if all that is meant by capitalism is the use of market mechanisms to determine supply and demand for specified goods and services. On the contrary, a belief in the mixed economy requires an appreciation of the virtues of competitive markets and the price system. Social democracy allows capitalist acts between consenting adults but does so only within a suitably circumscribed private sector. The issue is the *limits* of state interference. If the telecommunications infrastructure is under social control then subsidiary activities such as handset production or online services could, and in many cases should, be market-driven. The social need for innovation, the consumer demand for variety (say in telephone designs), and other reasons can quite convincingly be adduced in favour of market "liberalisation" to counterbalance the egalitarian values that would be embedded in a (re)nationalised telecommunications infrastructure. There is no space left to fill out further details. But the important point, and this is the main message of my paper, is that social democracy can, by advancing the case for a *balanced* pattern of ownership in the information age, resolve the "mounting tension"[34] between the novel concept of information as a commodity and the older ideal that treated it as a public good.

References

1. Fritz Machlup, *The Production and Distribution of Knowledge in the United States* (Princeton, NJ: Princeton University Press, 1962).

2. Daniel Bell, *The Coming of Post-Industrial Society: A Venture in Social Forecasting* (New York: Basic Books, 1973).

3. Youichi Ito, "Historical Comparisons of the Degrees of 'Johoka' (Informization): Implications for Modernization," *Keio Communication Review* 22 (2000): 3–29.

4. William H. Dutton, ed., *Society on the Line: Information Politics in the Digital Age* (Oxford: Oxford University Press, 1999).

5. David Trend, ed. , *Reading Digital Culture* (Oxford: Blackwell, 2001).

6. Manuel Castells, *The Rise of the Network Society* (Oxford: Blackwell, 1996).

7. Alistair S. Duff, *Information Society Studies* (London: Routledge, 2000).

8. Trevor Haywood, *Only Connect: Shaping Networks and Knowledge for the New Millennium* (London: Bowker Saur, 1999).

9. Anthony Giddens, *The Third Way: The Renewal of Social Democracy* (Cambridge: Polity Press, 1998).

10. John C. Cort, *Christian Socialism: An Informal History* (Maryknoll, NY: Orbis Books, 1988), 178–221.

11. John Rawls, *A Theory of Justice* (Oxford: Oxford University Press, 1973).

12. John Rawls, *Justice as Fairness: A Restatement*, edited by Erin Kelly (Cambridge, MA: The Belknap Press of Harvard University Press, 2001).

13. Rawls 2001, 31.

14. Rawls 2001, 42–43.

15. Rawls 2001, 111.

16. Rawls 1973, 3.

17. Rawls 2001, 136.

18. Rawls 2001, 115.

19. Rawls 2001, 44.

20. R. H. Tawney, *Equality* 4 ed. (London: Allen and Unwin, 1964), 40.

21. Tawney, 113.

22. Mairead Browne, "The Field of Information Policy: I. Fundamental Concepts," *Journal of Information Science* 23 (4) (1997): 261–275; Ian Rowlands, "Patterns of Author Cocitation in Information Policy: Evidence of Social, Collaborative, and Cognitive Structure," *Scientometrics* 44 (3) (1999): 533–546.

23. Marc U. Porat, *The Information Economy: Definition and Measurement* (Washington, DC: US Department of Commerce, 1977), 207.

24. Porat, 8.

25. Porat, 9.

26. Porat, 206.

27. Peter Hernon and Harold C. Relyea, "Information Policy," in Allen Kent, ed., *Encyclopedia of Library and Information Science* vol. 48 supplement II (New York: Marcel Dekker, 1991), 188.

28. E.g. David Hutchison, *Media Policy: An Introduction* (Oxford: Blackwell, 1999), although compare Mike Feintuck, *Media Regulation, Public Interest and the Law* (Edinburgh: Edinburgh University Press, 1999).

29. Robert H. Burger, *Information Policy: A Framework for Evaluation and Policy Research* (Norwood, NJ: Ablex Publishing), 3.

30. Ministry of Post and Telecommunications, *White Paper 2000 Communications in Japan: Expanding Frontier, IT in the 21st Century* (Tokyo: MPT).

31. Tony Fitzpatrick, "Critical Cyberpolicy: Network Technologies, Massless Citizens, Virtual Rights," *Critical Social Policy* 20 (3) (2000): 375–407.

32. Nick Moore, "Confucius or Capitalism? Policies for an Information Society," in Brian D. Loader, ed., *Cyberspace Divide: Equality, Agency and Policy in the Information Society* (London: Routledge, 1998), 149–160.

33. Rawls 2001, 136–140.

34. Michael E.D. Koenig, "Information Policy: the Mounting Tension (Value Additive versus Uniquely Distributable 'Public Good')," *Journal of Information Science* 21 (3) (1995): 229–231.

Bibliography

Bell, Daniel. *The Coming of Post-Industrial Society: A Venture in Social Forecasting.* New York: Basic Books, 1973.

Browne, Mairead. "The Field of Information Policy: I. Fundamental Concepts," *Journal of Information Science* 23 (4) (1997): 261–275.

Burger, Robert H. *Information Policy: A Framework for Evaluation and Policy Research.* Norwood, NJ: Ablex Publishing, 1993.

Castells, Manuel. *The Rise of the Network Society.* Oxford: Blackwell, 1996.

Cort, John C. *Christian Socialism: An Informal History.* Maryknoll, NY: Orbis Books, 1988.

Duff, Alistair S. *Information Society Studies.* London: Routledge, 2000.

Dutton, William H., ed. *Society on the Line: Information Politics in the Digital Age.* Oxford: Oxford University Press, 1999.

Feintuck, Mike. *Media Regulation, Public Interest and the Law.* Edinburgh: Edinburgh University Press, 1999.

Fitzpatrick, Tony. "Critical Cyberpolicy: Network Technologies, Massless Citizens, Virtual Rights," *Critical Social Policy* 20 (3) (2000): 375–407.

Giddens, Anthony. *The Third Way: The Renewal of Social Democracy.* Cambridge: Polity Press, 1998.

Haywood, Trevor. *Only Connect: Shaping Networks and Knowledge for the New Millennium.* London: Bowker Saur, 1999.

Hernon, Peter, and Relyea, Harold C. "Information Policy," in Allen Kent, ed., *Encyclopedia of Library and Information Science* vol. 48 supplement II. New York: Marcel Dekker, 1991, 176–204.

Hutchison, David. *Media Policy: An Introduction.* Oxford: Blackwell, 1999.

Ito, Youichi. "Historical Comparisons of the Degrees of 'Johoka' ('Informization'): Implications for Modernization," *Keio Communication Review* 22 (2000): 3–29.

Koenig, Michael E..D. "Information policy: the Mounting Tension (Value Additive versus Uniquely Distributable 'Public Good')," *Journal of Information Science* 21 (3) (1995): 229–231.

Machlup, Fritz. *The Production and Distribution of Knowledge in the United States.* Princeton, NJ: Princeton University Press, 1962.

Ministry of Post and Telecommunications. *White Paper 2000 Communications in Japan: Expanding Frontier, IT in the 21st Century.* Tokyo: MPT, 2000.

Moore, Nick. "Confucius or Capitalism? Policies for an Information Society," in Brian D. Loader, ed., *Cyberspace Divide: Equality, Agency and Policy in the Information Society* (London: Routledge, 1998), 149–160.

Porat, Marc U. *The Information Economy: Definition and Measurement.* Washington, DC: US Department of Commerce, 1977.

Rawls, John. *A Theory of Justice.* Oxford: Oxford University Press, 1973; first published 1971.

Rawls, John. *Justice as Fairness: A Restatement*, edited by Erin Kelly. Cambridge, MA: The Belknap Press of Harvard University Press, 2001.

Rowlands, Ian. "Patterns of Author Cocitation in Information Policy: Evidence of Social, Collaborative, and Cognitive Structure," *Scientometrics* 44 (3) (1999): 533–546.

Tawney, R. H. *Equality.* 4 ed. London: Allen and Unwin, 1964; first published 1931.

Trend, David, ed., *Reading Digital Culture.* Oxford: Blackwell, 2001.

19

INTERNET USER DEPENDENCE AND THE DUTY OF LOYALTY

Ian R. Kerr

We are losing control over ourselves. Our lives are no longer our own. We are bargaining ourselves away. The nature of this Faustian bargain in our brave new economy is straightforward: we are offered convenience and the speed of Hermes in exchange for complete exposure to everything we say and do online.

The bargain is not always irrational. Ours is not a blind faith. When we place our trust in online service providers (OSPs)[1] and other information intermediaries there are, usually, built-in legal safeguards. Our trust is founded on a number of promises. It is founded on contractual representations that our personal information and private communications will *not* be collected, used or disclosed to third parties without our knowledge and consent. But are these promises—and the legal mechanisms used to enforce them — sufficient to protect our privacy interests? Or is there a need for other safeguards that transcend the world of private ordering?

"Try This!"

Dig, if you will, a picture. Suppose that someone whose name you would not recognize has just sent you an e-mail styled, "Try This!" As it turns out, you do not even know that this e-mail has been sent to you because your e-mail account has been disabled. After trying to login to download your e-mail, an automated message appears indicating that you have exceeded your available disk quota. You are told to contact Supernet, your OSP. After spending 20 minutes trying to circumvent the automated voice system, you finally speak to a real person who assigns you a file number and dispatches a technician to investigate the matter. Off to work you go, trusting that your service provider will resolve the problem in a professional manner. Later that day, while you are at work, the technician begins to comb through all of your e-mail without your knowledge — something that you had supposedly consented to in the fine print of your *Terms of Service* agreement. She is searching for files with large attachments that can be deleted so as to free some memory and thereby re-enable your account.

During her search, the technician happens upon the "Try This!" message and notices that it contains a few very large attachments with suspicious sounding names. Suspecting child pornography, the technician opens the attachments. Sure enough, the "Try This!" message, sent to you without your knowledge or consent, contains images depicting young children engaged in sexual activity with adults. Horrified and angered by the images—and assuming all along that you are culpable—the technician informs her supervisor, who in turn contacts the police. The police request an electronic copy of the illicit file. Supernet decides to cooperate. Consequently, Supernet forwards the "Try This!" message and several of your other private communications to the police without telling you.

It merits taking pause to draw specific attention to the fact that, because your account had been automatically disabled, the illicit "Try This!" file (the existence of which remains unknown to you) has not yet been delivered to your inbox. Knowing this and knowing that there is no case against you without it, the police have instructed Supernet to resend the pornographic e-mail to you so that it will finally be in your possession. On this basis, the police will then be able to obtain a search warrant, seize your computer and arrest you. Supernet complies. You are subsequently arrested, tried and convicted for the possession of child pornography.

Right about now, you can stop imagining. All of this is in fact quite real.[2] In a decision rendered by the Alberta Court of Queen's Bench, subsequently affirmed by the Alberta Court of Appeal, it was held that Supernet's search of the customer's inbox, its decision to open the customer's e-mail without his consent, the police's instruction to copy and forward this mail to them without telling the customer, and the further police instruction to resend the illicit file to the user, *did not* unjustly interfere with the customer's reasonable expectation of privacy.[3]

Narratives such as this help to illustrate the incredible power that OSPs and other online information intermediaries hold over their customers and clients. OSPs are by default the gatekeepers of informational privacy on the Internet. By providing online services such as e-mail, Web site space, or portals to various online consortiums, OSPs gain access to and control over a plethora of personal information and private communications belonging to each of its many users. Each user is therefore dependent on their OSP not only for the proper storage, maintenance and management of personal information and private communications but, also, for determining whether and when that personal information may be disclosed to third parties. In other words, the safeguarding of user information is largely dependent on the benevolence and good judgment of OSPs.

A Chilling Possible World

One might try to discern a kind of moral from the above narrative. Perhaps those of us concerned about personal privacy ought to make an effort not to depend so heavily on information intermediaries. Or, at the very least, perhaps we should not store our personal information and private communications in digital spaces that we do not ourselves control. A good moral though this may be, it is not especially helpful. OSPs almost always require the disclosure of personal information as a precondition of the use of their services.[4] As well, most information intermediaries collect and log digital copies of every informational transaction that takes place on their system. Thus, even if you download all of your mail, delete it from the server, and store all of your communications on your own private disk space, anything that you send through the system is almost certain to be copied and archived by your information intermediary.[5] The only realistic means of circumventing this practical reality is through the use of anonymizer and encryption technologies.[6]

Individuals are bound to experience a further loss of control when the Internet takes the shape of some of its current visionaries and power brokers. For example, Larry Ellison (current Chair and CEO of Oracle Networks) and Scott McNealy (current Chair and CEO of Sun Microsystems) are not merely predicting but are also pushing-with-all-of-their-might for a networked world in which information is no longer stored on individual hard drives or company owned servers but, instead, is stored on more powerful Internet servers, manipulated through personal information management applications, and accessed through inexpensive Internet appliances.[7] In this chilling possible world, desktop computers become extinct and professional "*information management*" becomes the big money maker. The scheme is to supplant personal computers (PCs) with Internet appliances thereby shifting most of the sophistication away from the user and toward the network end. Internet appliances will contain very little hardware and almost no software — just a basic input/output system allowing a complete operating system to be downloaded every time the basic Internet appliance is switched on. Given their simplicity, Internet appliances will rely almost exclusively on lightening fast, centralized networks (owned, operated and controlled by companies like Oracle and Sun).[8]

The rhetoric in support of the shift to Internet appliances is premised on user convenience. Why spend time and money buying and installing software, obtaining upgrades, configuring hard drives, managing disk space, or fine tuning settings on your PC when those tasks could easily be delegated to an network administrator? In an appliance-based world, it is said, network users will no longer need to carry around heavy equipment or deal with complicated hardware and software problems. Given the projected ubiquity of the Internet appliance, users will simply need to carry a "*smart card*" that allows them access to the network from wherever they happen to be. Because all software programs are downloaded from the network, and because everyone's personal data files and backups are stored on servers connected to the system, it will be possible for an Internet appliance user to gain access to their information from anywhere in the world, as if sitting in front of their own machine.

To date, the main obstacle preventing the shift from a PC to an appliance-based computing universe seems to be the limitations of broadband and other high-speed Internet technologies.[9] Surprisingly little concern has been expressed about the fact that centralized (rather than end-to-end) computing will require all of our personal information and private communications to reside on Larry Ellison's, Scott McNealy's, or some other information manager's computers, leaving it solely in their control and, therefore, vulnerable to misuse, illicit trade or even theft.[10] If this chilling possible world is fully realized, we will have lost all control over our personal data and private communications. In such a world we will become completely and utterly dependent on the benevolence and good judgment of OSPs and other information managers.

Fidelity

Because OSPs have access to and an ability to make copies of most if not all personal information and private communications that pass through their systems, they are already *de facto* personal information managers. The possibility of online privacy is therefore dependent on a user's ability to trust an OSP with their personal information and private communications. One might therefore ask: what are the moral and legal foundations for such trust?

The relationship between an OSP and an Internet user is contractual in nature.[11] That is, it is based on an exchange of promises. The success of such a relationship is therefore founded in the moral notion of *fidelity*— the faithful adherence to one's promises. Where fidelity is concerned, one does not owe a duty except insofar as one has promised. Contractual relationships that are entered into *at arm's length* generally require nothing more than a fidelity to those promises voluntarily assumed by either party. Consequently, it is thought that Internet users can reasonably rely on their OSPs to do as they have pledged, but nothing more. Where the moral institution of promising falls short and an unfaithful OSP fails to fulfill its promises, the user has legal recourse through the law of contract.

Is fidelity a sufficient moral foundation to ensure online privacy?

Thus far, many OSPs have poor track records when it comes to living up to self-imposed privacy obligations. Consider, for example, the case of Aquacool_2000.[12] As a subscriber to Yahoo!'s online services, Acquacool_2000 was promised that his OSP is "committed to safeguarding his privacy online." When he signed up for Yahoo! services, he was further promised that he would be notified at the time of data collection or transfer if his personal data was to be shared with a third party. He was also promised that he would then have the option of *not* permitting the transfer. As the Yahoo! *Privacy Policy* states:

> This Privacy Policy will let you know: what personally identifiable information is being collected about you; how your information is used; who is collecting your information; with whom your information may be shared; what choices are available to you regarding collection, use, and distribution of your information....[13]

At the bottom of its *Privacy Policy* and throughout its Web site, Yahoo! also displayed the TRUSTe certificate, a logo which is familiar to many Internet users.[14]

By featuring the TRUSTe seal throughout its Web site, Yahoo! made a representation to Aquacool_2000 and to all of its other subscribers that it will comply with strict privacy policies and procedures and that it will not disclose personal information to third parties without prior permission or some other legal justification.

In fact, Yahoo! even set up technological measures to further encourage trust amongst its subscriber base. In order to facilitate a frank exchange of information on its message boards, Yahoo! constructed an architecture that allowed message board participants to select a *nome de plume* and thereby communicate pseudonymously. This further assurance of online privacy helped create a very lively online discussion. Relying on the express promise that their personal information would be kept confidential, online interlocutors felt free to speak their minds and trade important information on a number of important and sensitive issues.

Trusting all of these safeguards, Aqucool_2000 decided one day to throw himself into a heated debate online about a publicly traded corporation known as AnswerThink Consulting Group Inc. After Aquacool_2000 posted a number of critical remarks about its management team, AnswerThink came down heavy on Yahoo!, threatening the world's largest OSP with litigation if it did not unmask the identity of its public critic. When push-came-to-shove, Yahoo! caved. Not only did it break all of its promises to Aquacool_2000 by disclosing his personal information to Answerthink, it did so without ever telling him. Had Aquacool_2000 at least been notified, he would have had the opportunity to seek a protective order to enforce his constitutionally protected right to speak anonymously.[15] His inability to do so resulted not only in a potentially frivolous defamation suit against him; it also resulted in the immediate termination of his employment. As it turns out, Aquacool_2000 was an AnswerThink employee.

The case of Aquacool_2000 illustrates that the moral institution of fidelity and the law of contract will not always ensure our privacy online. As this case demonstrates, when it comes to keeping promises, OSPs such as Yahoo! often have competing considerations. Even if they do not engage in data-mining or otherwise profit in the information trade, when faced with the prospect of a third party lawsuit, a court order, or a request from the police, OSPs will often disclose rather than protect the informational interests of their users.

It is important to realize that, even if all OSPs kept all of their promises, the moral institution of fidelity would still prove insufficient as a means of ensuring online privacy. This is because not all OSPs promise to protect the privacy interests of Internet users to begin with, nor are they always obliged to. In fact, some OSPs make it clear right from the outset that their users should have a low expectation of privacy.[16] Some OSPs even go so far as to provide notice that they are actively monitoring user accounts and that they will voluntarily disclose user information and communications in a variety of circumstances.[17]

Given that some OSPs will break their promises with impunity and other OSPs make no such promises to begin with, fidelity seems insufficient as a moral foundation for ensuring online privacy.

The Duty of Loyalty

The duty of fidelity can be juxtaposed to the duty of loyalty. As we have seen, fidelity simply means keeping one's promises. The duty of loyalty is quite different. Historically, its foundations are derived from the *status of the relationship* rather than any of the undertakings voluntarily assumed by the parties.[18] Consequently, where loyalty is morally required, the duties entailed by the relationship are said to pre-exist any specific promises that are pledged.[19] Because the duty of loyalty derives from the nature of the relationship rather than from any promises voluntarily assumed by the parties, it follows that a duty of loyalty is not necessarily discharged simply by keeping one's promises.[20] The duty of loyalty demands something more.

One special instance of the duty of loyalty that has been carefully developed and adapted by the courts of common law is known as the fiduciary obligation. The rationale underlying the fiduciary concept is quite straightforward. Where one party has come to trust another, there is some danger that the trusted party may decide to serve its own ends rather than those of the trusting party. In order to avoid such mischief, the fiduciary obligation protects those who *by virtue of their relationship* have come to depend on others.

Professor Weinrib once characterized the fiduciary obligation as the law's realization of the economic importance of fostering incentive by protecting relationships of interdependence:

> A sophisticated industrial and commercial society requires that its members be integrated rather than autonomously self-sufficient, and through the concepts of commercial and property law provides mechanisms of *interaction and interdependence*. The fiduciary obligation ... constitutes a means by which those mechanisms are protected.[21]

According to Professor Weinrib, the basic policy underlying the fiduciary obligation is the desire to preserve and promote the integrity of socially valuable relationships that arise as a result of human interdependency. An interactive and interdependent society mandates the monitoring of trusting relationships in order to avoid their potential for abuse. According to Professor Weinrib, the hallmark of a fiduciary relationship is that one party has the leeway to affect the legal position of the other, putting the latter at the mercy of the former.

Other scholars have held that a fiduciary's discretion can usually be understood as part of a wider category of power held by the trusted party that includes any access that they might have to the trusting party's assets:

> "Discretion," by itself, is not the significant fact. In this context we are concerned with the abuse of the relationship. For this purpose discretion merely indicates that the trusted party has access to assets and, hence, the opportunity to abuse.... [T]rust which leads to the trusted party gaining "access" to assets will attract the fiduciary obligation. The presence of "discretion" is merely an indication in a particular case that such trust exists. It is the potential for the abuse of that trust which requires the obligation.[22]

The most commonly cited examples of traditional status-based fiduciary relationships, where one party gains access to another's assets include: trustee/beneficiary, solicitor/client, principal/agent, director/corporation, partner/partner, employer/employee, guardian/ward, doctor/patient, parent/child and confessor/penitent.[23] However, courts have come to recognize that a variety of other relationships are also constructed on the same foundation of trust and loyalty as were the traditional status-based fiduciary relationships. In recognition of the inherent danger of unduly restricting fiduciary doctrine — especially given the fact that the fiduciary doctrine aims to protect, preserve and encourage a number of socially and commercially valuable relationships—courts have chosen *not* to limit the fiduciary obligation to the fixed category of status-based fiduciary relationships.

In a nutshell, the duty of loyalty requires the trusted party to act in the best interests of the trusting party. Seen from another perspective, the duty of loyalty forbids the trusted party from furthering its own self-interest where doing so would be detrimental to the best interests of the trusting party. If a conflict of interests arises, the duty of loyalty demands the trusted party to remain faithful to the trusting party, despite its own reluctance to do so. To use one of our narratives from above as an example, if Yahoo! had owed a duty of loyalty to Aquacool_2000, that duty would require Yahoo! to keep its promise (not to disclose Aquacool_2000's personal information) in spite of the threat of litigation by AnswerThink.

Under what circumstances, if any, might an OSP be said to owe a duty of loyalty to its users?

The courts of common law have in some instances been willing to impose such a duty when the following four indicia of a fiduciary relationship can be adequately demonstrated:

1. The trusted party has scope for the exercise of some discretion or power;
2. The trusted party can unilaterally exercise that power or discretion so as to affect the trusting party's legal or practical interests;
3. The trusting party is peculiarly vulnerable to or at the mercy of the party holding the discretion or power; and
4. The trusting party is entitled to expect that the trusted party will act in his or her interests and for the purposes of the relationship.[24]

It is quite plain that a number of the constituent elements outlined above are fully present in many OSP-user relationships. As we have seen, Internet users are very often in a relationship of dependence with their service providers. The current architectures of the networked world allow OSPs access to Internet users' personal information and private communications in a manner unparalleled by even the most powerful financial institutions or arms of government. Access to these informational assets allows OSPs to exercise power to the benefit or detriment of its users. Aquacool_2000, for example, lost his job as a result of Yahoo!'s discretionary use of his informational assets. When Supernet exercised its discretion, Dale Weir went to jail. Therefore, to paraphrase Professor Weinrib, there are times when an OSP has the leeway to affect the legal position of its user, putting the latter at the mercy of the former. An OSP acting in bad faith has access to and therefore could: i) convert a user's private communications to its own or to another's advantage; ii) disclose confidential information to a competitor; or iii) turn over otherwise privileged evidence in the course of criminal or private litigation, etc.

At the same time — even if Yahoo! *did* hold itself out as willing to act in the best interests of its users— it is not clear that all OSPs always do so. To take an extreme example (mentioned above in footnote 17), an employer who provides Internet services does not generally undertake to do so exclusively for the benefit of its employees. Offering such services to employees is but a means to the corporation's own ends. Even the most benevolent employer (whose policy permits employees to utilize its Internet services for personal use) does not offer such services for the exclusive benefit of the employees. If an employee uses those services to illicit ends or in any other manner that is not in the best interests of the corporation, how could it possibly be said that the employer is obligated to use the evidence that it has gathered to serve the employee's benefit rather than serving the best interests of the corporation or its shareholders? In what meaningful sense can the employee be said to have expected a duty of loyalty from his employer that would trump its own corporate interests?

Conclusion

More and more, OSPs are in a position to observe and record everything that we say and do online. Increasingly, we are forced to rely on them not only to provide quality informational services but also to store and otherwise manage our private information. Because OSPs are in a position of control, we have come to depend on them to safeguard our personal information and private communications. This gives OSPs power and discretion: power to control our online behaviour; and discretion to alter our outcomes.

Currently, relationships between OSPs and Internet users are governed primarily by the moral institution of fidelity and the law of contract. Given that many OSPs will break their promises with impunity and other OSPs make no such promises to begin with, fidelity seems insufficient as a moral foundation for ensuring online privacy. Consequently, it has been suggested here that an alternative set of duties might be derived from the very nature of the relationship between some OSPs and their users. Where a fiduciary relationship can be established, it is possible to impose a duty of loyalty on some OSPs. Where a duty of loyalty is owing, an OSP must remain faithful to its users despite its own reluctance to do so.

It has also been suggested that the possibility of imposing a duty of loyalty on OSPs who have created a reliance interest (by holding themselves out as acting in the best interests of their users) is an increasingly important consideration. While it would be wrongheaded to conclude that OSPs *always* owe a duty of loyalty (as if we could somehow generalize about a motley collection of private orderings) it would be equally misguided to conclude that OSPs *never* owe such a duty. The conclusion offered here is more modest than either of these two extremes. The only claim that has been made here is that *some* OSPs display all of the constituent elements of a fiduciary relationship and that we might therefore justifiably require those that do to act in the best interests of their users in some instances. In those instances, the OSP will be required to safeguard a user's personal information and private communications is spite of its reluctance to do so.

As we move with the speed of Hermes towards a world where Internet users have little or no control over there own information, the moral demand for OSP loyalty to trump commercial convenience ought to gain significance. Absent such a demand, we might be bargaining ourselves away.

Notes

1. In netspeak, a distinction has been drawn between "Internet Service Providers" (ISPs) and Application Service Providers" (ASPs). ISPs are utilized in order to gain access to the Internet — the client connecting to the ISPs' servers which provide the necessary uplink into cyberspace. ASPs make available assorted software applications, such as personal banking, once a user has *already* gained access to the Internet. Many ISPs, however, also provide application services like e-mail, and, as a result, frequently blur this distinction. There has been a tendency in several jurisdictions to treat ISPs— who merely provide access to the Internet and do not exercise any control over their users— as mere conduits of users' interaction. ISPs are thereby excluded from liability for the conduct of their users: see for example, *Cubby Inc.* v *Compuserve Inc.*, 776 FSupp 135 (SDNY 1991); *Zeran* v *America Online, Inc.*, 129 F3d 327 (4th Cir 1997); and also the *Communications Decency Act*. US Code. Vol. 47, sec. 230 (1996). The term "online service provider" is used throughout this article as a generic term to refer to any e-mail provider, bulletin board operator, auction host, anonymous emailer, commercial or amateur Web site, or any other provider of an online service who is not merely a conduit to Internet access but an entity that offers a service in exchange for, among other things, the ability to collect and store their users' personal information or private communications according to certain *Terms of Service*.

2. The above narrative is based on the actual case of *R* v *Weir*, 1998 AJ No 155, (ABQB 1998) and *R* v *Weir*, 2001 AJ No 869, (ABCA 2001). Similar cases have arisen in the United States: *US* v *Maxwell*, 45 MJ 406 (CAAF 1996).

3. It is important to note that, in the actual Alberta case, Dale Weir, the recipient of the "Try This!" e-mail, was not an innocent person who was framed by the sender of the e-mail. On the facts set out in *Weir*, the addressee of the message was a consumer of child pornography. Though this revelation certainly makes it more difficult to sympathize with Mr. Weir about the fact that his personal information was ultimately disclosed, the manner in which Weir's private communications were discovered and disclosed should be troubling to everyone. There was no subpoena, no search warrant — no prior judicial authorization of any sort. Supernet simply made a unilateral decision to sift through Weir's private account and then to disclose its finding without notice or any other form of due process.

4. Ian R. Kerr, "The Legal Relationship Between Online Service Providers and Internet Users," 35 *Canadian Business Law Journal* 419, 421–423 (2001).

5. Ibid., 423.

6. See, e.g., www.zeroknowledge.com; www.pgp.com. In spite of the relative accessibility and affordability of such products, most people have not yet adopted their use on a regular basis. As security tightens in the so-called 'War Against Terrorism,' it is unclear what the future holds with respect to the use of these technologies as a means of enhancing Internet user privacy. Given that Zeroknowledge Systems has recently discontinued carriage of the Freedom Network, its basic anonymizer software [see D.

McCullagh. Leading Anonymity System to End. <http://www.wired.com/news/business/0,1367,47337,00.html> (October 2001).], it appears as though these techniques for ensuring user privacy could become less and less available.

7. Fried, I. Ellison's NIC Co. to Team with Sun. <http://news.cnet.com/news.0-1006-200-6375843.html> (June 2001); Bartlett, M. Net Appliances Sales May be Set for Take-Off. <http://www.newsbytes.com/news/01/063710.html> (March 2001).

8. Rimer, D.H., and Noglows, P. Internet Appliances and Universal Access. http://www.iword.com/iword41/iword41.html (1999).

9. Hopper, G.S. Who Needs a PC? Why Internet Appliances Will Succeed. <http://www.allnetdevices.com/industry/industry/2000/06/21/who_needs.html> (June 2000); Streitfeld, D. "For a Dead Idea, the 'Network Computer is Downright Sprightly'," *Washington Post,* 12 June 2000, sec. H, p.3.

10. Schock, J. Death to Desktop!. <http://www.jasonschock.com/writings/dtd/index.php3> (April 2001).

11. Kerr, 423.

12. See Plaintiff's complaint, paragraph 6, originally filed at United States District Court Central District of California. <http://www.epic.org/anonymity/aquacool_complaint.pdf> (May 2000). This suit, *Aquacool_2000* v *Yahoo!* [hereinafter *Aquacool_2000*], was ultimately dropped for undisclosed reasons. Aquacool_2000 is not alone in his plight. Other online posters' identities have similarly been sought after by corporations upset over the content of their posts. For example, in *Hvide* v *ACLU*, 770 So 2d 1237 (Fla Dist Ct App 3d 2000) the court upheld an order for Yahoo! and America Online, Inc. to reveal the identities of the eight anonymous defendants accused of posting allegedly defamatory messages. Also, in the Canadian cases of *Philip Services Corp.* v. *John Doel,* Court File No. 4592/98 (Ont Gen Div 1998) and *Irwin Toy* v *Doe*, OJ No. 3318 (Ont Sup Ct 2000). OSPs were ordered to reveal the identities of their, respective, clients alleged to have posted defamatory comments.

13. Yahoo! Privacy Policy. <http://docs.yahoo.com/info/privacy> (April 1994) [hereinafter *Yahoo! Privacy Policy*].

14. TRUSTe is an independent, nonprofit privacy initiative dedicated to building users' trust and confidence on the Internet and accelerating growth of the Internet industry. TRUSTe has developed a third-party oversight "seal" program that alleviates users' concerns about online privacy, while meeting the specific business needs of each of its licensed Web sites. Were Yahoo! to breach its privacy commitments, it would lose its certification. Thus far, it remains certified. See particular verification for Yahoo!Truste Validation Page. <http://www.truste.org/validate/361> (May 2000). See also Truste. <http://www.truste.org/> (April 2000).

15. The U.S. Supreme Court has firmly held that the First Amendment protects anonymous speech. See *McIntyre* v *Ohio Elections Commission,* 514 US 334 (SC 1995).

16. For example, Verio's *Acceptable Use Policy* spells out to its users that: "In general, the Internet is neither more nor less secure than other means of communication, including mail, facsimile, and voice telephone service, all of which can be intercepted and otherwise compromised. As a matter of prudence, however, Verio urges its subscribers to assume that all of their on-line communications are insecure. Verio cannot take any responsibility for the security of information transmitted over Verio's facilities." [See Verio Acceptable Use Policy. <http://home.verio.com/company/aup.cfm> (May 2000).]

17. This is often the case with employers who provide Internet services to their employees, since employers generally have a greater duty to control the conduct of their employees.

18. RT Allen, "When Loyalty No Harm Meant," 43 *Review of Metaphysics* 281 (Dec 1989)

19. Karen Hanson, "The Demands of Loyalty," 16 *Idealistic Studies* 195 (1986).

20. Conversely, though parties to a

contract by definition owe a duty of fidelity to one another, they do not necessarily owe each other a duty of loyalty.

21. Ernest J. Weinrib, "The Fiduciary Obligation," 25 *University of Toronto Law Journal* 1, 11 (1989) emphasis added.

22. Robert Flannigan, "The Fiduciary Obligation," 9 *Oxford Journal of Legal Studies* 285, 308 (1989).

23. Ibid., 294.

24. *Frame* v *Smith,* 42 DLR 4th 81, 97 (SCC 1987); and *Hodgkinson* v *Simms* (1994), 117 DLR 4th 161, 179-180 (SCC 1994).

20

Clashes Between Businesses and Consumers Over Unsolicited Commercial E-Mails

Byung S. Lee and *Wonhi Synn*

Introduction

Businesses want to utilize e-mail as a low-cost advertising tool to reach millions of consumers, while consumers have been frustrated with unsolicited commercial e-mails (UCE) they don't want themselves or their children to look at. Consumer groups advocate an opt-in system for consumers, in which consumers have to take an affirmative action to receive commercial e-mails from specific companies. On the other hand, business leaders are in support of an opt-out system, meaning that consumers should notify the sender not to send anymore UCE to them.

Consumer groups believe that e-mail marketing should be permission-based to protect the sanctity of the home and to value privacy of consumers. Businesses argue that only well-known established companies could rely on the opt-in approach to contact consumers, not small or start-up companies unless they have a deep pocket to promote their products or services through the traditional media. The Federal Trade Commission has been mainly concerned about UCE when it was used to disseminate false or misleading information about products or services offered for sale on the Internet.

The solution to the ongoing clash between consumers and businesses may be found by enforcing current laws, introducing new legislation or taking a bottom-up approach of self-regulation. This paper is based on a survey of businessmen and ordinary consumers to find which of the three approaches is appropriate in dealing with UCE, or how to make a good compromise between the competing interests at stake.

Literature review

Internet direct mail has many advantages over traditional paper direct mail: speedy delivery, an immediate response, potential targeting of a particular audience, a global medium, low cost, and viral marketing, which relies on recipients forwarding the message to other like-minded individuals. In a word, it works as well as or better than regular direct mail, in many instances.[1] Because of these advantages, e-mail has become an important communications tool, often surpassing the telephone for many forms of business and personal.[2]

Sending out additional e-mails after setting up an infrastructure incurs only minimal costs, so a handful of responses from millions of e-mail recipients could bring profit to the marketer. The low economic disincentives[3] to mass mailing would lead to marketers abusing e-mail as a marketing tool, inundating users with commercial messages, so-called "carpet bombing." Sending unsolicited bulk e-mail — usually commercial — to Internet users who have not given permission to send it has been called pejoratively "spamming."[4] As a good example, two lawyers from Scottsdale, Arizona, went beyond sending an e-mail to individual recipients in 1994, posting a solicitation for legal services on thousands of Usenet news groups and targeting those wishing to earn a "Green Card."[5]

Reputable companies can recruit opt-in clients from a broad existing base of clients by having them visit their Web sites for ads or promotional materials. Also they can rely on traditional mass media for promotion and marketing. But financially weak companies, especially when they started recently or plan to start, would think they have to be given a chance to make an initial contact with potential consumers because consumers usually go to a well-known business rather than surveying the market before making their purchase decision.[6]

The Direct Marketing Association and other advertising forces who have wanted spamming to continue were in a battle with Internet consumer advocates who want spamming to cease.[7] In response to increasing complaints from Internet Service Providers (ISPs), privacy advocates and consumers, however, businesses have changed their attitude. For example, 16 online marketers set up the Responsible Electronic Communication Alliance (RECA), which suggested that the member companies adopt the single opt-in system and offer consumers clear and conspicuous notice of what they're signing up for and the ability to remove themselves quickly from any mailing list. This change may be also attributed to pressure on businesses from the Federal Trade Commission (FTC) to develop self-regulatory practices.[8]

Small companies — often financially weak — however, may still argue that the opt-out commercial messages are not necessarily randomly sent to customers, and all consumers are not sophisticated enough to choose an opt-in,[9] in addition to invoking the right to free commercial speech under the First Amendment protection.

Consumers who receive spam do not like it because it typically offers something that is of little or no interest to the recipient.[10] According to one survey, about 80 percent of American Web users received spam, about 10 percent read it, and 4 percent claimed to retaliate.[11,12] Some may delete UCE as soon as they find the messages are not relevant to their interest or may hate junk mail and delete it as soon as possible without giving a slight glance. Others might try e-mail filters to separate junk mail from what they want to read. But no filter software is perfect, so the e-mail users have to delete junk mail still delivered into their e-mail box and check for important mail sent to the junk mail box. The improving technology also could not be a perfect solution in face of marketers who are getting more sophisticated.[13]

The direct opt-out postal mail has been accepted as a legitimate marketing tool for a long time. When direct market experts warn against spamming, therefore, they need to point out differences between unsolicited e-mail and postal bulk mail as a marketing tool: The recipient bears the cost of e-mail, and spamming is against longtime Internet standards of "netiquette."[14]

As consumers have to spend more and more time[15] downloading and deleting UCE and may have to use software to sift out unneeded UCE, their frustration level will increase. If the situation is to deteriorate with more companies joining this spamming bandwagon, people may abandon a spam-clogged Internet instead of wading through unwanted advertisements.

When people discuss controlling Internet content or user activity to protect the Internet, ISPs have become the ideal target because they are more visible than most users who get services from them.[16] Some may argue that if ISPs post an electronic "No Trespass" sign, advertisers will be forced to negotiate with ISPs for the right to post advertisements on private property. Such a requirement would reintroduce the idea of property rights and allow only valuable UCE to survive in the marketplace (*CAUCE*). But putting the onus on online providers is not practical and possible without adequate legislation.[17] If ISPs are allowed to set up their own standards, direct marketers have to comply with the policies of 3,000 different standards, not a practical option.[18] Also some ISPs are willing to cooperate with spammers to sell lucrative contracts that expressly permit customers to send unsolicited commercial e-mail.[19]

Unsolicited bulk e-mail poses a serious threat to the integrity, safety, and efficient, reliable operation of the Internet.[20] To prevent their system from being clogged by spam and to reduce complaints from their clients about spam, ISPs have tried to solve the problem on their own. Since what is spam or not, has not been clearly defined, lawsuits were inevitable. Harris Interactive, Inc., a market research firm, sued online service providers and an anti-spam organization after the ISPs blocked the firm's e-mails to their subscribers, based on information from the organization. Harris Interactive failed to get a temporary restraining order that would have forced an anti-spam organization to take the company off a list of e-mail spammers. But the firm could successfully make ISPs unblock access to their subscribers in 2000.[21] In one case, 24/7 Media Inc. had successfully pleaded with a judge to slap a temporary restraining order on the anti-spam organization that put it on the spammer list.[22] Another restraining order against the same anti-spam list provider was issued for Yesmail.com, an opt-in mail provider.[23]

Legislation could be another approach. There are 18 states that enacted spam legislation (*Spam Laws: United States: State Laws*). The states' efforts to clamp down on spam were not always successful. A California law aimed at reining in unsolicited bulk e-mail was deemed unconstitutional in June 2000, because it violated the dormant Commerce Clause of the U.S. Constitution by placing inconsistent restrictions on interstate use of the Internet. A Washington law suffered the same fate in March 2000. At the federal level, however, there are no laws even though spam bills have been introduced into the Senate and House. Some bills that intended to rein in unsolicited commercial e-mail did not pass because the Senate and House took different positions towards direct e-mail marketing.[24] Even if a similar bill is to be enacted, it still has to overcome the First Amendment issues to survive.[25]

Chung[26] found in his 1999 study that federal statute and bills were more generous to Internet commercial messages than state statues and bills. He added that bills introduced for protecting consumers' privacy might be unconstitutional if they have a blanket ban over unsolicited commercial electronic e-mail since advertisers could send informational commercial e-mails to recipients.

Marcus[27] admitted that the Internet is a more "democratic" medium, which deserves more First Amendment protection than other media, and commercial speech is protected through the First Amendment. But he still believed that regulation on spam could be constitutional, because spam as intrusive commercial messages is sent over the Internet to a captive viewer — not a democratic model — and the government may have an interest in preventing the cost shifting that occurs in intrusive Internet advertising and in making the Internet a more "aesthetic" place. Whether the Supreme Court would accept this reasoning remains to be seen.

A general consensus exists about a need for regulations on UCE, but when it comes to the level and means of regulation, people's viewpoints diverge. Business people may want an opt-out system while consumer advocate groups want an opt-in system and, sometimes, even a double opt-in.[28] In fear of a consumer backlash, businesses are slowly moving to a single opt-in, but still want to interpret the term more liberally, so they could use a passive opt-in,[29] rely on viral marketing, or rent an opt-in list from outsiders.

Three approaches can be taken to regulate rampant e-mail marketing: 1) Individual actors attempting to shape behavior through the promotion of a code of conduct or through social and monetary pressures with vehicles such as boycotts, 2) finding approaches within the bounds of current legal doctrine, such as using trespass law to regulate abuse of marketers of ISP's resources, 3) or new legislation.[30]

Method

This study employed Q methodology as an appropriate analysis tool since Q methodology enables "measurement of anything subjective to the person." The methodology provides a "basis for measurement of feelings, attitudes, opinions, thinking, fantasy, and all else of a subjective nature."[31]

A Q-population was generated from an extensive review of online and offline articles, books, and comments from people surveyed. The first group of statements represents the position anti-spammers would take; the second group of statements reflects the position of those who would favor spam.

The two groups of statements were further divided into five subgroups of "Opinions on UCE" "Burden vs. benefits," "Prior permission," "Regulations," and "Reasons for regulations." The number of these statements was reduced to 40 in total as a Q-sample, but each cell was designed to keep at least two statements. As shown in Table 1, some subgroups have more statements than others do, reflecting the complexity of issues the subgroups represent.

Twenty people successfully sorted 40 statements on a 9-point most-agree/most-disagree Q-sort rank scale during September 2001. (See Figure 1).

Among 20 people, there were seven managers, two people involved in health education or public health, a teacher, a finance professor, a college student, a coach, a technician, a business analyst, an investment advisor, a business consultant, a salesman, an administration assistant and an engineer.

Their ages ranged from 20 to 51. Thirteen people had a dial-up connection at home; five with a broadband connection such as a cable or DSL (digital subscriber lines) connection; and two with no Internet connection. At work, 14 people have a broadband connection, such as a cable or other faster Internet connection; three, dial-up; one, no connection; and the remaining two, giving no response. Fourteen perceived themselves as savvy Internet users while six as non-savvy users. (See Appendix I).

Responses were entered into the MQMethod program for Macintosh,[32] which intercorrelated individual responses to each statement in a 20×20 correlation matrix. Factors were extracted using the principal component solution. After Varimax rotation, 3-factor solution was selected based on ease of interpretation, with 16 people aligned significantly with only one of three factors and one person, with two factors.

Table 1.
The structure of Q-sample statements

	Anti-spammers	*Spammers*
Opinions on UCE	1, 3, 5, 7, 9	2, 4, 6, 8, 10
Burden vs. benefits	11,12, 15, 17	13, 14, 16, 18
Prior permission	19, 20, 21, 22	23, 24, 25, 26
Regulations	27, 28 29, 30, 31	32, 33, 34, 35, 36
Reasons for regulations	37, 40	38, 39

Figure 1. Q-sort distribution

-4	-3	-2	-1	0	1	2	3	4	Rank score
3	4	5	5	6	5	5	4	3	Frequency

Findings

Three extracted factors, or types, accounted for 54 percent of variance in the respondent set. There was a moderate negative correlation between factors 1 and 2 and a slight positive relationship between factors 2 and 3, as shown in Table 2.

Table 2
Correlation Between Factors

	F1	*F2*	*F3*
F1	1	-0.49	- 0.03
F2	-0.49	1	0.21
F3	-0.03	0.21	1

Z-scores were converted into Q-sort rank scores by taking all the Q sorts significantly loaded on each type and averaging them together into a single Q-sort.33 Six consensus statements, on which all three types uniformly agreed or disagreed, emerged in analysis. (See Table 3).

Respondents in three types all admitted that participants in the global Internet as a community needed to abide by certain rules (29)[34] and tended to mildly disagree that few reputable marketers use UCE to advertise goods and services (39) and all consumers are not technologically capable of signing up for an opt-in (24). They tended to be neutral about advertisers sending their UCE to those who have an ongoing business or personal relationship with the advertisers (23), commercial e-mailers' shifting costs to e-mail recipients (11), and e-mailers' UCE unscrupulously targeting consumers (5).

This study tried to understand types, or factors, by "interpreting statements which characterize the factor, i.e., statements scored +4, +3, -3, and -4,"[35] those sorters strongly agreed or disagreed. These statements also were checked to see whether they distinguished each type from the other two.

Table 3
Consensus Statements

Statements	*Z-scores*	*Q-sort Rank Scores*
5) Unsolicited commercial e-mailers don't have any idea whether their audience is interested in what they offer.	0.31, -0.04, -0.39	1, 0, -1
11) Unsolicited commercial e-mailers think it's really neat they can reach a million people for free, but they do so by shifting the costs onto others.	0.06, 0.20, 0.01	0, 1, 0
23) The advertisers should be allowed to e-mail unsolicited advertisements if they have an ongoing business or personal relationship with the recipient.	-0.34, 0.16, 0.05	-1, 1, 0
24) Consumers who don't know about a certain technology or aren't familiar enough with it to sign up for an opt-in mailing list will miss information they might want to read.	-0.45, -0.09, -0.84	-2, 0, -2
29) The global Internet is a community. Like any community, participation in it implies certain rules and obligations.	1.03, 0.80, 1.28	3, 2, 3
39) There are very few reputable marketers using unsolicited commercial e-mails to advertise goods and services.	-0.37, -0.73, -0,43	-1, -1, -1

Type 1: UCE objectors

Seven sorters—three males (25 percent of male respondents) and four females (50 percent of female respondents)—were aligned with only this factor, explaining 21 percent of variance, a biggest type. Their average age was 34. They were a health area worker, a teacher, a college student, a technician, a coach and a materials manager. Five had a dial-up connection at home; one has a broadband connection; another one, no connection. At work, four had a broadband connection, such as cable or DSL; the others indicated "dial-up," "no connection," or "no response." Five perceived themselves as savvy Internet users, while two thought otherwise.

This type was significantly different from others in the sorting of statements 2, 3, 6, 8, 9, 15, 19, 22, 25, and 38, as shown in Tables 4 and 5. Sorters in this group believed that the global Internet as a community needs certain rules and obligations (29). For them, the Internet is not a public place (1, 2), so UCE violates their privacy (3). They didn't want to suffer the junk e-mail flood unless they actually requested receiving it (19), nor they wanted to bother with filtering it (15). Sorter 9 commented on statement 19, "Ringing my telephone, entering my e-mail inbox and knocking on my front door should be reserved for family, friends and those that are invited." This sorter's feeling was further expressed by his comment on statement 15, "I shouldn't have to put a security gate at my home, call blocking on my phone or a filter on my e-mail."

Sorters of this type believed that marketers don't have any constitutional right to send unsolicited e-mails to them (4). The sorters treated e-mail marketing differently from traditional marketing, such as Internet Web ads (8) or traditional media marketing (9). They thought marketers don't have any right to contact

Table 4
Statements Type 1 Strongly Agreed On

Statements	*Rank Score*	*Z-score*
15)** It is unfair to burden the consumer with the task of filtering large numbers of unwanted commercial messages.	4	2.07
19)** You shouldn't be forced to suffer the e-mail junk flood unless and until you actually request it.	4 1	84
22)** It is a bad idea to give commercial e-mailers the right to have one free shot at a recipient and then put on the shoulder of the recipient the burden of requesting removal his or her name from their list.	4	1.82
3)** Unsolicited commercial e-mailing violates my privacy.	3	1.56
1) I think e-mail as a personal space in which I interact with friends and colleagues. Unsolicited commercial e-mail pops up in my face, intruding on that private zone.	3	1.27
9)** Consumers are marketed to at every turn—TV, radio, newspaper, billboards, etc. Could we have at least e-mails to ourselves?	3	1.14
29) The global Internet is a community. Like any community, participation in it implies certain rules and obligations.	3	1.03

Note. ** indicates a distinguishing statement for this type at a significant level of $p< .01$.

Table 5
Statements Type 1 Strongly Disagreed On

Statements	*Rank Score*	*Z-score*
8)** People are bombarded with constant advertisements, such as banners, when surfing the Internet. Commercial e-mailing is the part of Internet advertising I am willing to accept.	-4	-1.81
38)** Unsolicited commercial e-mailers are providing a service by distributing information that could help their recipients make informed decisions.	-4	-1.63
2)** The Internet is a public resource since it was created in part with taxpayer monies, and an e-mail address is a matter of public record, like a street address.	-4	-1.54
4) Sending unsolicited commercial e-mail is a constitutional right as part of commercial speech.	-3	-1.34
13) Only big companies can reach Internet users through traditional media. So, small companies without financial resources should be allowed to use unsolicited commercial e-mail.	-3	-1.25
6)** When commercial e-mail is appropriate and useful to the recipient, it is welcomed, unsolicited or not.	-3	-1.18
25)** It is ok to send an unsolicited e-mail if an e-mailer tells customers how the e-mailer got their e-mail address and provides a link to a Web page that spells out a privacy policy.	-3	-1.05

Note. ** indicates a distinguishing statement for this type at a significant level of $p < .01$.

them without being invited even if the marketers offer e-mail recipients opt-out options (22), or inform the recipients of their privacy policy or of how they got the recipients' address (25). Small companies without financial resources could not be an exception here (13).

The sorters didn't believe the benefits of getting commercial information through UCE (6, 38). This type's opinion on UCE was well reflected by Sorter 6's comment on statement 38. She wrote "Unsolicited commercial e-mail is not a 'service.' It is an 'inconvenience.'"

Type 2: Market believers

Six sorters— 5 males (42 percent of responding males) and one female (13 percent of females)—were aligned with this type, explaining 20 percent of variance. Their ages were 39 on average. This type included three managers, a finance professor, a business analyst and an investment advisor. Four had a dial-up connection and two, a DSL connection at home. At work, five had a broadband connection, such as cable or DSL; and one, a dial-up connection. One half of them perceived themselves as savvy users while the other half thought otherwise.

Type 2 sorters were significantly different from other types in sorting statements 1, 3, 6, 9, 10, 28, 32, 33, 34, 35, and 40, as shown in Table 6 and 7. They didn't believe that UCE is a serious problem, at least not more serious than other marketing tools, such as TV, radio, newspaper, billboards ads, etc (9). Sorters of this type would welcome commercial e-mails as far as they are appropriate and useful to them (6). They agreed that commercial e-mailers have the right to

Table 6
Statements Type 2 Strongly Agreed On

Statements	*Rank Score*	*Z-score*
10)** I can delete the commercial e-mail just as quickly as I can throw away a piece of junk mail or change the channel on the television to avoid advertisements.	4	1.57
35)** In general, government regulation of unsolicited commercial e-mail should be considered as a last resort.	4	1.53
33)* Balancing businesses' need to reach new customers against users' desire not to be bothered can be reached by market mechanism.	4	1.50
34)** Legislation to restrict unsolicited commercial e-mails, even if it passes in the United States, would be difficult to enforce within the country and wouldn't apply elsewhere.	3	1.46
32)** Legislation should not stifle or inhibit the freedom of business that uses unsolicited commercial e-mails.	3	1.40
6)* When commercial e-mail is appropriate and useful to the recipient, it is welcomed, unsolicited or not.	3	1.20
36) Filtering could be done by Internet service providers before unsolicited commercial e-mail is delivered to the user's computer.	3	1.20

Note. * indicates a distinguishing statement for this type at a significant level of $p< .05$; **, at $p< .01$.

throw one free shot to consumers if they offer an opt-out option for them (22).

They disagreed that e-mail is a personal place (1) and UCE violates users' privacy (3). They believed that UCE is more of a technological problem rather than a social one (30), and that UCE problem can be solved by simply using the delete key (10) or Internet service providers' filtering (36). Sorter 4 commented on statement 10, "I do it all the time and I'm really not bothered by it."

Their worry was the government's intervention. They believed that legislation should not stifle or inhibit the freedom of business that uses UCE (32) because they believed that the market mechanism could balance businesses' need to reach new customers against users' desire not to be bothered (33). Sorter 1 said on statement 33, "Consumers can and will ultimately decide when unsolicited e-mails have gone too far by boycotting 'offensive' companies and patronizing services of firms that can effectively combat it." They didn't worry about the possibility of the Internet being abandoned by people because of UCE (40). Sorter 18 commented on statement 40 that UCE's threat is "no more than print or TV advertising."

This group believed that government regulation of UCE should be considered as a last resort (35). Sorter 18 commented on statement 33, "Markets generally provide a more efficient solution than government." Also legislation to restrict UCE, even if it passes in the United States, would be difficult to enforce within the county and wouldn't apply elsewhere (34). Therefore, they disagreed that legislation is a first step that could significantly reduce UCE volume, even though it cannot totally eliminate UCE (28).

Table 7
Statements Type 2 Strongly Disagreed On

Statements	*Rank Score*	*Z-score*
3)** Unsolicited commercial e-mailing violates my privacy.	-4	-1.61
1)** I think e-mail as a personal space in which I interact with friends and colleagues. Unsolicited commercial e-mail pops up in my face, intruding on that private zone.	-4	-1.47
40)** Over time, unless the growth of unsolicited commercial e-mails isn't stopped, it will destroy the usefulness and effectiveness of e-mail as a communication tool.	-4	-1.27
9)** Consumers are marketed to at every turn—TV, radio, newspaper, billboards, etc. Could we have at least e-mails to ourselves?	-3	-1.26
30) Junk e-mail issue is more of a social problem than a technical one. Junk commercial e-mail won't be ended by technical solutions, but by legislative solutions.	-3	-1.25
22) It is a bad idea to give commercial e-mailers the right to have one free shot at a recipient and then put on the shoulder of the recipient the burden of requesting removal his or her name from their list.	-3	-1.22
28)** Legislation cannot totally eliminate unsolicited commercial e-mail, but it is a first step that could significantly reduce its volume.	-3	-1.21

Note. ** indicates a distinguishing statement for this type at a significant level of $p < .01$.

Type 3: Proper UCE advocates

Type 3, the smallest of the three types, was composed of two males (17 percent of male respondents) and one female (13 percent of female respondents). Their average age was 46. They worked as a district manager, a business consultant, and an administration assistant. Two had a dial-up connection at home, and one, a cable connection. At work they all had a broadband connection. They all perceived themselves as savvy users.

Sorters under Type 3 believed that the Internet participants should abide by certain rules and obligations (29). Since the Internet is a public resource (2), they thought, it is ok for the business to send its customers e-mails, including unsolicited ones if they are relevant and beneficial to the recipients (26) or accompany an opt-out option (22). They didn't believe that the marketers shift costs to e-mail recipients through UCE (12) and that UCE is far more likely than postal advertisements to be inappropriate or personally offensive (7).

They didn't believe that legitimate businesses and organizations are increasingly using UCE to recruit new customers (37), but still had a concern that a rampant growth of UCE will destroy the usefulness and effectiveness of e-mail as a communication tool (40). They wanted marketers not to rent the e-mail list to other companies (21).

Rather than legislation, they preferred technology in solving unwanted commercial e-mails (18), such as filtering them by the Internet service providers (36).

Sorters of this type opposed legislation that would create a separate Internet network to deal with unsolicited

Table 8
Statements Type 3 Strongly Agreed On

Statements	Rank Score	Z-score
40)** Over time, unless the growth of unsolicited commercial e-mails isn't stopped, it will destroy the usefulness and effectiveness of e-mail as a communication tool.	4	1.73
26) If a business just sold a VCR to a customer, it is ok for the business to e-mail the customer about new movie releases as useful information to the customer.	4	1.69
2)** The Internet is a public resource since it was created in part with taxpayer monies, and an e-mail address is a matter of public record, like a street address.	4	1.49
36) Filtering could be done by Internet service providers before unsolicited commercial e-mail is delivered to the user's computer.	3	1.41
21)** A company that collects e-mail addresses should be allowed to use them, but it should not rent the e-mail list to others.	3	1.31
29) The global Internet is a community. Like any community, participation in it implies certain rules and obligations.	3	1.29
18) Someone could develop filtering software that could recognize the consumer's preferences and filter out e-mails that would be of no interest to the user.	3	1.24

Note. ** indicates a distinguishing statement for this type at a significant level of $p < .01$.

commercial e-mails (31), because it is too expensive, according to sorter 8. This type perceived junk e-mail as more of a technical problem, rather than a social one, opposing any legislative solutions (30). This group also disagreed that legislation should not stifle or inhibit the freedom of business that uses UCE.

Discussion and Conclusion

One consensus statement among three groups was "The global Internet is a community. Like any community, participation in it implies certain rules and obligations" (29). But the statement means a different thing to each group in reality, which was revealed in their different understanding of what is the Internet for, what kind of messages may be sent over the Internet, and what kind of rights marketers should have on the Internet.

For UCE objectors, the Internet is not a public place (1, 2) while market believers (1) and proper UCE advocates (2) perceived it as a public place. Naturally, UCE objectors thought UCE invades their privacy (3) and UCE is not entitled to constitutional protection given to commercial speech (4). On the other hand, market believers did not believe that UCE violates the recipient's privacy (3).

UCE objectors treated the e-mail marketing differently from other traditional mass media marketing vehicles (8, 9) while market believers treated the e-mail the same as other marketing medium (9).

For UCE objectors, dealing with unsolicited e-mail junk and filtering large numbers of unwanted commercial messages were a burden and suffering

Table 9
Statements Type 3 Strongly Disagreed On

Statements	*Rank Score*	*Z-score*
31)** Legislation should be introduced so that unsolicited commercial e-mails could be handled through a separate Internet network; there is no justification for forcing third parties to bear the load of unsolicited advertising.	-4	-1.69
37) Legitimate businesses and organizations are increasingly using unsolicited commercial e-mail to recruit new customers.	-4	-1.68
7)* Unsolicited commercial e-mail is far more likely than postal advertisements to be inappropriate or personally offensive.	-4	-1.65
32) Legislation should not stifle or inhibit the freedom of business that uses unsolicited commercial e-mails.	-3	-1.30
22) It is a bad idea to give commercial e-mailers the right to have one free shot at a recipient and then put on the shoulder of the recipient the burden of requesting removal his or her name from their list.	-3	-1.29
12)* Unsolicited commercial e-mailing is bad because it allows one person to profit at another's expense. Let's make commercial enterprises bear the costs of what they do to make money.	-3	-1.27
30) Junk e-mail issue is more of a social problem than a technical one. Junk commercial e-mail won't be ended by technical solutions, but by legislative solutions.	-3	-1.27

Note. * indicates a distinguishing statement for this type at a significant level of $p< .05$; **, at $p< .01$.

(15, 19), while market believers thought they could delete unwanted messages easily (10). Proper UCE advocates also did not recognize any sacrifice consumers have to face because of UCE (12).

UCE objectors were against the idea of giving commercial e-mailers the right to unsolicited e-mail (22) because UCE is not appropriate and useful to the recipient (6), giving no benefits to consumers (38). On the other hand, market believers believed consumers would welcome even unsolicited commercial messages if they are appropriate and useful (6). Proper UCE supporters had the same idea that businesses should be allowed to send useful information (26). Proper UCE supporters observed that commercial e-mail is not more likely than traditional postal ads to be inappropriate or personally offensive to consumers (7), nor legitimate business and organizations are increasingly using UCE (37).

UCE objectors would not accept UCE even if e-mailers reveal how they acquired recipients' e-mail addresses and explain their privacy policy for the recipients (25). Small companies could not be an exception and should not be treated more favorably in the market than bigger companies (13). But market believers and proper UCE advocates supported the idea of giving commercial e-mailers the right to have one free shot (22).

Market believers and proper UCE supporters understood UCE as a technical problem rather than a social one, so they suggested that technical solutions should be pursued instead of legislation (30). For example, market believers and proper UCE advocates pointed to filtering of UCE by ISPs (36). Proper UCE advocates also believed that filtering software could accommodate even personal preferences in the future (18).

The difference between market believers and proper UCE advocates existed in their prediction. For market believers, without restriction on UCE, e-mail will still be a useful and effective communication tool (40), but not so with proper UCE advocates (40). UCE advocates also indicated renting the list to others as an area of concern (21).

Market believers vigorously opposed any kind of legislation. They referred to legislation as a last resort (35) because they believed the market mechanism alone can balance interests of consumers and businesses (33). According to them, legislation would not be effective in America and elsewhere (34) and would not decrease the UCE volume (28). Even if the legislation is introduced, it should not stifle and inhibit the freedom of businesses that use unsolicited commercial e-mails (32).

Proper UCE advocates did not show a strong negative feeling towards legislation, except for one that would create another Internet network only for commercial e-mails (31). One strange response was that proper UCE advocates disagreed that legislation should not stifle or inhibit the freedom of business that uses unsolicited commercial e-mails (32). It seems that they might interpret "should" as an expression of "what is probable or expected," not as "duty, obligation or necessity."[32]

The difference among the three groups could be based on their different experience in reality. UCE objectors were mainly composed of consumers while market believers made up of mostly business managers, and proper UCE advocates, a small portion of managers. Also females were more likely to belong to UCE objectors than the other two groups. Among eight females, four were found among UCE objectors while the other two groups had only one each. Sorters' perception of their being savvy users seemed to have little relationship with their type.

There is a difference in age among the three groups: UCE objectors were younger than market believers and proper USE supporters. At the same time, UCE objectors were less likely to have a broadband connection than the other two groups. UCE objectors had broadband in the case of 14 percent at home and 57 percent at work, while market believers' respective percentage went up to 33 percent and 83 percent and proper USE supporters' percentage, 33 percent and 100 percent respectively. Age and the connection speed could be a factor to separate UCE objectors from the other two groups. Considering the small number of the sorters, further study is recommended to verify this relationship.

In conclusion, there were three different groups that have different opinions toward UCE: UCE objectors, who were in support of consumers' privacy on one extreme; market believers who wanted to support a *laissez-faire* policy on the other extreme; and proper UCE advocates who are in support of UCE as far as it is beneficial to consumers in between, but much closer to market believers than UCE objectors.

Considering the fundamental difference among the three groups—especially UCE objectors and market believers—even in understanding of the concept of the Internet and e-mail, the big gap among the groups could not be easily narrowed. This wide gap is also reflected in the current atmosphere of stalemate. For a few years, the House and Senate could not successfully come up with a bill on the commercial e-mail use, and diverging opinions exist among scholars about whether a new bill on the use of commercial messages, even if enacted, could pass constitutional free speech muster.

One hope is that proper UCE advocates might play a leading role in having the other two groups shift their positions towards proper UCE advocates.

Appendix 1. Rotated Factor Matrix for Three Factor Solution

ID	*Sex*	*Occupation*	*Age*	*Savvy user*	*Connection at home*	*Connection at work*	*Factor Loadings*		
							Type 1	*Type 2*	*Type 3*
6	f	health education	27	yes	dial-up	broadband	0.77	-0.07	0.14
9	m	public health	45	yes	dial-up	broadband	0.83	-0.20	0.06
10	f	teacher	46	no	broadband	broadband	0.56	0.04	0.21
11	f	college student	20	no	dial-up	no response	0.58	-0.02	-0.19
13	f	materials manager	42	yes	dial-up	dial-up	0.69	-0.37	-0.09
15	m	athletic coach	27	yes	no connection	broadband	0.78	-0.25	0.08
20	m	medicine technician	31	yes	dial-up	no connection	0.73	-0.29	-0.03
1	m	product dev. mgr	31	yes	broadband	broadband	-0.26	0.79	0.06
4	f	business analyst	36	yes	dial-up	broadband	0.29	0.67	0.07
16	m	finance professor	51	no	broadband	broadband	-0.14	0.62	0.30
17	m	service manager	29	no	dial-up	broadband	-0.25	0.76	-0.08
18	m	investment advisor	49	no	dial-up	broadband	-0.28	0.83	0.09
19	m	operations manager	39	yes	dial-up	dial-up	-0.21	0.72	0.11
7	m	district manager	45	yes	dial-up	broadband	-0.06	0.13	0.95
8	m	business consultant	50	yes	broadband	broadband	-0.07	0.11	0.96
14	f	administration assistant	43	yes	dial-up	broadband	0.30	-0.18	0.46
3	m	salesman	29	yes	dial-up	dial-up	0.53	-0.45	-0.01
2	f	office manager	31	yes	broadband	broadband	-0.07	0.24	-0.14
5	f	process engineer	28	no	dial-up	no response	-0.08	0.34	0.10
12	m	program manager	47	yes	no connection	broadband	0.04	0.14	0.33
		% of explained variance					21%	20%	12%

Note. Defining variates are shown in bold; mixed loaders, underlined.

(Appendix II) Statements and Rank Scores

Statements	*Type and Rank Scores*		
	Type 1	*Type 2*	*Type 3*
1) I think of e-mail as a personal space in which I interact with friends and colleagues. Unsolicited commercial e-mail pops up in my face, intruding on that private zone.	3	-4	2
2) The Internet is a public resource since it was created in part with taxpayer monies, and an e-mail address is a matter of public record, like a street address.	-4	0	4
3) Unsolicited commercial e-mailing violates my privacy.	3	-4	-1
4) Sending unsolicited commercial e-mail is a constitutional right as part of commercial speech.	-3	0	-2

Statements	*Type and Rank Scores* Type 1	Type 2	Type 3
5) Unsolicited commercial e-mailers don't have any idea whether their audience is interested in what they offer.	1	0	-1
6) When commercial e-mail is appropriate and useful to the recipient, it is welcomed, unsolicited or not.	-3	3	1
7) Unsolicited commercial e-mail is far more likely than postal advertisements to be inappropriate or personally offensive.	1	-2	-4
8) People are bombarded with constant advertisements, such as banners, when surfing the Internet. Commercial e-mailing is the part of Internet advertising I am willing to accept.	-4	2	1
9) Consumers are marketed to at every turn — TV, radio, newspaper, billboards, etc. Could we have at least e-mails to ourselves?	3	-3	-1
10) I can delete the commercial e-mail just as quickly as I can throw away a piece of junk mail or change the channel on the television to avoid advertisements.	-1	4	1
11) Unsolicited commercial e-mailers think it's really neat they can reach a million people for free, but they do so by shifting the costs onto others.	0	1	0
12) Unsolicited commercial e-mailing is bad because it allows one person to profit at another's expense. Let's make commercial enterprises bear the costs of what they do to make money.	2	-1	-3
13) Only big companies can reach Internet users through traditional media. So, small companies without financial resources should be allowed to use unsolicited commercial e-mail.	-3	0	-2
14) Low-cost unsolicited commercial e-mail would be a good deal for the consumer because inflated advertising costs are not passed on through product pricing.	-2	1	0
15) It is unfair to burden the consumer with the task of filtering large numbers of unwanted commercial messages.	4	-1	1
16) Software that examines e-mail will easily filter out unwanted e-mails.	0	1	0
17) The means of filtering large numbers of unwanted messages are imperfect and cost money.	2	-1	2
18) Someone could develop filtering software that could recognize the consumer's preferences and filter out e-mails that would be of no interest to the user.	1	2	3
19) You shouldn't be forced to suffer the e-mail junk flood unless and until you actually request it.	4	-2	2
20) Most unsolicited commercial e-mailers will not respect the user's request to put his or her name off their list.	1	-2	-2
21) A company that collects e-mail addresses should be allowed to use them, but it should not rent the e-mail list to others.	-2	-1	3
22) It is a bad idea to give commercial e-mailers the right to have one free shot at a recipient and then put on the shoulder of the recipient the burden of requesting removal his or her name from their list.	4	-3	-3
23) The advertisers should be allowed to e-mail unsolicited advertisements if they have an ongoing business or personal relationship with the recipient.	-1	1	0
24) Consumers who don't know about a certain technology or aren't familiar enough with it to sign up for an opt-in mailing list will miss information they might want to read.	-2	0	-2
25) It is ok to send an unsolicited e-mail if an e-mailer tells customers how the e-mailer got their e-mail address and provides a link to a Web page that spells out a privacy policy.	-3	1	0

Statements	*Type and Rank Scores* Type 1	Type 2	Type 3
26) If a business just sold a VCR to a customer, it is ok for the business to e-mail the customer about new movie releases as useful information to the customer.	-2	2	4
27) Strict advertising laws could inhibit commercial e-mailers who want to give false promises.	0	-2	-1
28) Legislation cannot totally eliminate unsolicited commercial e-mail, but it is a first step that could significantly reduce its volume.	2	-3	2
29) The global Internet is a community. Like any community, participation in it implies certain rules and obligations.	3	2	3
30) Junk e-mail issue is more of a social problem than a technical one. Junk commercial e-mail won't be ended by technical solutions, but by legislative solutions.	1	-3	-3
31) Legislation should be introduced so that unsolicited commercial e-mails could be handled through a separate Internet network; there is no justification for forcing third parties to bear the load of unsolicited advertising.	-1	-2	-4
32) Legislation should not stifle or inhibit the freedom of business that uses unsolicited commercial e-mails.	-2	3	-3
33) Balancing businesses' need to reach new customers against users' desire not to be bothered can be reached by market mechanism.	-1	4	2
34) Legislation to restrict unsolicited commercial e-mails, even if it passes in the United States, would be difficult to enforce within the country and wouldn't apply elsewhere.	2	3	-2
35) In general, government regulation of unsolicited commercial e-mail should be considered as a last resort.	0	4	1
36) Filtering could be done by Internet service providers before unsolicited commercial e-mail is delivered to the user's computer.	0	3	3
37) Legitimate businesses and organizations are increasingly using unsolicited commercial e-mail to recruit new customers.	0	2	-4
38) Unsolicited commercial e-mailers are providing a service by distributing information that could help their recipients make informed decisions.	-4	0	0
39) There are very few reputable marketers using unsolicited commercial e-mails to advertise goods and services.	-1	-1	-1
40) Over time, unless the growth of unsolicited commercial e-mails isn't stopped, it will destroy the usefulness and effectiveness of e-mail as a communication tool.	2	-4	4

Notes

1. Roberts, Stevan, Michelle Feit, and Robert, W Bly. 2001. Internet Direct Mail: The complete guide to successful e-mail marketing campaigns. Chicago: NTC Business Books, xii-xiii. MacPherson, Kim. 2001. Permission-based e-mail marketing that works!, Chicago: Dearborn Trade, 3 & 13.

2. Roberts, Feit, and Bly, 4–5.

3. E-mail marketing is also known as digital direct marketing. It is popular among marketers, because it is about 20 times less expensive than typical offline catalog campaigns. It is also one of the best ways to keep customers coming back, though there are privacy concerns (Sindell 2000, 113).

4. Casey, Timothy. 2000. ISP liability survival guide: Strategies for managing copyright, spam, cache, and privacy regulations. New York: Wiley Computer Publishing, 136–137.

5. Marcus, Joshua. 1998. Commercial speech on the Internet: Spam and the First

Amendment. <http://www.ipwatchdog.com/spamlawrev.html>.

6. Afuah, Allan, and Christopher L. Tucci. 2001. *Internet business models and strategies: Text and cases.* Boston: MaGraw-Hill Irwin, 36.

7. Woodward, Victor. 1998. E-mail spam vs. the First Amendment. *Dominopower Magazine.* August. <http://dominopower.com/issues/issue199808/spam001.html>.

8. Rosencrance, Linda. 2000. E-mail marketers announce anti-spam standards. *CNN.com,* 26 September. <http://www.cnn.com/2000/TECH/computing/09/26/anti-spam.standards.idg/index.html>. Junnarkar, Sandeep. 2000. Online marketers propose privacy standards. CNET.com., 25 September. < http://news.cnet.com/news/0-1005-200-2862059.html>.

9. Railsback, Kevin; Yager, Tom, Jan. 22, 2001. *Infoworld,* 54.

10. MacPherson, Kim. 2001. Permission-based e-mail marketing that works!, Chicago: Dearborn Trade, 15.

11. Some anit-spammers may send huge messages that can clog the Internet servers that allowed spam or crash them. Other spam haters have been known to send continuous faxes to spammers' fax machines in the middle of the night. (Roberts, Feit, Bly, 147).

12. Catlett, Jason. 1997. Comments on junkbusters concerning consumer on-line privacy-p954807. <http://www.ftc.gov/bcp/privacy/wkshp97/comments2/junkbust.htm>.

13. Thibodeau, Patrick. 2000. Survey: Spam perceptions may be hurting e-commerce. Computerworld, 13 April. <http://www.computerworld.com/cwi/story/0,1199,AV47_STO43858,00.html>.

14. Roberts, Feit, Bly, 145-147.

15. According to a market researcher, 40 percent of an individual's incoming e-mail is going to be spam within the next five years, up from 10 percent in 2000 (Armstrong 2000).

16. Casey, xv.

17. Marcus.

18. Miller, Kate. 2001. Congress considers legislation to limit spam. Computerworld, 27 March. <http://www.computerworld.com/cwi/story/0,1199,NAV47_STO59032,00.html>.

19. Olsen, Stefanie. 2001. MSN filter sparks subscriber ire. CNET News.com, 6 April. <http://news.cnet.com/news/0-1005-200-5531362.html>.

20. Casey, 186.

21. Disabatino, Jennifer. 2000a. Pollster sues over placement on spam list. *Computerworld,* 1 August. <http://www.computerworld.com/cwi/story/0,1199,NAV47_SO47848,00.html>.

22. Disabatino.

23. Evans, James. 2000. Judge blocks Yesmail.com blacklisting. *IDG News Service,* 18 July. <http://www.computerworld.com/cwi/story/0,1199,NAV47_STO47268,00.html>.

24. In the 106th Congress (1999–2000), the House of Representatives passed the Unsolicited Electronic Mail Act of 2000 (H.R. 3113), but it died from inaction in the Senate. The "CAN SPAM" Act of 2000 (S. 2542) was a companion bill to H.R. 3113, although it differed from the House bill in significant respects. Several other spam-related bills were also introduced in the 106th Congress (*Spam Laws: United States: Federal*). The Unsolicited Electronic Mail Act of 2001 was introduced this year and had cleared the House committees, but expected tough opposition from the Direct Marketing Association (DMA) and some members of Congress. They said the bill could spark numerous lawsuits and empower ISPs to set their own anti-spam standards, which could become national standards (Ross 2001a and 2001b). The Senate introduced a more lenient bill, which would require UCE to have a valid return address to facilitate consumers' removal from spam lists.

25. Hansen, Evan. 2000. Court kills key parts of bulk e-mail law. *Computerworld,* 9 June. <http://news.cnet.com/news/0-1005-200-2047482.html>.

26. Chung, Hwi-man. 1999. Ban spam?: Exploring the legal issues and constitution-

ality of federal and state statutes and bills regulating junk e-mail. Paper presented at the law division of the Association for Education in Journalism and Mass Communications, 4–7 August at New Orleans, Louisiana.

27. Marcus.

28. Rosencrance.

29. Some people used the term permission-based instead of opt-in because when an Internet user completes and submits a form, a "yes" to the "opt-in" box is already pre-checked instead of the user checking it off (Roberts, Reit, and Bly, 74–75).

30. Loren, Lydia P. Learning cyberlaw in cyberspace. <http://cyberspacelaw.org/loren/index.html>.

31. Stephenson, W. 1967. *The Play Theory of Mass Communication.* Chicago: University of Chicago Press, 11.

32. MQMETHOD is a public domain program, which readers can retrieve from the following Web site: <http://www.rz.unibw-muenchen.de/~p41bsmk/qmethod/addfls.htm>. The program is also available in PC and Unix versions at this URL.

33. Brown, Steven R.1980. *Political subjectivity: Applications of Q Methodology in political science.* New Haven, CT: Yale University, 23.

34. For easy reference, the related statement number was put in the parentheses from here on.

35. Brown, 23–24.

Bibliography

Afuah, Allan, and Christopher L. Tucci. 2001. *Internet business models and strategies: Text and cases.* Boston: MaGraw-Hill Irwin.

Armstrong, Larry. 2000. Making mincemeat out of unwanted e-mail. *Businessweek online,* 18 December. <http://www.businessweek.com/2000/00_51/b3712216.htm>.

Brown, Steven R.1980. *Political subjectivity: Applications of Q Methodology in political science.* New Haven, CT: Yale University.

Casey, Timothy. 2000. *ISP liability survival guide: Strategies for managing copyright, spam, cache, and privacy regulations.* New York: Wiley Computer Publishing.

Catlett, Jason. 1997. Comments on junkbusters concerning consumer on-line privacy-p954807. <http://www.ftc.gov/bcp/privacy/wkshp97/comments2/junkbust.htm>.

CAUCE: Coalition Against Unsolicited Commercial E-mail. <http://www.cauce.org/legislation/index.shtml>.

Chung, Hwi-man. 1999. Ban spam?: Exploring the legal issues and constitutionality of federal and state statutes and bills regulating junk e-mail. Paper presented at the law division of the Association for Education in Journalism and Mass Communications, 4–7 August at New Orleans, Louisiana.

Disabatino, Jennifer. 2000a. Pollster sues over placement on spam list. *Computerworld,* 1 August. <http://www.computerworld.com/cwi/story/0,1199,NAV47_SO47848,00.html>.

______. 2000b. Pollster loses restraining-order request in spamming case. *Computerworld,* 9 August. <http://www.computerworld.com/cwi/story/0,1199,NAV47_STO48350,00.html>.

______. 2000c. Harris Interactive drops suit against Microsoft. *Computerworld,* 8 September. <http://www.computerworld.com/cwi/story/0,1199,NAV47_STO49888,00.html>.

______. 2000d. Marketing firm gets restraining order against spamming list operator. *Computerworld,* 17 November. <http://www.computerworld.com/cwi/story/0,1199,NAV47_STO54174,00.html>.

Evans, James. 2000. Judge blocks Yesmail.com blacklisting. *IDG News Service,* 18 July. <http://www.computerworld.com/cwi/story/0,1199,NAV47_STO47268,00.html>.

Gove, Philip B., ed. 1981.*Webster's third new international dictionary of the English language unabridged.* Springfield, MA: Merriam-Webster.

Haney, Clare. 2000. Harris Interactive drops

ISP lawsuits. *Computerworld*, 13 September. <http://www.computerworld.com/cwi/story/0,1199,NAV47_STO50088,00.html>.

Hansen, Evan. 2000. Court kills key parts of bulk e-mail law. *Computerworld*, 9 June. <http://news.cnet.com/news/0-1005-200-2047482.html>.

Junnarkar, Sandeep. 2000. Online marketers propose privacy standards. CNET.com., 25 September. < http://news.cnet.com/news/0-1005-200-2862059.html>.

Loren, Lydia P. Learning cyberlaw in cyberspace. <http://cyberspacelaw.org/loren/index.html>.

MacPherson, Kim. 2001. Permission-based e-mail marketing that works!, Chicago: Dearborn Trade.

Marcus, Joshua. 1998. Commercial speech on the Internet: Spam and the First Amendment. <http://www.ipwatchdog.com/spamlawrev.html>.

Miller, Kate. 2001. Congress considers legislation to limit spam. *Computerworld*, 27 March. <http://www.computerworld.com/cwi/story/0,1199,NAV47_STO59032,00.html>

MQMethod 2.06 for the Macintosh. <http://www.rz.unibw-muenchen.de/~p41bsmk/qmethod>.

Olsen, Stefanie. 2001. MSN filter sparks subscriber ire. CNET News.com, 6 April. <http://news.cnet.com/news/0-1005-200-5531362.html>.

Railsback, Kevin; Yager, Tom, Jan. 22, 2001. *Infoworld*, 54–55.

Roberts, Stevan, Michelle Feit, and Robert, W Bly. 2001. *Internet Direct Mail: The complete guide to successful e-mail marketing campaigns.* Chicago: NTC Business Books.

Rosencrance, Linda. 2000. E-mail marketers announce anti-spam standards. *CNN.com*, 26 September. <http://www.cnn.com/2000/TECH/computing/09/26/antispam.standards.idg/index.html>.

Ross, Patrick. 2001a. House panel votes against spam. *CNET News.com*, 21 March. <http://news.cnet.com/news/0-1005-200-5206615.html>.

______.2001b. Spam bill clears House committee. *CNET News.com*, 28 March. <http://news.cnet.com/news/0-1005-200-5335487.html>

Sindell, Kathleen. 2000. *Loyalty marketing for the Internet age: How to identify, attract, serve, and retain customers in an e-commerce environment.* Chicago: Dearborn Trade.

Spam Laws: United States: Federal Laws: 107th Congress: Summary. <http://www.spamlaws.com/federal/summ107.html>.

Spam Laws: United States: State Laws: Summary. <http://www.spamlaws.com/state/summary.html>.

Stephenson, W. 1967. *The Play Theory of Mass Communication.* Chicago: University of Chicago Press.

Thibodeau, Patrick. 2000. Survey: Spam perceptions may be hurting e-commerce. *Computerworld*, 13 April. <http://www.computerworld.com/cwi/story/0,1199,AV47_STO43858,00.html>.

Woodward, Victor. 1998. E-mail spam vs. the First Amendment. *Dominopower Magazine.* August. <http://dominopower.com/issues/issue199808/spam001.html>.

21

An Ethics for the Electronic World: the Ethics of Dialogue

Maria Antonieta Lopes Vigário

Abstract

Nowadays there is a need for a universal ethics. The consideration of human beings as participants in the communication community gives the philosophical background to the professional commitments of information professionals. It also implies a profound consideration of all possible partners in the discourse of ethics, giving rise to a multicultural community. The respect for human rights is also a feature of this way of thinking about the ethical problems posed in the building of a fair information society.

The experience of an ethical discussion based upon rational arguments might be a way to educate people around the world, helping them to consider themselves as partners in the setting of an ethics where everyone has responsibilities. The rules of argumentation, based on rationality, might make a contribution to the sharing of this discourse of ethics around the electronic community.

The participation in an ethical discussion based upon rational argumentation gave to Portuguese information professionals and users of information services the responsibility for setting up a code of professional ethics. This experience of building something new together, after four years of debate, enhances the importance of this kind of ethics.

Introduction

My communication deals with several concepts that are the background and foundation of my professional commitments:

- The aim to join efforts between people to build something together.
- The respect for each person as they are.

- This study aims to find the best way to enhance dialogue between different cultures.

Having some freedom, and being aware of the difficulties arising from the spreading of information and communication technologies, I thought that the best way was to start a joint reflection on ethical issues in my professional life.

These issues became so important for me that it became the subject of my PhD dissertation.

A Story

After these preliminary remarks, allow me to tell you a story:

As part of my professional duties, I became interested in information ethics. The real concern at that time, and it remains the same, was the respect for human rights in daily life.

I became aware that Professional Ethics was a new issue for Portuguese information professionals. After my MSc, I started a Commission for Ethics with a group of friends who were working in different information fields.

This work revealed the different perspectives of these professionals. We were a group of six people from the three Portuguese professional associations. The main idea was to discover if Portuguese information professionals wanted a professional code of ethics and to find the best way to implement such a code.

Working with different professional associations at the same time is not an easy task, but the interest of professionals had to be gained. To prepare the members of the commission for the dialogue was the first part. Some agreements were made. First, we have to hear everyone and understand what they have to say about different concerns regarding professional ethics. Second, we respect Human Rights. Third, we have to be patient, to have hope, to trust people and, last of all, to write the code of ethics.

We held many meetings over the following four years. In those meetings, we studied in different ways— we needed to apply our ideas of correctness to different professional contexts, and imagine what would be the difficulties of others and their answers to the ethical issues.

We used questionnaires to discover professionals' level of interest in ethics. We organised an international meeting on professional ethics for information professionals. The communications of that meeting and the results of the surveys were published. After this, we organised different professional meetings around Portugal.

The Process

During the meetings, we started by explaining the difference between morals and ethics. The second task was to present the most important issues in professional ethics for information professionals. After a break, case studies were presented to the participants. Discussions were held about the most appropriate ways to deal with the conflicts and problems posed in the case studies.

To enhance the discussion, Jürgen Habermas' rules of argumentation were applied. The golden rule was that everyone should participate. We told the attendees that their opinions as human beings, as participants in a practical discourse, were the most important factors involved in the discussion.

Secondly, taking part in this practical discourse imposes the use of rationality. Participants had to present reasons to support their claims that their opinions were the most correct. The problem of emotional opinions and prejudices was overcome by reason.

The solving of daily problems in professional life was covered because everyone has his/her professional duties as a background — the experience of interaction between information professionals and the users of information services. The dialogue with others from different contexts enhanced the discussions.

The rules of argumentation were observed. The autonomy of each person was respected because everyone participated as he/she liked and had the right to question any bit of work already done by others, so as to understand the reasons behind any assertion.

It is argumentation between several reasons which improves personal truth. This supposes an ideal community of communication, within which the experience of thinking assumes its relevance and credibility. When someone thinks, they are presenting arguments and counter-arguments to reach the truth.

The rules for argumentation are rational, and presuppose that they are to be observed by others. These rules are part of people's personal reasoning and they are also used by any human being in a situation of dialogue with others.

This rational argumentation has, following Alexy[1] and according to Habermas,[2] rules which must be observed:

The minimal logic and semantic rules:

1.1 No speaker may contradict himself;

1.2 Every speaker who applies predicate F to object A must be prepared to apply F to all other objects resembling A in all relevant objects;

1.3 Different speakers may not use the same expression with different meanings.

In procedural terms:

2.1 Every speaker may assert only what he really believes;

2.2 A person who disputes a proposition or norm not under discussion must provide a reason for wanting to do so.

In process terms, argumentative speech is a process of communication that, in light of its goals of reaching a rationally motivated agreement, must satisfy improbable conditions:

3.1 Every subject with the competence to speak and act is allowed to take part in the discourse;

3.2 a. Everyone is allowed to question any assertion whatever;

b. Everyone is allowed to introduce any assertion whatever in the discourse;

c. Everyone is allowed to express his attitudes, desires and needs.

These are good rules to begin a dialogue with, aren't they? My point is that these rules were applied among Portuguese information professionals and users of information services who participated in the meetings organized by the Commission of Ethics in Portugal. And I wonder if they might be applied in the context of electronic information.

The final product of this process is the code of ethics for information professionals in Portugal, which has been built following the rules of ethical discourse quoted above and, in which, everyone who wanted to participate had the opportunity to do so.

Joining the efforts of professionals from different professional associations and from different professional contexts is also related to the idea of a real communication community grounded in the ideal communication community presented by this ethics.

As has been said previously, this is only an explanation of what the concept of ethics means nowadays in this networked society, and in a multicultural professional reality.

As Apel[3] claims:

> For justice, in conjunction with co-responsibility, belongs to the universally valid moral condition of the coexistence and co-operation of different cultures in the face of the common problems of humankind.

The rationality of arguments with the consideration of all affected by rules give to this ethics the possibility of being considered universal.

As this kind of ethical reasoning worked well as the basis for professional commitments, I wonder if it should also be applied to a broader context. I understand the different counter-arguments against this ethics.

Is This an Ethics Without Content?

Firstly, the content. Dialogue has value in itself, but what is this dialogue about? Where are the concerns regarding the content of the ethical decision? Where is justice?

It seems that this "Ethics of Dialogue" is only a process, a set of rules to speak out our ethical concerns, and the decisions will be made by the ethics of responsibility. And it is the other way around too! The people who are participants in the discourse of ethics consider others—all those participating in the same discourse. First of all, because they are arguing, they claim the validity of certain moral duties with regard to all possible discourse partners. That is an inter-subjective validity. People who are arguing the validity of a moral duty think also about the side effects of an action—the consequences morally relevant for everyone. Afterwards, they consider themselves, as well as others, as co-responsible for the discovery and solution of all moral problems. That is why this ethics is of dialogue.

It seems like a rational framework for discourse, but does it lack any real application? The news is that this framework was applied in a broad professional context and it worked. Why shouldn't it be tried in an even broader context?

The content of the rules to be set and then discussed among these partners in the discourse was determined by professional concerns. How can it be applied to a broader context—namely to the virtual world of the Internet and computer communication? This requires the respect of different cultures and different interests. It means that this ethics needs a multi-cultural dialogue all over the world if it is to be applied.

I understand very well that this is a difficult task. But achieving this within Portugal was not easy, yet we succeeded! It is difficult, but not impossible.

The difficulty arises when we realise that people using the computer communication technologies have their own backgrounds, have diverse motives and lack common goals—it is a different kind of reality.

To reach an intercultural dialogue among people is not an easy task. But they can be motivated by need. The need to have a better environment might be a good reason to start thinking about others as co-participants in the discourse of ethics.

Morality and Ethics

There are different mentalities, different cultural values and moralities. The difference between morality and ethics gives us the possibility of understanding why this kind of ethical reflection may be useful for the multi-cultural dialogue. Moral judgements and ethical reflections are different yet sometimes the two overlap. Moral judgement belongs to the culture within which we are born. There are different moralities and sometimes the search for agreement is very difficult. Even in a profession like ours, there are many cultures to be respected and different persons have different motives for embracing a moral framework. It can be said that moral judgements are culture dependent.

The ethical reasoning has a rational basis. It is a philosophical discipline—when we speak about ethics we are referring to a particular kind of rationality. In the ethics being considered, we are not proposing an ideal of happiness for everyone, because we have to understand and respect different personal choices. We ask for a different kind of agreement. It is not goodness that we are looking for, but the correctness of our actions.

Rationality is assumed to be common to all human beings. That's why they are considered as partners in the discourse. So, the arguments in favour or against any rule should have a rational fundament.

We can agree that rational thinking is not in fashion, that there are many other vectors in human life than rationality. Nevertheless, the capacity to think is the basis for decision making, the possibility for dialogue among people and it is, in Aristotelian terms, the specific of human kind.

To set up a universal ethics for the communication community means to attribute value to rational thinking. It is of great value for all human beings. If we give up our rational thinking we lose the bond that can unite us.

Thinking rationally about different ethical problems. Solving ethical issues rationally. These two aims can be achieved through the ethics of discourse.

Nevertheless, the problem remains. How might ethics of discourse be a foundation for Human Rights in this multicultural society?

Human Rights in a Multi-Cultural Society

The validity of certain moral claims and duties with regard to all possible discourse partners gives to the "ethics of discourse" the grounding for it to be considered as a foundation for human rights.

The different needs of different cultures are considered if the rationality of argumentation is observed. The procedural norms of discourse ethics give a basis for a communicative understanding among people around the world.

This assumption is based on the common rationality of all human beings. Nevertheless, there is a problem. We can consider all possible discourse partners as equals only in the discourse. Or should we take this consideration of the importance of all possible partners as the beginning of a universal consideration of all others? The relation of the discourse of ethics to practical life leads to the consideration of all as subjects of rights.

Looking for a consensus in basic values presupposes authenticity. It means that, whoever participates in discourse, following the methodological rules, should be aware that they are in a serious participation. The participation implies the presence of all other human beings as participants in looking for a consensus in morally relevant problems.

And what of those who do not want to participate? People who give up thinking, or people who are against the participation of others? They should be convinced that respecting human beings is in their best interest, because they will benefit in the long run. Firstly, because they will also be considered as discourse partners and it is better for them to be considered as participants than to be called tyrants. However, this argument is not a sufficient one regarding the brute force of tyranny.

In spite of all discourse, it is possible for a person to observe the discourse rules and to be interested in correctness, and yet still not agree with the equality of human rights. Nevertheless, as Alexy[4] says,

> discourse theory does not know any conversational restraint, but it demands that only arguments examinable by all they concern may be admitted, if, as with the human rights, a solution to a conflict of interests is called for. Accordingly a racist who denies the equality of the human rights for religious, metaphysical, or magical reasons is by definition no participant in an ideal discourse. His existence can therefore not devalue the argument of consensus.

The Pedagogical Role

How to spread these concerns? How to interest persons in the morally relevant problems they can face?

Those who participate in solving ethical problems have to be aware of their educational role. This is a reason to stress the pedagogical role of this ethics.

What can we do if someone refuses to participate? And what happens to people who give up thinking about ethics? People have freedom to think and to act. Whatever they want to do, they are considered as ideal participants in the communication community. Nevertheless, they have to be aware of their lack of responsibility if they give up thinking about ethics. So, the best way is to spread information about ethical decision-making and about the rules to be observed during this task. The basic relationship between information ethics and human rights should become common knowledge among information professionals and users of information services.

User Training

To introduce information professionals to ethical decision-making within their professional commitments is important, but it is not enough. The information user should be aware of the different ethical issues regarding the collection, storage and management of information devices and contents.

Why? Because what we are looking for is a better world, where each person is considered as a subject of ethical thinking and a participant in a community where others should be respected.

To attain an environment within which everyone has the possibility of being respected, it is necessary to spread the foundations of human rights.

There are many people interested in understanding why some set of rules must be applied. For instance, why should anyone be truthful instead of a liar? The answer is that, as Kant says, if you lie once, nobody can trust you anymore and, if you cannot trust others, how can you live in a decent world?

Giving to different people the right to express themselves is a way to enhance the discourse of ethics and, in an electronic environment, spreading the idea of participation to build a set of rules to prevent misconduct might be a powerful tool.

Summary

There are processes which are not only processes. They are based on important assumptions. They are also based upon the fundamentals of human beings, their rationality, desires and needs. To propose an ethical process for human dialogue within electronic communications is a risk. The risk of being considered a dreamer. The risk of speaking without being understood. Or worse: "Who are you to point out the best way to hold a dialogue?"

I'm an information professional from a peripheral country of the European Union: Portugal. And I took the risk of trying to set up something with the help of others. Giving participation to all possible partners in the discourse of ethics. Considering all human beings who could be affected by our professional commitments.

And now I remain with my heart and thought in the present moment. It is possible to have people all over the world speaking freely about their concerns, preventing misconduct, reaching for a better world for everyone, and building it together. Maybe I'm a dreamer, but I'm not the only one.

References

1. Alexy, R. (1998). "Justice and Discourse (Discourse Theory and Human Rights)." In: Alves, J.L. (editor), Ética e o Futuro da Democracia. Proceedings of the International Symposium on "Ethics and the Future of Democracy," Lisbon 94, European Capital of Culture, May 25-28, 1994, Portuguese Society of Philosophy, Sociedade Portuguesa de Filosofia, 133-142. Lisboa: Edições Colibri.

2. Habermas, J. (1995). *Moral Consciousness and Communicative Action.* Oxford: Polity Press, Blackwell's Publishers Limited, 2nd. ed. p. 87–89.

3. Apel, K.O. (1999). "Justice in a Multicultural Society." In: Kearney, R., & Dooley, M. (editors), *Questioning Ethics: Contemporary Debates in Philosophy.* London: Routledge. p. 147

4. Alexy, 142.

Bibliography

Alexy, R. (1998). "Justice and Discourse (Discourse Theory and Human Rights)." In: Alves, J.L. (editor), *Ética e o Futuro da Democracia. Proceedings of the International Symposium on "Ethics and the Future of Democracy," Lisbon 94, European Capital of Culture, May 25–28, 1994, Portuguese Society of Philosophy, Sociedade Portuguesa de Filosofia,* 133–142. Lisboa: Edições Colibri

Apel, K.O. (1980). *Towards a Transformation of Philosophy.* London: Routledge & Kegan Paul Ltd.

Apel, K.O. (1999). "Justice in a Multicultural Society." In: Kearney, R. & Dooley, M. (editors), *Questioning Ethics: Contemporary Debates in Philosophy.* London: Routledge

Habermas, J. (1995). *Moral Consciousness and Communicative Action.* Oxford: Polity Press, Blackwell's Publishers Limited, 2nd. ed.

About the Contributors

Stephen Almagno: Stephen Almagno was a professor of library and information science at the University of Pittsburgh from 1971 to 2001. During that time his major research and teaching areas were historical bibliography, humanities, and information ethics. With Dr. Toni Carbo he established the Information Ethics course and program in the School of Information Sciences. After retiring from the University of Pittsburgh, he became Chief Operations Officer at the Antonianum in Rome, Italy.

Spyridoula M. Armeni: Spyridoula M. Armeni is pursuing her Ph.D. at the Computer Engineering and Informatics Department of Patras University in Greece. Her research area is watermarking and digital images. She is the author or co-author of several articles published in international conferences in the field of watermarking.

J.J. Britz: J.J. Britz is an associate professor in the School of Information Technology at the University of Pretoria. He specializes in the field of information ethics and is currently involved in two research projects on South Africa: the determination of information poverty and a moral reflection on the protection of consumer data. Professor Britz is also a visiting professor at the University of Wisconsin, Milwaukee, and the University of Amsterdam.

Netiva Caftori: Netiva Caftori has been a professor of women's studies and computer science at Northeastern Illinois University for the past 20 years. She is a three time recipient of the excellence award for research and service. In 2003 she is writing a computer security book as part of her sabbatical leave. Her other research interests include universal access and effective use of computers in education. She is also an avid artist. Dr. Caftori studied at Tel-Aviv University and the University of Illinois at Chicago from which she received her three degrees. She has served for the past six years on the international board of Computer Professionals for Social Responsibility (CPSR).

David Wildon Carr: David Wildon Carr is an associate professor in the School of Information and Library Science at the University of North Carolina at Chapel Hill. His teaching responsibilities include materials selection, humanities and social science reference, cultural institutions, field experience, information and culture, and advising. He was given an award for outstanding teaching in 2000-2001 and was the faculty advisor for "Libraries and Librarianship: Past, Present, and Future," at the University of Oxford, May 20–June 2, 2001.

Dimitrios Christodoulakis: Dimitrios Christodoulakis is a full professor in the Computer Engineering and Informatics Department of Patras University where he has been a professor since 1984. He has been scientific coordinator on various research and development projects in the following areas: knowledge and database systems, hypertext and multimedia, and natural language processing. He is the author or co-author of over 70 articles published in international journals, and editor and co-editor of conference proceedings and journals.

Bill Crowley: Bill Crowley, a long-term practitioner turned educator, is associate professor, Graduate School of Library and Information Science, Dominican University. His degrees are in history (B.A., Hunter College), library service (M.S., Columbia University), English/folklore (M.A., Ohio State University), and higher education (Ph.D., Ohio University). Bill has published in both higher education and library and information science literatures, addressing such topics as government information policies, present and future status of the academic librarian, library legislative activism, and the competition between "library" and "information" in graduate education.

David Doss: David Doss is an associate professor and the chair of the Department of Applied Computer Science at Illinois State University. He is co-principal investigator of the Survivability-Over-Security (SOS) Research Group. He is also a retired lt. commander in the U.S. Navy.

Alistair S. Duff: Alistair S. Duff has been a lecturer at Napier University, Edinburgh, since 1994. He is deputy program leader on the M.Sc. Journalism program offered by Napier University's School of Communication Arts. He has also been active in setting up events such as the annual Epixtech Information Society Lecture and a Teaching the Information Society Symposium.

Deborah Ginsberg: Deborah Ginsberg is Electronic Services Librarian at Illinois Institute of Technology. Deborah's B.A. is in Russian Studies from Brown University. She gradated cum laude from the University of Illinois College of Law and practiced for five years. Her MLIS is from Dominican University where she worked as a graduate assistant. She also has a BFA from the School of the Art Institute of Chicago. Deborah's practice has included a clerkship with Justice Warren Wolfson.

J.B. Hill: J.B. Hill is the head of reference at Sims Memorial Library at Southeastern Louisiana University. He received a master's of library science degree from George Peabody College, Vanderbilt University, and a M.A. in of economics from Mankato State University. He currently serves on several state and national library committees, as well as the editorial board of *The Serials Librarian*. He is a frequent presenter and author on library issues relating to reference and serials.

Jeffrey Huber: Jeffrey Huber is an associate professor in the School of Library and Information Studies at Texas Woman's University and associate director of research in the Houston Academy of Medicine–Texas Medical Center Library. He is an internationally recognized authority concerning HIV/AIDS information.

Ursula Iliffe: Ursula Iliffe holds a B.A. degree in humanities from Nene University College. After extensive experience in medical survey research, she was employed as research associate on the Privacy in the Digital Library project at Loughborough University.

Eric W. Johnson: Eric W. Johnson is the Interim library director at Sims Memorial Library at Southwestern Louisiana University. He holds an MLS and an M.A. in English from Southern Connecticut State University.

Ian R. Kerr: Ian R. Kerr has received a B.Sc. from the University of Alberta and an M.A., an Ll.B and a Ph.D. from the University of Western Ontario and is a member of the Bar of Ontario. He is a professor of law at the

University of Ottawa, where he holds the Canada Research Chair in Ethics, Law and Technology. His primary areas of interest lie in the intersection of media, technology, private law and applied ethics. He has numerous published writings in academic books and journals on ethics and electronic information, internet regulation, e-commerce, internet service provider liability, online defamation, and privacy and anonymity. He is also special counsel to the Technology Law Practice Group at the law firm of Nelligan O'Brien Payne LLP.

A. Dale King: A. Dale King is professor of business at Lenoir-Rhyne College in Hickory, North Carolina. She holds a Ph.D. in administration, cognate area in business, from Colorado State University and her dissertation topic was "Owners'/Managers' and Educational Administrators' Perceptions of Small Business Needs."

J. Wayne King: J. Wayne King is a professor of business at Lenoir-Rhyne College in Hickory, North Carolina. He holds a Ph.D. in administration, cognate in business, from Colorado State University and his dissertation topic was "Postsecondary Institutions' Role in Meeting the Training Needs of High Technology Industries."

Wallace C. Koehler, Jr.: Wallace C. Koehler, Jr., is a professor in the Library and Information Science program at Valdosta State University in Georgia. He earned an M.S. in information science from the University of Tennessee and a Ph.D. from Cornell University. His research interests include information ethics and web metadata and related topics.

Byung S. Lee: Byung S. Lee is an associate professor in journalism and communication at Elon University, where he has taught web publishing and design, polling, research and presentation, senior seminar and print journalism courses. His awards include a Poynter Institute Visual Journalism Educators Seminar fellowship, a Pew Center Civic Journalism 2000 fellowship, and an American Society of Newspaper Editors' Institute for Journalism Excellence fellowship. His main research interests include new technology and communication ethics.

Sofia F. Lioli: Sofia F. Lioli works at the Computer Technology Institute on linguistic projects. She received her diploma in pedagogy from the Department of Primary Education at the University of Patras, Greece. She specialized in teaching issues of primary schools.

Tom Mendina: Tom Mendina is the chairman of the Ethics of Electronic Information in the 21st Century Symposium. He is assistant to the Dean of Libraries at the University of Memphis, where his responsibilities include library development, marketing, and external relations. He has held positions at the University of Texas–Austin and Yale University libraries.

Lester J. Pourciau: Lester J. Pourciau was appointed director of libraries at what was then Memphis State University in August of 1970. He retired in 1999. Les continues to serve as a deputy chair of the International Organizing Committee for the Crimea Conference. He was the recipient of the Distinguished Alumnus Award from the Graduate Library School at Louisiana State University in 1988, and received the Distinguished Alumni Award from the Graduate School of Library and Information Science at Indiana University in 1999. He is the founder of the Ethics of Electronic Information in the 21st Century Symposium.

Barbara Rockenbach: Barbara Rockenbach is the instructional services librarian at the Arts Library at Yale University. She has her MLIS from the University of Pittsburgh, where she was the first Information Ethics Fellow. She started at Yale University in 1997 as the Kress Fellow in Art Librarianship. She in an active member in ARLIS/NA (Art Libraries Society of North America), as chair of the Public Policy Committee. She has several publications in the *Journal of Information Ethics*, the *Journal of Scholarly Publishing*, and *Art Documentation*.

Bryan Smith: Bryan Smith is a senior investigator with the Survivability-Over-Security (SOS) research group as well as an information system security professional. His areas of research focus mainly on the issues of personal privacy and the protection of critical infrastructure. This includes work previously done on the Carnivore system as well as current grant funded research in the area of public key infrastructures.

Retha Snyman: Retha Snyman is a senior lecturer in the Department of Information Science at the University of Pretoria. She lectures on information and knowledge management, bibliographic control, and research methodology. She serves on various national and international professional committees. She has presented papers at local and international conferences and she is also the author or co-author of a number of journal articles.

Paul Sturges: Paul Sturges is professor of library studies at Loughborough University, UK. He researches and writes on a wide range of topics across the field of information and library science, and has undertaken consultancy, lectured, and participated in conferences in over 30 countries. The second edition of the *International Encyclopedia of Information and Library Science*, of which he and John Feather are editors, will be published by Routledge in 2003.

Wonhi Synn: Wonhi Synn is associate professor of business administration at the Martha and Spencer Love School of Business, Elon University, where he has been teaching for the past 12 years. His research interests include business ethics, performance evaluations, technology in financial markets, and case research. He holds a Ph.D. in business administration from the State University of New York at Buffalo.

Feili Tu: Feili Tu is assistant professor in the School of Library and Information Science at San Jose State University. Her area of expertise in both research and teaching is in medical informatics and health sciences librarianship. Her research centers on health information services, consumer health literacy, and medical informatics and the use of information technology and the internet to deliver high quality health information and services to health professionals and the general public.

Maria Antonieta Lopes Vigário: Maria Antonieta Lopes Vigário works in the Information and Documentation Service of the Foundation for Science and Technology in Lisbon, Portugal. She holds a M.Sc. in information management and a Ph.D. in information sciences from the University of Sheffield, UK. She was the coordinator of the Committee of Ethics for Information Professionals in Portugal.

William Yurcik: William Yurcik is a senior system engineer at the University of Illinois at Urbana–Champaign and is co-principal investigator of the Survivability-Over-Security (SOS) research group, where his investigations include system survivability, networked group communications, and computer security ethics. Prior to his academic career, he worked for more than 10 years as a network professional with organizations such as the Naval Research Laboratory, FEDSIM, MITRE, and NASA. He was awarded NASA's highest civilian award for coordinating NASA's remote sensing capabilities with the U.S. Air Force during Operation Restore Hope in Somalia.

Nancy Zimmerman: Nancy Zimmerman is an associate professor in the College of Library and Information Science at the University of South Carolina where she teaches courses in educational services in libraries, introduction to the information professions, school library media, and children's and young adult materials and services. Her research is in the areas of education for librarianship and information ethics. She is president of the American Association of School Librarians, and a councilor-at-large of the American Library Association.

INDEX

"Age of Paper" 49
Age of Reason 31
Alibris 90
Almagno, Stephen: first professor in the U. S. to teach Information Ethics 8; full professor of Library and Information Science at Pittsburgh 8; as hero 25; as visiting International Lecturer at Pittsburgh 8
Amazon.com 86
American Library Association: accredited master's programs 98, 100, 125; *Code of Ethics* 19, 76, 88, 121; Reference and Users Association 121
American Psychiatric Association 34
appliance-based computing universe 168
archiving 76
Aquacool_2000 169
Association for Library and Information Science Education 100, 125
Association of College and Research Libraries 61
Association of Records Managers and Administrators 62
Auden, W. H., "The Protestant Mystics" 21
authentication via watermarking 145

banner advertisements 85
Barber, Bernard, *The Logic and Limits of Trust* 48
BarnesandNoble.com 86
Berry, Thomas, *The Great Work—Our Way into the Future* 22
beta testing 150
bibliographic network, international 109
Blanchard, Kenneth, *The Power of Ethical Management* 134
British Library Association 19
Buber, Martin 19
Burnett, Frances Hodgson, *The Secret Garden* 74

Carbo, Toni, dean, University of Pittsburgh School of Information Sciences 5, 6, 8, 16
Carter, Stephen, *Integrity* 20
ChannelOne 83
child pornography 167
civil liberties 40
Code of Professional Conduct (British Library Association) 19
commercialization 82
community 45, 187, 196
computer intrusions 149
confidentiality 76
consumer health information 119
copyright protection 145
Crimea Conference 55
cultural pragmatism 94
culturally-defined meaning 32
cybercrime 140
cyberplagiarism 133

Dalai Lama, *Ethics for the New Millennium* 20
Data Protection Acts of 1984 and 1998 (UK) 77
data protection officers 80
deontological codes 60
deregulation of telecommunications infrastructure 162
deviance 30
difference principle (Rawls) 158
Direct Marketing Association 178

e-commerce 84, 85
e-mail: as advertising tool 177; as personal place 185; pornographic 167; unsolicited bulk e-mail 179
Eastern Europe, absence of legal infrastructure 58
Encyclopedia Britannica 82
entropic information context 49
Esdaile, Arundell, *Manual of Bibliography* 7, 17
ethics, ethical: according to the dictionary 39; codes of ethics 60, 62, 72, 76; of dialog, 199; dilemmas 111; discussion 196; fabric 46; reasoning 199; in reference service 121; reflection

28; as a scientific discipline 135; and universal bibliographic control 108; values 46
Ethics of Electronic Information in the 21st Century (EEI21-MEMPHIS) symposium 3, 6

"fee vs. free" 88, 91
fidelity (legal) 169, 173
fiduciary obligation 171
filtering software 78
fingerprinting 145
First Amendment protection 180
FirstSearch 90
freedom of expression 110
Friends of the library, St. Charles Public Library 87

Gates Library Foundation 83
Gay Pride Day 33
globalization: defined 96; globalized market environment 101
GNU Project 138
Gorman, Michael, *Our Enduring Values* 28

Habermas, Jurgen 197
Hammarskjold, Dag 20
homophobia 37
homosexuality 31, 33
honor codes 136
human rights 197, 200

information: access to 108, 111; censorship of 111; educators 104; entropic information context 49; as ethical 47; and interdisciplinarity 49; irrelevant 114; ownership 111; professions 19; quality 123; societies 154; world information organizations 63
Information Ethics course 28
information professionals 59
Information Science (Chinese journal) 54
institutional ethos 46, 51
intellectual property rights 140
International bibliographic network 109
International Federation of Library Associations and Institutions 61, 115
International Franciscan-Dominican Research Centre 7
Internet: appliances 168; in China 53; free exchange of digital objects in 141; not immune from copyright 142; main channel for health information 123; not a panacea for information 131; philosophy of 138; not a public place 183; security 148; service providers 178; two main trends 145; in the Ukraine 55; unregulated universe of information 120; Worm of 1998 149

Journal of Homosexuality 36
Journal of Information Ethics 9

Kant, Immanuel 60, 139, 146
Kaplan, Abraham 105
King, Martin Luther 21
Kinghorn, John Rye, *Parable* 17
knowledge 52
knowledge managers 99

language: control function 112; irrelevant 114; and reality 113; universal 113
law of contract 173
Lesbian Health Foundation 36
liberty principle 157
librarian, librarianship: job title 100; public 103, 120; school 102; survival of 95; and trust 48
library, libraries: agreements with booksellers 86; commercialized 84; as a cultural institution 52; digital 76; indirect advertisements 83; missions 66; practitioners 104; reference 120; as a sanctuary 125; vendor partnerships 125
Library Bill of Rights 19
Library Hi Tech News 57
Lipset, Seymour Martin 97
Loughborough University, Department of Information Science 79
LOUIS Library Consortium (Louisiana) 84

madness 31
Mandela, Nelson 21
"market believers" 184
medical data 119
Medical Library Association 122, 125
Merton, Robert K. 97
metadata 115
Mintzberg, Henry 61
moral action 39
Muller, Robert 17
multicultural society 200

National Health Council 122
National Library of Medicine 126
New York Public Library online bookstore 87
9/11 40, 77
Nussbaum, Martha 17

online service providers 166
Owens Corning Corporate Library 95

Peale, Norman Vincent, *The Power of Ethical Management* 134
penetration testing 151
personal data 75
plagiarism in academe 132
Porat, Marc, *The Information Economy* 159
privacy 79
privatization 83
professional responsibility 48
Public Library Association 122

Rawls, John 156
Reagan, Ronald 155
reference librarianship in public libraries 120
regulatory association 61
Responsible Electronic Communication Alliance 178
Rilke, Rainer Maria 4
Rockenbach, Barbara: first Information Ethics Fellow at Pittsburgh 18; "Information Ethics at the University of Pittsburgh" 16
rules of argumentation 198
Russian National Public Library for Science and Technology 57

schools of library and information science 104
Second World War 162
Security Administrator for Analyzing Networks 150
Severson, Richard, *The Principles of Information Ethics* 134
Shraiberg, Yakov 55
"smart card" 168
social democracy, principles 155
Society of American Archivists 62
South Caucasian Regional Library Conference 56
Soviet countries, former (Former Soviet Union) 53, 75
spam 178
state interference, limits 163
Stokes, Roy 4, 7, 17
Stonewall riots 33

Teilhard de Chardin, Pierre 16, 27
text watermarking 143
Thatcher, Margaret 155
Third Way 155
Thomas Goodrich Eliensis— Remy/Remigius Guedon 143
trade unions 62
trust: enduring 51; ethos of 48; as key word 41; and knowledge 52; relationship 47, 81, 125
truth 47

uncertainty and the transfer of knowledge 50
UNESCO 115
United States Department of Defense 57, 149
United States Department of State 57
United States Library Awareness Program 77
Universal Declaration of Human Rights 21
University of Pittsburgh School of Information Sciences 6, 7, 16, 18, 26
University of Virginia honor code 133

values: American 9; core, for bibliographic control 110

watermarking, types 144
World Health Organization 34
World Intellectual Property Organization 140
WorldCat 90
Wuerl, Donald 7

Yahoo! 169